It Works!

GMAT® SENTENCE CORRECTION

PREPARATION THAT WORKS FOR YOU

DEBORAH PHILLIPS

It Works! Publishing

Copyright © 2013 Deborah Phillips
All rights reserved. This includes the right to reproduce any portion of this book in any form.
ISBN: 0615919413
ISBN-13: 9780615919416

Contents

Preface ... i

THE LESSONS

1	Problems with NOUNS, PRONOUNS, and POSSESSIVES	3
2	Problems with AGREEMENT	21
3	Problems with PARALLELISM	37
4	Problems with COMPARISONS	53
5	Problems with VERBS	69
6	Problems with MODIFIERS	85
7	Problems with SENTENCES	101
8	Problems with WORDINESS	117
9	Problems with AWKWARDNESS	135
10	Problems with DICTION	151
11	Problems with IDIOMS	169
12	Problems with CLARITY	185

THE GMAT-STYLE TESTS

TEST 1	201
TEST 2	219
TEST 3	237
TEST 4	255
TEST 5	273
TEST 6	291

Preface

The purpose of this book is to prepare test-takers for the sentence correction questions on the GMAT® (Graduate Management Admissions Test). The sentence corrections questions are one of the types of questions found in the Verbal Section of the GMAT®.

The GMAT Test

DESCRIPTION OF THE GMAT TEST
The GMAT consists of three sections. These three sections are the Analytical Writing section, the Quantitative section, and the Verbal section.

DESCRIPTION OF THE VERBAL SECTION
The Verbal section will most likely consist of 41 questions to be answered in 75 minutes. The questions in the Verbal section will be made up of a mixture of reading comprehension questions, critical reasoning questions, and sentence correction questions.
    Out of the probable 41 questions in the Verbal section, there will most likely be between twelve and fourteen Sentence Correction questions. To finish the section within the allotted time, you should plan on spending between around 90 seconds per question in this section.

DESCRIPTION OF THE SENTENCE CORRECTION QUESTIONS
Each sentence correction question consists of a statement and five answer choices labeled (A) through (E). All or part of the initial statement is underlined, and answer choice (A) is the same as the underlined part of the statement. The test-taker must choose the answer that is the most correct and stylistically acceptable in formal written English. The test-taker chooses answer (A) if the initial statement is grammatically correct and stylistically preferable as it is. The test-taker chooses one of the other answers if any of these answers is more grammatically correct or more stylistically preferable.
    Here is a sample of a sentence correction question:

> After Theodore Roosevelt's mother and first wife died on the same day in 1884, Roosevelt vowed to permanently remain out of politics to mourn the loss.
>
> (A) vowed to permanently remain out of politics to mourn
> (B) vowed to remain permanently out of politics in order to mourn
> (C) had vowed to permanently remain out of politics for the purpose of mourning
> (D) had vowed to remain out of politics permanently in order to mourn
> (E) vowed to remain out of politics permanently to mourn

You should note that part of the initial statement is underlined and that answer (A) is exactly the same as the underlined part of the statement. You should also note that answers (B) through (E) contain various possible corrections for the underlined part of the statement. The correct answer choice to this question is answer (E).

Preface | i

THE POINTS TESTED IN THE SENTENCE CORRECTION QUESTIONS
These questions test a combination of formally correct grammar and simple, elegant style. Two or more distinct points are often tested in a single question.

The most common formally correct grammar points that are tested are nouns, pronouns, possessives, agreement, parallelism, comparisons, verbs, modifiers, and sentences. The most common simple, elegant style points that are tested are wordiness, awkwardness, diction, idioms, and clarity.

The points listed above are based on an exhaustive study of the points tested on official released GMAT tests. Any point that appears on this list has appeared numerous times on official released versions of the test.

This Book

THE APPROACH
The approach used in this book is a systematic, skill-building methodology, one that begins with a simple presentation of skills in the lessons and ends with tests that consist of GMAT-style questions at the difficulty level of the actual test.

In each lesson, one skill is presented using examples containing easier language than the language found on a GMAT to ensure that the targeted skill is clear. A skills practice exercise follows each skill presentation, using language that is at the difficulty level of the GMAT but is in a single-sentence format that makes the practice easier than GMAT-style questions. The materials then progress to GMAT-style skills practice exercises that are at the level of the actual test but cover only the material from that particular lesson. Thorough explanations follow each skills practice exercise and each GMAT-style practice exercise.

After all the individual lessons have been mastered, GMAT-style tests are presented. These GMAT-style tests contain questions that cover points from each of the lessons. These questions are at the difficulty level of the GMAT and contain the same selection of skills as the GMAT. Thorough explanations follow each skills practice exercise and each GMAT-style test.

THE CONTENTS
The book includes a lesson section and a test section. The lesson section includes twelve individual lessons *(Nouns, Pronouns, and Possessives, Agreement, Parallelism, Comparisons, Verbs, Modifiers, Sentences, Wordiness, Awkwardness, Diction, Idioms, and Clarity)*. Each of these lessons includes a presentation, a skills practice exercise with thorough explanations, and a GMAT-style practice exercise with thorough explanations. The test section includes six GMAT-style tests with twelve questions in each *(Test 1, Test 2, Test 3, Test 4, Test 5, and Test 6)* with thorough explanations for each correct and incorrect answer.

THE QUESTION STRATEGY
It is important to use the appropriate strategy when approaching a sentence correction question. Keep in mind that each question consists of a statement and five answer choices, that all or part of the statement is underlined, that the five answer choices are various restatements of the underlined section of the statement, and that answer (A) is always the same as the underlined section in the statement, indicating that this is the answer to choose if the underlined part of the statement is correct as it is.

As you read the statement, focus on the underlined part and look for any problems you can spot. It is important to understand that you cannot completely ignore the part of the sentence that is not underlined because something in the part that is not underlined may be causing problems in the underlined part. It is also important to understand that there may be (and probably will be) more than one problem in the underlined part. Finally, it is important to understand that the problems in the underlined part could be related to grammatical correctness or to style. Perhaps you can spot the issues in the following statement:

> After Theodore Roosevelt's mother and first wife died on the same day in 1884, Roosevelt vowed *to permanently remain* out of politics to mourn the loss.

Perhaps you can spot the issue with the modifier *permanently* that is incorrectly positioned between *to* and *remain*, and perhaps you cannot.

As you read the answers, the most powerful tool you can use is to compare the answers to determine what is being tested. Study the following set of answers from the sample question:

(A) *vowed* to permanently remain out of politics to mourn
(B) *vowed* to remain permanently out of politics in order to mourn
(C) *had vowed* to permanently remain out of politics for the purpose of mourning
(D) *had vowed* to remain out of politics permanently in order to mourn
(E) *vowed* to remain out of politics permanently to mourn

In this set of answers, you should note *vowed* in answers (A), (B), and (E) and *had vowed* in answers (C) and (D) and understand that this question is testing verb tenses

Now study the same set of answer choices with different sections in italics.

(A) vowed to *permanently* remain out of politics to mourn
(B) vowed to remain *permanently* out of politics in order to mourn
(C) had vowed to *permanently* remain out of politics for the purpose of mourning
(D) had vowed to remain out of politics *permanently* in order to mourn
(E) vowed to remain out of politics *permanently* to mourn

In this set of answers, you should note the various positions of *permanently* in answers (A), (B), (C), (D), and (E) and understand that this question is testing the position of the modifier *permanently*.

Finally, study these answer choices with a third set of sections in italics.

(A) vowed to permanently remain out of politics *to mourn*
(B) vowed to remain permanently out of politics *in order to mourn*
(C) had vowed to permanently remain out of politics *for the purpose of mourning*
(D) had vowed to remain out of politics permanently *in order to mourn*
(E) vowed to remain out of politics permanently *to mourn*

In this set of answers, you should note *to mourn* in answers (A) and (E), *in order to mourn* in answers (B) and (D), and *for the purpose of mourning* in answer (C) and understand that this question is testing the idea of purpose and how it can be expressed most concisely, without being overly wordy.

Simply by studying the answers in this way, you can determine that this question is testing verbs, modifiers, and wordiness. It is very common for a sentence correction question on the GMAT to test three different concepts, in this case the two concepts of verbs and modifiers that deal with grammatical correctness and the one concept of wordiness that is stylistic.

THE DEVICES USED IN THE EXPLANATIONS
The following devices are used in the explanations throughout this book:
- A ⬚box⬚ is used to indicate incorrect part(s) of an incorrect answer.
- *Italics* are used to indicate a part of a sentence or response that should be noticed.
- **Bold** is used to indicate the correct part(s) of a correct answer.

Study the sample question and answer choices to see how they would be marked:

After Theodore Roosevelt's mother and first wife died on the same day in 1884, Roosevelt vowed to permanently remain out of politics to mourn the loss.

(A) vowed *to* ⬚permanently⬚ *remain* out of politics to mourn
(B) vowed to remain permanently out of politics ⬚in order to mourn⬚
(C) ⬚had vowed⬚ *to* ⬚permanently⬚ *remain* out of politics ⬚for the purpose of mourning⬚
(D) ⬚had vowed⬚ to remain out of politics permanently ⬚in order to mourn⬚
(E) **vowed** to remain out of politics **permanently to mourn**

In answers (A) and (C), the box around ⬚permanently⬚ indicates that this modifier is incorrectly positioned between the two parts of the infinitive *to* and *remain,* making these answers incorrect. In answers (B), (C), and (D), there is a box around either ⬚in order to mourn⬚ or ⬚for the purpose of mourning⬚ to indicate that these parts of the answers are incorrect, in this case because they are overly wordy. In answers (C) and (D), the verb ⬚had vowed⬚ is boxed because it is in the incorrect tense. The word *After* in the original statement is in italics because it is the key word to indicate that the verb tense is incorrect. Answer (E) is the correct answer, with the correct verb tense **vowed**, the correctly positioned modifier **permanently**, and the more concise (and less wordy) **to mourn** each in bold to indicate that these parts of the answer are either grammatically correct or stylistically preferable.

THE STUDY PLAN
As you work your way through each of the twelve lessons, work slowly and carefully. Make sure that you understand each point that is made because each point has appeared on the GMAT numerous times and will most likely appear on the test when you take it. Highlight those points that are causing you problems, and make a list of those points to review the day before the test. Challenge yourself not just to find the correct answers to the questions but to find each of the points that are covered in the explanations. You should plan on spending one-to-two hours on each of the lessons to master it.

As you work your way through each of the six tests, first try each test under time pressure, with twenty minutes to answer the twelve questions on each test. Then, prior to checking the answers and explanations, go over each question more slowly and carefully to see if you can spot (and perhaps underline) each of the issues in a particular question and its answers. Challenge yourself not just to find the correct answers to the questions but to find each of the points that are covered in the explanations. You should plan on spending one-to-two hours on each of the tests to master it.

THE LESSONS

Lesson 1: Problems with NOUNS, PRONOUNS, and POSSESSIVES

Nouns are words that represent either a person, place, thing, or idea; **pronouns** are words that replace nouns; **possessives** are words that show what a noun possesses, or owns. Problems with nouns, pronouns, and possessives generally occur in the following situations on the GMAT:
1. when subject pronouns *(I, he, she, we, they)* and object pronouns *(me, him, her, us, them)* are confused
2. when incorrect forms of third person possessive pronouns *(his, hers, its, theirs)* or third person reflexive pronouns *(himself, herself, themselves)* are used
3. when reflexive pronouns *(myself, yourself, himself, herself, ourselves, yourselves, themselves)* are used incorrectly
4. when countable nouns (nouns that can be counted, such as *books, tables,* and *friends)* and uncountable nouns (nouns that cannot be counted, such as *water, money,* or *happiness)* are confused
5. when countable quantifiers *(many, few, fewer, number)* and uncountable quantifiers *(much, less, amount, a great deal)* are confused
6. when the relative pronoun *which* is used to refer to a complete idea rather than a specific noun

EXAMPLE 1: This example shows confusion between subject and object pronouns.

INCORRECT: Just *between* you and I, the story they told the police seems quite improbable.
CORRECT: Just *between* you and me, the story they told the police seems quite improbable.

In the incorrect example, the subject pronouns *you* and *I* follow the preposition *between*. In the correct example, the object pronouns **you** and **me** follow the preposition *between*.

- -

EXAMPLE 2: This example shows an incorrectly formed reflexive pronoun.

INCORRECT: After winning their first trophy, the members of the cheerleading squad congratulated *theirselves*.
CORRECT: After winning their first trophy, the members of the cheerleading squad congratulated **themselves**.

In the incorrect example, the reflexive pronoun *theirselves* is formed incorrectly. In the correct example, the reflexive pronoun **themselves** is formed correctly.

- -

EXAMPLE 3: This example shows an incorrectly used reflexive pronoun.

INCORRECT: The *manager* sent a letter which pertained to all of the other workers and *myself*.
CORRECT: *I* sent a letter which pertained to all the other workers and **myself**.

In the incorrect example, the reflexive pronoun *myself* is used incorrectly because it is used as an object but does not refer to the subject *manager*. In the correct example, the reflexive pronoun **myself** is used correctly because it is an object that does refer to the subject *I*.

- -

EXAMPLE 4: This example shows confusion between countable and uncountable nouns.

INCORRECT: Do you have some good *advices* for me?
CORRECT: Do you have some good **advice** for me?

In the incorrect example, the uncountable noun *advice* is used incorrectly as a countable plural noun *advices*. In the correct example, **advice** is used correctly as an uncountable noun.

- -

EXAMPLE 5: This example shows confusion between countable and uncountable quantifiers.

INCORRECT: The advertisement boasted that the new product had *less fat* and *less calories*.
CORRECT: The advertisement boasted that the new product had *less fat* and fewer *calories*.

In the incorrect example, the uncountable quantifier *less* is used correctly with the uncountable noun *fat*, but *less* is used incorrectly with the countable noun *calories*. In the correct example, the uncountable quantifier *less* is used correctly with the uncountable noun *fat*, and the countable quantifier **fewer** is used correctly with the countable noun *calories*.

- -

EXAMPLE 6: This example shows the relative pronoun *which* referring to a complete idea.

INCORRECT: *All of their debt has been paid off*, which *makes the couple feel happy.*
CORRECT: *All of their debt has been paid off*, and that *makes the couple feel happy.*

In the incorrect example, the relative pronoun *which* refers to the complete idea *all their debt has been paid off* rather than a specific noun. In the correct example, *which* has been replaced with the conjunction **and** and the demonstrative pronoun **that**, which can refer to a complete idea such as *all their debt has been paid off*.

SKILLS PRACTICE: Find the problems with **nouns**, **pronouns**, and **possessives** in the following sentences. (The number in parentheses indicates the number of problems you should find.) Then, study the explanations on the pages that follow.

1. In 1952, an aspiring 21-year-old money manager named Warren Buffet placed a small advertisement in an Omaha newspaper inviting people to attend a class on investing, which he figured would be a good way to accustom hisself to appearing before an audience. *(2)*

2. Plato and Aristotle and others discussed language among themselves in the fourth and third centuries B.C., and their discussions have had great impact on you and I since we have inherited several central categories of grammatical analysis, such as nouns and verbs, from themselves. *(3)*

3. Corporations have been preoccupied with the experiences, qualification, and achievement of individuals; however, corporations need to focus themself on the successes of teams of workers rather than on the accomplishments of any individual. *(3)*

4. Brokerage firms lend money on margin, which means that they will lend you monies equal to a percentage of the value of the security in your account. *(3)*

5. Although no detailed theory of the origin of comets is accepted by all astronomers, a great deal of them now believe that comets were created in the early days of the solar system from residual planetary matters in the outer, colder part of the solar system and less of them are detractors of this theory. *(3)*

6. Danish invasion into England during the ninth century introduced the Scandinavian term "Yule" for Christmas, which explains its' use in later medieval and Tudor England. *(3)*

7. Hurricane Andrew, the small but ferocious hurricane which slammed into South Florida in 1992 and then continued northwest across the Gulf of Mexico to strike Louisiana, left deaths and destructions in its path and caused damages costing $25 billion to repair. *(3)*

8. The Robot Research Project (RRP) was completed in record time, with all the work accomplished by the research team and myself but with much but not all of the credit going to us since a certain unnamed manager who had actually contributed little if anything to the project took a great amount of the accolades for her. *(3)*

EXPLANATIONS (I = incorrect, C = correct)

1. In 1952, an aspiring 21-year-old money manager named *Warren Buffet placed a small advertisement in an Omaha newspaper inviting people to attend a class on investing,* which he figured would be a good way to accustom hisself to appearing before an audience.

    - The relative pronoun *which* is used incorrectly. This relative pronoun should be used to refer to a specific noun and not to a complete idea such as *Warren Buffet placed a small advertisement in an Omaha newspaper inviting people to attend a class on investing.*
        I: *which*
        C: **something that**

    - The reflexive pronoun *hisself* is incorrectly formed.
        I: *hisself*
        C: **himself**

    -

2. Plato and Aristotle and others discussed language among themselves in the fourth and third centuries B.C., and their discussions have had *great impact* on you and *I* since *we* have inherited several central categories of grammatical analysis, such as nouns and verbs, from *themselves*.

    - The noun *impact* is used incorrectly. This noun can be used only as a countable noun and cannot be used as an uncountable noun, as it is here.
        I: *great impact*
        C: **a great impact**

    - The subject pronoun *I* is used incorrectly. The subject pronoun *I* and the object pronoun *me* should not be confused. In this situation, the object pronoun *me* is needed because it is the object of the preposition *on*.
        I: *I*
        C: **me**

    - The reflexive pronoun *themselves* is used incorrectly. This reflexive pronoun should be used as an object only when it refers to the subject. Since the subject is *we* (and not *they*), the reflexive pronoun *themselves* cannot be used.
        I: *themselves*
        C: **them**

    -

3. Corporations have been preoccupied with the |experiences|, |qualification|, and achievement of individuals; however, corporations need to focus |themself| on the successes of teams of workers rather than on the accomplishments of any individual.

- The noun |experiences| is used incorrectly. The noun *experience* can be countable or uncountable, and the countable *(an experience =* "a particular encounter"*)* and uncountable *(some experience =* "knowledge and wisdom gained from one's encounters"*)* versions of this noun have different meanings. The meaning that fits into this context is the uncountable meaning, so the countable plural *experiences* is incorrect.
  - I: *experiences*
  - C: **experience**

- The noun |qualification| is used incorrectly. This noun can be used only as a countable noun and cannot be used as an uncountable noun, as it is here.
  - I: *qualification*
  - C: **qualifications**

- The reflexive pronoun |themself| is incorrectly formed.
  - I: *themself*
  - C: **themselves**

---

4. *Brokerage firms lend money on margin,* |which| *means that they will lend you* |monies| *equal to a percentage of the value of the* |security| *in your account.*

- The relative pronoun |which| is used incorrectly. This relative pronoun should be used to refer to a specific noun and not to a complete idea such as *Brokerage firms lend money on margin*.
  - I: *which*
  - C: **and this**

- The noun |monies| is used incorrectly. The noun *money* can be countable or uncountable, and the countable *(monies =* "specific currencies"*)* and uncountable *(some money =* "medium of exchange"*)* versions of this noun have different meanings. The meaning that fits into this context is the uncountable meaning, so the countable plural *monies* is incorrect.
  - I: *monies*
  - C: **money**

- The noun |security| is used incorrectly. This noun can be countable or uncountable, and the countable *(securities =* "financial investments"*)* and uncountable *(some security =* "freedom from danger"*)* versions of this noun have different meanings. The meaning that fits into this context is the countable meaning, so the uncountable noun *security* is incorrect.
  - I: *security*
  - C: **securities**

5. Although no detailed theory of the origin of comets is accepted by all *astronomers*, *a great deal* of them now believe that comets were created in the early days of the solar system from residual planetary *matters* in the outer, colder part of the solar system and *less* of *them* are detractors of this theory.

- The uncountable quantifier *a great deal* is used incorrectly. An uncountable quantifier should not be used with the countable noun *astronomers*.
    I: *a great deal*
    C: **a large number**

- The noun *matters* is used incorrectly. The noun *matter* can be countable or uncountable, and the countable *(a matter* = "situation") and uncountable *(some matter* = "substance") versions of this noun have different meanings. The meaning that fits into this context is the uncountable meaning, so the countable plural *matters* is incorrect.
    I: *matters*
    C: **matter**

- The uncountable quantifier *less* is used incorrectly. An uncountable quantifier should not be used with the with the pronoun *them*, which refers to the countable noun *astronomers*.
    I: *less*
    C: **fewer**

- -

6. *Danish invasion* into England during the ninth century *introduced* the Scandinavian *term "Yule" for Christmas*, *which* explains *its'* use in later medieval and Tudor England.

- The noun *invasion* is used incorrectly. This noun can be used only as a countable noun and cannot be used as an uncountable noun, as it is here.
    I: *Danish invasion*
    C: **The Danish invasion**

- The relative pronoun *which* is used incorrectly. This relative pronoun should be used to refer to a specific noun and not to a complete idea such as *Danish invasion...introduced the...term "Yule" for Christmas*.
    I: *which*
    C: **and this**

- The possessive pronoun *its'* is incorrectly formed.
    I: *its'*
    C: **its**

- -

7. Hurricane Andrew, the small but ferocious hurricane which slammed into South Florida in 1992 and then continued northwest across the Gulf of Mexico to strike Louisiana, left *deaths* and *destructions* in its path and caused *damages* costing $25 billion to repair.

- The noun *deaths* is used incorrectly. The noun *death* can be countable or uncountable, and the countable *(a death* = "a specific loss of life"*)* and uncountable *(some death* = "a mass amount of loss of life"*)* versions of this noun have different meanings. The meaning that fits into this context is the uncountable meaning, so the countable plural *deaths* is incorrect.
    I: *deaths*
    C: **death**

- The noun *destructions* is incorrect. The noun *destruction* can be used only as an uncountable noun and cannot be used as an countable plural noun *destructions*, as it is here.
    I: *destructions*
    C: **destruction**

- The noun *damages* is used incorrectly. The noun *damage* can be countable or uncountable, and the countable *(damages* = "legal compensation"*)* and uncountable *(some damage* = "loss, injury"*)* versions of this noun have different meanings. The meaning that fits into this context is the uncountable meaning, so the countable plural *damages* is incorrect.
    I: *damages*
    C: **damage**

- -

8. The Robot Research Project (RRP) was completed in record time, with all the *work* accomplished by the research team and *myself* but with much but not all of the credit going to us since a certain unnamed *manager* who had actually contributed little if anything to the project took a great *amount* of the *accolades* for *her*.

- The reflexive pronoun *myself* is used incorrectly. A reflexive pronoun should be used as an object only when it refers to the subject. Since the subject is *work* and not *I*, the reflexive pronoun *myself* cannot be used as an object.
    I: *myself*
    C: **me**

- The uncountable quantifier *amount* is used incorrectly. An uncountable quantifier should not be used with the countable noun *accolades*.
    I: *amount*
    C: **number**

- The object pronoun *her* is used incorrectly. A reflexive pronoun should be used as an object when it refers to the subject. Since the subject is *manager* and the object pronoun *her* refers to the subject, a reflexive pronoun should be used.
    I: *her*
    I: *her*
    C: **herself**

GMAT-STYLE SKILLS PRACTICE: Choose the letter of the answer to each question that best reflects the style and accuracy of standard written English. Then, study the explanations on the pages that follow.

1. President Lincoln, under considerable pressure from abolitionists, saw his main objective as saving the Union; he therefore trod carefully in negotiations <u>between them and himself so as not to offend slaveholding border states, something</u> he felt he needed to do to maintain the Union.

    (A) between them and himself so as not to offend slaveholding border states, something
    (B) between he and them so as not to offend slaveholding border states, something
    (C) between he and them so as not to offend slaveholding border states, which
    (D) between him and them so as not to offend slaveholding border states, something
    (E) between them and himself so as not to offend slaveholding border states, which

2. Before the Roman conquest, the Iberian Peninsula was inhabited by <u>numerous peoples of diverse origins and unrelated linguistic affiliations, though in many cases researchers knew relatively little information about themselves</u> today.

    (A) numerous peoples of diverse origins and unrelated linguistic affiliations, though in many cases researchers knew relatively little information about themselves
    (B) numerous peoples of diverse origins and unrelated linguistic affiliations, though in much cases researchers knew relatively little information about them
    (C) a great deal of people of diverse origins and unrelated linguistic affiliations, though in much cases researchers knew relatively little informations about them
    (D) numerous peoples of diverse origins and unrelated linguistic affiliations, though in many cases researchers knew relatively little information about them
    (E) a great deal of people of diverse origins and unrelated linguistic affiliations, though in many cases researchers knew relatively little information about themselves

3. William Randolph Hearst's parents purchased the *San Francisco Examiner* for their son to provide him with a voice when he ran for the U.S. Senate, something he did more to accede to his parents' wishes than for himself.

   (A) their son to provide him with a voice when he ran for the U.S. Senate, something he did more to accede to his parents' wishes than for himself
   (B) their son to provide himself with a voice when he ran for the U.S. Senate, something he did more to accede to his' parents' wishes than for himself
   (C) theirs son to provide him with a voice when he ran for the U.S. Senate, something he did more to accede to his' parents' wishes than for him
   (D) their son to provide him with a voice when he ran for the U.S. Senate, which he did more to accede to his parents' wishes than for himself
   (E) their son to provide himself with a voice when he ran for the U.S. Senate, which he did more to accede to his parents' wishes than for him

4. It is ironic that lightning kills more people in the developed world and less in the underdeveloped world since it is one of the forces of nature against which humans have some protections.

   (A) less in the underdeveloped world since it is one of the forces of nature against which humans have some protections
   (B) fewer in the underdeveloped world since it is one of the forces of nature against which humans have some protection
   (C) less in the underdeveloped world since its one of the forces of nature against which humans have some protection
   (D) fewer in the underdeveloped world since its one of the force of nature against which humanity has some protection
   (E) fewer in the underdeveloped world since it's one of the few force against which humanity has some protections

5. The famous painting *Washington Crossing the Delaware* by Emanuel Leutze demonstrates a certain number of artistic licenses, in items such as the boat, and this was in reality much larger.

    (A) number of artistic licenses in items such as the boat, and this was
    (B) amount of artistic license in items such as the boat, and this was
    (C) number of artistic license in items such as the boat, which was
    (D) amount of artistic licenses in items such as the boat, which was
    (E) amount of artistic license in items such as the boat, which was

6. On January 17, 1950, seven men dressed themselves in Halloween masks, drove themselves to Brinks headquarters, forced their way in, and stole millions of dollars, a robbery that put themselves in the headlines and provided themselves with notoriety for decades to come.

    (A) dressed themselves in Halloween masks, drove themselves to Brinks headquarters, forced their way in, and stole millions of dollars, a robbery that put themselves in the headlines and provided themselves
    (B) dressed themselves in Halloween masks, drove them to Brinks headquarters, forced their way in, and stole millions of dollars, a robbery that put them in the headlines and provided themselves
    (C) dressed themselves in Halloween masks, drove themselves to Brinks headquarters, forced their way in, and stole millions of dollars, a robbery that put them in the headlines and provided them
    (D) dressed them in Halloween masks, drove them to Brinks headquarters, forced their way in, and stole millions of dollars, a robbery that put them in the headlines and provided them
    (E) dressed themselves in Halloween masks, drove themselves to Brinks headquarters, forced their way in, and stole millions of dollars, a robbery that put themselves in the headlines and provided them

EXPLANATIONS

1. This question tests **nouns**, **pronouns**, and **possessives**.

   President Lincoln, under considerable pressure from abolitionists, saw his main objective as saving the Union; *he therefore trod carefully in negotiations* <u>between them and himself so as not to offend slaveholding border states, something</u> *he felt he needed to do to maintain the Union.*

   (A) *between* them and himself so as not to offend slaveholding border states, something
   - This answer contains the correct reflexive pronoun **himself** as object of the preposition *between*, since the object refers to the subject *he* of the verb *trod*. This answer also uses **something** to avoid the problem of the relative pronoun *which* referring to a complete idea that is found in some of the other answers. This answer is correct.

   (B) *between* he and them so as not to offend slaveholding border states, something
   - The subject pronoun *he* is used incorrectly. The subject pronoun *he* and the object *him* should not be confused. In this situation, the object pronoun *him* is needed because it is the object of the preposition *between,* and in fact, a reflexive pronoun should be used in place of the object pronoun because the object refers to the subject *he* of the verb *trod.*

   (C) *between* he and them so as not to offend slaveholding border states, which
   - The subject pronoun *he* is used incorrectly. The subject pronoun *he* and the object pronoun *him* should not be confused. In this situation, the object pronoun *him* is needed because it is the object of the preposition *between,* and in fact, a reflexive pronou should be used in place of the object pronoun because the object refers to the subject *he* of the verb *trod.*
   - The relative pronoun *which* is used incorrectly. This relative pronoun should be used to refer to a specific noun and not to a complete idea such as *he therefore trod carefully in negotiations.*

   (D) between *him* and them so as not to offend slaveholding border states, something
   - The object pronoun *him* is used incorrectly. A reflexive pronoun should be used as an object when it refers to the subject. Since the subject of the verb *trod* is *he* and the object pronoun *him* refers to the subject, a reflexive pronoun should be used.

   (E) between them and himself so as not to offend slaveholding border states, which
   - The relative pronoun *which* is used incorrectly. This relative pronoun should be used to refer to a specific noun and not to a complete idea such as *he therefore trod carefully in negotiations.*

2. This question tests **nouns**, **pronouns**, and **possessives**.

Before the Roman conquest, the Iberian Peninsula was inhabited by <u>numerous peoples of diverse origins and unrelated linguistic affiliations, though in many cases researchers knew relatively little information about themselves</u> today.

(A) numerous peoples of diverse origins and unrelated linguistic affiliations, though in many cases *researchers knew* relatively little information about *themselves*
- The reflexive pronoun *themselves* is used incorrectly. This reflexive pronoun should be used as an object only when it refers to the subject. Since the subject of the verb *knew* is *researchers* and not *people*, the reflexive pronoun *themselves* cannot be used.

(B) numerous peoples of diverse origins and unrelated linguistic affiliations, though in *much* cases researchers knew relatively little information about them
- The uncountable quantifier *much* is used incorrectly. An uncountable quantifier should not be used with the countable noun *cases*.

(C) *a great deal* of *peoples* of diverse origins and unrelated linguistic affiliations, though in *much* cases researchers knew relatively little *informations* about them
- The uncountable quantifier *a great deal* is used incorrectly. This uncountable quantifier should not be used with the countable noun *peoples*.
- The uncountable quantifier *much* is used incorrectly. This uncountable quantifier should not be used with the countable noun *cases*.
- The noun *informations* is incorrect. The noun *information* can only be used as an uncountable noun and cannot be used as an countable noun *informations*, as it is here.

(D) **numerous peoples** of diverse origins and unrelated linguistic affiliations, though in **many** *cases* **researchers knew relatively little information about them**
- This answer contains the correct countable quantifier **numerous** used with the logical plural countable noun **peoples**, the correct countable quantifier **many** used with the countable noun *cases*, the correct uncountable noun **information**, and the correct object pronoun **them**, which refers to the object *peoples*. This answer is correct.

(E) *a great deal* of *people* of diverse origins and unrelated linguistic affiliations, though in many cases researchers knew relatively little information about *themselves*
- The uncountable quantifier *a great deal* is used incorrectly. An uncountable quantifier should not be used with the countable noun *people*.
- The noun *people* is used incorrectly. The countable plural noun *people* has an alternate plural form *peoples* with a different meaning (*people* = "a group of individuals" and *peoples* = "various cultures"). The meaning that fits into this context is the meaning of *peoples*.
- The reflexive pronoun *themselves* is used incorrectly. This reflexive pronoun should be used as an object only when it refers to the subject. Since the subject of the verb *knew* is *researchers* and not *people*, the reflexive pronoun *themselves* cannot be used.

3. **This question tests nouns, pronouns, and possessives.**

William Randolph Hearst's *parents purchased* the *San Francisco Examiner* for <u>*their* son to provide *him* with a voice when *he* ran for the U.S. Senate, something *he* did more to accede to *his* parents' wishes than for *himself*.</u>

(A) their son to provide him with a voice when he ran for the U.S. Senate, something *he* did more to accede to his parents' wishes than for himself.
  - This answer contains the correct form of the possessive **their**, the correct object pronoun **him** when the subject is *parents*, the correct form of the possessive **his**, and the correct reflexive pronoun **himself** when the subject is *he*. This answer also avoids the problem of the relative pronoun *which* referring to a complete idea by using **something**. This answer is correct.

(B) their son to provide himself with a voice when he ran for the U.S. Senate, something he did more to accede to his parents' wishes than for himself.
  - The reflexive pronoun himself is used incorrectly. This reflexive pronoun should be used as an object only when it refers to the subject. Since the subject of the verb *purchased* is *parents* and not *he*, the reflexive pronoun *himself* cannot be used.
  - The possessive his is incorrectly formed. The correct form of this possessive is *his*.

(C) theirs son to provide him with a voice when he ran for the U.S. Senate, something he did more to accede to his parents' wishes than for him.
  - The possessive theirs is incorrectly formed. The correct form of this possessive is *their*.
  - The possessive his is incorrectly formed. The correct form of this possessive is *his*.
  - The object pronoun him is used incorrectly. A reflexive pronoun should be used as an object when it refers to the subject. Since the subject is *he* and the object pronoun *him* refers to the subject, a reflexive pronoun should be used.

(D) their son to provide him with a voice *when he ran for the U.S. Senate*, which he did more to accede to his parents' wishes than for himself.
  - The relative pronoun which is used incorrectly. This relative pronoun should be used to refer to a specific noun and not to a complete idea such as *when he ran for the U.S. Senate*.

(E) their son to provide himself with a voice *when he ran for the U.S. Senate*, which he did more to accede to his parents' wishes than for him.
  - The reflexive pronoun himself is used incorrectly. This reflexive pronoun should be used as an object only when it refers to the subject. Since the subject of the verb *purchased* is *parents* and not *he*, the reflexive pronoun *himself* cannot be used.
  - The relative pronoun which is used incorrectly. This relative pronoun should be used to refer to a specific noun and not to a complete idea such as *when he ran for the U.S. Senate*.
  - The object pronoun him is used incorrectly. A reflexive pronoun should be used as an object when it refers to the subject. Since the subject is *he* and the object pronoun *him* refers to the subject, a reflexive pronoun should be used.

4. This question tests **nouns**, **pronouns**, and **possessives**.

It is ironic that lightning kills more *people* in the developed world and <u>less in the underdeveloped world since it is one of the forces of nature against which humans have some protections</u>.

(A) *less* in the underdeveloped world since it is one of the forces of nature against which humans have some *protections*
- The uncountable quantifier *less* is used incorrectly. An uncountable quantifier should not be used to refer to the countable noun *people*.
- The noun *protections* is used incorrectly. The noun *protection* can be countable or uncountable, and the countable *(protections = "acts to prevent injury or harm")* and uncountable *(some protection = "a state where injury or harm is prevented")* versions of this noun have different meanings. The meaning that fits into this context is the uncountable meaning, so the countable plural *protections* is incorrect.

(B) fewer in the underdeveloped world since it is one of the forces of nature against which humans have some protection
- This answer contains the correct countable quantifier **fewer**, the correct subject and verb **it is**, the correct plural noun **forces**, and the correct uncountable noun **protection**. This answer is correct.

(C) *less* in the underdeveloped world since *its* one of the forces of nature against which humans have some protection
- The uncountable quantifier *less* is used incorrectly. An uncountable quantifier should not be used to refer to the countable noun *people*.
- The possessive adjective *its* is used incorrectly. The possessive adjective *its* and the subject and verb *it's* should not be confused. In this situation the subject and verb *it's* is needed.

(D) fewer in the underdeveloped world since *its* one of the forces of nature against which humanity has some protection
- The possessive adjective *its* is used incorrectly. The possessive adjective *its* and the subject and verb *it's* should not be confused. In this situation the subject and verb *it's* is needed.

(E) fewer in the underdeveloped world since it's one of the few *force* against which humanity has some *protections*
- The noun *force* is used incorrectly. The noun *force* can be countable or uncountable, and the countable *(a force = "a specific power")* and uncountable *(some force = "a mass of strength or power")* versions of this noun have different meanings. The meaning that fits into this context is the countable plural meaning, so the uncountable *force* is incorrect.
- The noun *protections* is used incorrectly. The noun *protection* can be countable or uncountable, and the countable *(protections = "acts to prevent injury or harm")* and uncountable *(some protection = "a state where injury or harm is prevented")* versions of this noun have different meanings. The meaning that fits into this context is the uncountable meaning, so the countable plural *protections* is incorrect.

5. This question tests **nouns**, **pronouns**, and **possessives**.

The famous painting *Washington Crossing the Delaware* by Emanuel Leutze demonstrates a certain <u>number of artistic licenses, in items such as the boat, and this was</u> in reality much larger.

(A) *number of* artistic *licenses* in items such as the *boat*, and *this* was
- The countable quantifier *number of* is used incorrectly. The countable quantifier should not be used with what should be the uncountable noun *license*.
- The noun *licenses* is used incorrectly. The noun *license* can be countable or uncountable, and the countable *(a license* = "certificate granting permission"*)* and uncountable *(some license* = "intentional deviation from a rule"*)* versions of this noun have different meanings. The meaning that fits into this context is the uncountable meaning, so the countable plural *licenses* is incorrect.
- The pronoun *this* is used incorrectly. This pronoun refers to a complete idea, but a relative pronoun that can refer to the single noun *boat* is needed.

(B) amount of artistic license in items such as the boat, and *this* was
- The pronoun *this* is used incorrectly. This pronoun refers to a complete idea, but a relative pronoun that can refer to the single noun *boat* is needed.

(C) *number of* artistic *license* in items such as the boat, which was
- The countable quantifier *number of* is used incorrectly. This countable quantifier should not be used with the uncountable noun *license*.

(D) *amount of* artistic *licenses* in items such as the boat, which was
- The noun *licenses* is used incorrectly. The noun *license* can be countable or uncountable, and the countable *(a license* = "certificate granting permission"*)* and uncountable *(some license* = "intentional deviation from a rule"*)* versions of this noun have different meanings. The meaning that fits into this context is the uncountable meaning, so the countable plural *licenses* is incorrect. The countable plural *licenses* is also incorrect when used with the uncountable quantifier *amount of*.

(E) amount of artistic license in items such as the *boat*, which was
- This answer contains the correct uncountable quantifier **amount of** with the logical uncountable noun **license** and also correctly uses the relative pronoun **which** to refer to the noun *boat*. This answer is correct.

6. This question tests **nouns, pronouns**, and **possessives**.

On January 17, 1950, seven *men* dressed themselves in Halloween masks, drove themselves to Brinks headquarters, forced their way in, and stole millions of dollars, a robbery that put themselves in the headlines and provided themselves with notoriety for decades to come.

(A)   dressed themselves in Halloween masks, drove themselves to Brinks headquarters, forced their way in, and stole millions of dollars, a robbery that *put* themselves in the headlines and *provided* themselves
  - The reflexive pronoun themselves following *put* is used incorrectly. A reflexive pronoun should be used as an object only when it refers to the subject. Since the subject of the verb *put* is *that* (which refers to *robbery*) and not *men*, the reflexive pronoun *themselves* cannot be used following *put*.
  - The reflexive pronoun themselves following *provided* is used incorrectly. A reflexive pronoun should be used as an object only when it refers to the subject. Since subject of the verb *provided* is *that* (which refers to *robbery*) and not *men*, the reflexive pronoun *themselves* cannot be used following *provided*.

(B)   dressed themselves in Halloween masks, *drove* them to Brinks headquarters, forced their way in, and stole millions of dollars, a robbery that put them in the headlines and *provided* themselves
  - The object pronoun them following *drove* is used incorrectly. A reflexive pronoun should be used as an object when it refers to the subject. Since the subject of the verb *drove* is *men* and the object pronoun *them* refers to the subject, a reflexive pronoun should be used following *them*.
  - The reflexive pronoun themselves following *provided* is used incorrectly. A reflexive pronoun should be used as an object only when it refers to the subject. Since the subject of the verb *provided* is *that* (which refers to *robbery*) and not *men*, the reflexive pronoun *themselves* cannot be used following *provided*.

[(C)]   *dressed* themselves in Halloween masks, *drove* themselves to Brinks headquarters, forced their way in, and stole millions of dollars, a robbery that *put* them in the headlines and *provided* them
  - This answer contains the correct reflexive pronoun **themselves** as object of *dressed* and *drove* and the correct object pronoun **them** as object of *put* and *provided*. This answer is correct.

(D)   *dressed* them in Halloween masks, *drove* them to Brinks headquarters, forced their way in, and stole millions of dollars, a robbery that put them in the headlines and provided them
  - The object pronoun them following *dressed* is used incorrectly. A reflexive pronoun should be used as an object when it refers to the subject. Since the subject of the verb *drove* is *men* and the object pronoun *them* refers to the subject, a reflexive pronoun should be used following *dressed*.
  - The object pronoun them following *drove* is used incorrectly. A reflexive pronoun should be used as an object when it refers to the subject. Since the subject of the verb *drove* is *men* and the object pronoun *them* refers to the subject, a reflexive pronoun should be used following *them*.

(E)   dressed themselves in Halloween masks, drove themselves to Brinks headquarters, forced their way in, and stole millions of dollars, a robbery that *put* themselves in the headlines and provided them
  - The reflexive pronoun themselves following *put* is used incorrectly. A reflexive pronoun should be used as an object only when it refers to the subject. Since the subject of the verb *put* is *that* (which refers to *robbery*) and not *men*, the reflexive pronoun *themselves* cannot be used following *put*.

Lesson 2: Problems with AGREEMENT

> **Agreement** involves making sure that related items in a sentence match in terms of number (singular and plural) and gender (masculine and feminine). The most common types of agreement problems on the GMAT are problems related to number (singular and plural) in the following situations:
> 1. when a pronoun does not agree with the noun it refers to
> 2. when a possessive does not agree with the noun it refers to
> 3. when a noun does not agree with a noun that it logically should agree with
> 4. when a subject does not agree with a verb
> 5. when the subject is a relative pronoun *(who, which, that)* and the verb does not agree with the referent of the relative pronoun

EXAMPLE 1: This example shows a pronoun that does not agree with the noun it refers to.

INCORRECT:　The legislators had conflicting ideas on the *law* and had vigorous debates before voting on *them*.
CORRECT:　　The legislators had conflicting ideas on the *law* and had vigorous debates before voting on it.

In the incorrect example, the plural pronoun *them* is incorrect because it refers to the singular noun *law*. In the correct example, the singular pronoun **it** correctly refers to the singular noun *law*.

- -

EXAMPLE 2: This example shows a possessive that does not agree with the noun it refers to.

INCORRECT:　Each *animal* in the local zoo has a habitat appropriate to *their* lifestyle.
CORRECT:　　Each *animal* in the local zoo has a habitat appropriate to its lifestyle.

In the incorrect example, the plural possessive *their* is incorrect because it refers to the singular noun *animal*. In the correct example, the singular possessive **its** correctly refers to the singular noun *animal*.

- -

EXAMPLE 3: This example shows a noun that does not agree with a noun it logically should agree with.

INCORRECT: The teacher told the assembled *students* that they should take out their *textbook* and read Chapter 10.

CORRECT: The teacher told the assembled *students* that they should take out their **textbooks** and read Chapter 10.

In the incorrect example, the singular noun *textbook* does not make logical sense when it is used with the plural noun *students*. In the correct example, the plural noun **textbooks** does make logical sense when it is used with the plural noun *students*.

- -

EXAMPLE 4: This example shows a verb that does not agree with the subject.

INCORRECT: Of all the cars in the lot, only *one* of the latest models *have* all the features that buyers require.

CORRECT: Of all the cars in the lot, only *one* of the latest models **has** all the features that buyers require.

In the incorrect example, the plural verb *have* does not agree with the singular subject *one*. In the correct example, the singular verb **has** does agree with the singular subject *one*.

- -

EXAMPLE 5: This example shows a verb that does not agree with the referent of the relative pronoun subject.

INCORRECT: Hunter Medical Center is constructing several new *buildings* in the current location *that is going* to improve the center's ability to serve the community.

CORRECT: Hunter Medical Center is constructing several new *buildings* in the current location *that* **are going** to improve the center's ability to serve the community.

In the incorrect example, the singular verb *is going* does not agree with the relative pronoun subject *that*, which refers to the plural noun *buildings*. In the correct example, the plural verb **are going** does agree with the relative pronoun subject *that*, which refers to the plural noun *buildings*.

SKILLS PRACTICE: Find the problems with **agreement** in the following sentences. (The number in parentheses indicates the number of problems you should find.) Then, study the explanations on the pages that follow.

1. A healthy spine has three gentle curves that makes them resilient and ensures a balanced center of gravity. *(3)*

2. Believing that beards and long hair were too easy to grab, Alexander the Great ordered all of his troops to shave their face and head. *(2)*

3. Because Romance languages, which are a descendant of Vulgar Latin, has remained in close contact over the centuries, its subgroups are more difficult to identify than the subgroups of the Germanic language is. *(4)*

4. In order to produce electrical nerve impulses, neurons must be triggered by a stimulus, which are anything inside or outside the body that evoke a physical or psychological response. *(2)*

5. Spain's wealth from their American colonies from the 15th century to the end of the 18th century remained mostly in the hands of the aristocracy and the monarchy and were not effective in creating a merchant class with any political power. *(2)*

6. Pottery fragments, or a potsherd, serves as a major key in dating a lost culture and in reconstructing their living and trading patterns. *(3)*

7. To escape the worst effects of bad weather, big algae grows offshore beyond the line of breaking waves, but even there it is vulnerable to wave damage. *(2)*

8. Andorra is a tiny country in the Pyrenees mountains which have no income taxes and allow foreign nationals to hold "passive residential status" if it spends 183 days per year in country, place a deposit of 21,000 Euros in the national bank, and pay an annual levy of 6,024 Euros. *(4)*

EXPLANATIONS (I = incorrect, C = correct)

1. A healthy *spine* has three gentle *curves that* makes them resilient and ensures a balanced center of gravity.

   - The singular verb *makes* does not agree with the subject *that*, which refers to the plural noun *curves*.
     - I: *makes*
     - C: **make**

   - The plural pronoun *them* does not agree with the singular noun *spine*.
     - I: *them*
     - C: **it**

   - The singular verb *ensures* does not agree with the subject *that*, which refers to the plural noun *curves*.
     - I: *ensures*
     - C: **ensure**

- -

2. Believing that *beards* and long hair were too easy to grab, Alexander the Great ordered all of his *troops* to shave their face and head.

   - The singular noun *face* does not make sense when used with the plural nouns *beards* and *troops*.
     - I: *face*
     - C: **faces**

   - The singular noun *head* does not make sense when used with the plural nouns *beards* and *troops*.
     - I: *head*
     - C: **heads**

- -

3. Because Romance *languages*, which are a descendant of Vulgar Latin, has remained in close contact over the centuries, its subgroups are more difficult to identify than the *subgroups* of the Germanic language is.

   - The singular noun *descendant* does not make sense when used with the plural noun *languages*.
     - I: *a descendant*
     - C: **descendants**

   - The singular verb *has* does not agree with the plural subject *languages*.
     - I: *has*
     - C: **have**

   - The singular possessive *its* does not agree with the plural noun *languages*, to which it refers.
     - I: *its*
     - C: **their**

Lesson 2: Problems with AGREEMENT

- The singular verb *is* does not agree with the plural subject *subgroups*.
    - I: *is*
    - C: **are**

- -

4. In order to produce electrical nerve impulses, neurons must be triggered by a *stimulus, which are* anything inside or outside the *body that evoke* a physical or psychological response.

    - The plural verb *are* does not agree with the subject *which*, which refers to the singular noun *stimulus*.
        - I: *are*
        - C: **is**

    - The plural verb *evoke* does not agree with the subject *that*, which refers to the singular noun *body*.
        - I: *evoke*
        - C: **evokes**

- -

5. *Spain's wealth* from *their* American colonies from the 15th century to the end of the 18th century remained mostly in the hands of the aristocracy and the monarchy and *were* not effective in creating a merchant class with any political power.

    - The plural possessive *their* does not agree with the singular noun *Spain*, to which it refers.
        - I: *their*
        - C: **its**

    - The plural verb *were* does not agree with the singular subject *wealth*.
        - I: *were*
        - C: **was**

- -

6. Pottery *fragments*, or a *potsherd*, *serves* as a major key in dating a lost *culture* and in reconstructing *their* living and trading patterns.

    - The singular noun *potsherd* does not make sense when used with the plural noun *fragments*.
        - I: *a potsherd*
        - C: **potsherd**
    - The singular verb *serves* does not agree with the plural subject *fragments*.
        - I: *serves*
        - C: **serve**

    - The plural possessive *their* does not agree with the singular noun *culture*, to which it refers. To correct this error, you can change *their* to *its*.
        - I: *their*

          C: **its**

- -

7.   To escape the worst effects of bad weather, big *algae* |grows| offshore beyond the line of breaking waves, but even there |it is| vulnerable to wave damage.

   • The singular verb *grows* does not agree with the plural subject *algae*.
          I: *grows*
          C: **grow**

   • The singular subject and verb |it is| does not agree with the plural noun *algae*.
          I: *it is*
          C: **they are**

- -

8.   Andorra is a tiny *country* in the Pyrenees mountains *which* |have| no income taxes and |allow| foreign *nationals* to hold "passive residential status" if |it spends| 183 days per year in country, place *a* |deposit| of 21,000 Euros in the national bank, and pay *an annual levy* of 6,024 Euros.

   • The plural verbs |have| and |allow| do not agree with the subject *which*, which refers to the singular noun *country*.
          I: *have...allow*
          C: **has...allows**

   • The singular subject and verb |it spends| does not agree with the plural noun *nationals*.
          I: *it spends*
          C: **they spend**

   • The singular noun |deposit| does not make sense when used with the plural noun *nationals*.
          I: *a deposit*
          C: **deposits**

   • The singular noun |levy| does not make sense when used with the plural noun *nationals*.
          I: *an annual levy*
          C: **annual levies**

Lesson 2: Problems with AGREEMENT

GMAT-STYLE SKILLS PRACTICE: Choose the letter of the answer to each question that best reflects the style and accuracy of standard written English. Then, study the explanations on the pages that follow.

1. From an early age, herring perfect the art of synchronized swimming because <u>they depend upon them for its survival</u>.

    (A) they depend on them for its survival
    (B) they depend on it for their survival
    (C) they depend on it for its survival
    (D) it depends on them for its survival
    (E) it depends on it for their survival

2. <u>A bat's wings are a membrane of skin that link their enormously long fingers with the hind legs.</u>

    (A) A bat's wings are a membrane of skin that link their enormously long fingers with the hind legs.
    (B) A bat's wings are membranes of skin that links its enormously long finger with the hind leg.
    (C) Bats' wings are membranes of skin that links its enormously long fingers with the hind legs.
    (D) Bats' wings are a membrane of skin that link their enormously long finger with the hind leg.
    (E) Bats' wings are membranes of skin that link their enormously long fingers with the hind legs.

3. The extra blood in those who live at high altitudes consist primarily of red corpuscles, which carry the hemoglobin needed to absorb oxygen.

   (A) those who live at high altitudes consist primarily of red corpuscles, which carry
   (B) those who lives at high altitudes consist primarily of red corpuscles, which carry
   (C) those who live at high altitudes consists primarily of red corpuscles, which carry
   (D) those who lives at high altitudes consists primarily of red corpuscles, which carries
   (E) those who live at high altitudes consists primarily of red corpuscles, which carries

4. Instead of using bats or rackets, ancient Chinese of the Han Dynasty played a version of badminton using their feet to kick the shuttlecock.

   (A) bats or rackets, ancient Chinese of the Han Dynasty played a version of badminton using their feet
   (B) bats or rackets, ancient Chinese of the Han Dynasty played a version of badminton using his feet
   (C) bats or rackets, ancient Chinese of the Han Dynasty played a version of badminton using his foot
   (D) a bat or racket, ancient Chinese of the Han Dynasty played a version of badminton using their feet
   (E) a bat or racket, ancient Chinese of the Han Dynasty played a version of badminton using his foot

5. Patronymics, or last names derived from the father's first name, was widely employed in Scandinavian countries for centuries; fathers would pass his first name on to his sons, to which -*sen* in Denmark and Norway and -*son* in Sweden were added.

    (A) last names derived from the father's first name, was widely employed in Scandinavian countries for centuries; fathers would pass their first names on to their sons
    (B) a last name derived from the father's first name, were widely employed in Scandinavian countries for centuries; fathers would pass their first names on to their sons
    (C) last names derived from fathers' first names, was widely employed in Scandinavian countries for centuries; fathers would pass his first name on to his sons
    (D) last names derived from fathers' first names, were widely employed in Scandinavian countries for centuries; fathers would pass their first names on to their sons
    (E) a last name derived from the father's first name, were widely employed in Scandinavian countries for centuries; fathers would pass his first name on to his sons

6. An individual's personal values and morals and the social context in which it occurs determine whether a particular behavior is seen as ethical or unethical.

    (A) it occurs determine
    (B) they occur determine
    (C) it occurs determines
    (D) they occur determines
    (E) it occur determine

EXPLANATIONS

1. This question tests **agreement**.

   From an early age, *herring* perfect the art of synchronized *swimming* because they depend upon them for its survival.

(A) they depend on *them* for *its* survival
   - The plural pronoun *them* does not agree with the singular noun *swimming*, to which it refers.
   - The singular possessive *its* does not agree with the plural noun *herring*, to which it refers.

(B) they depend on it for their survival
   - This answer contains the correct plural pronoun **they** to refer to *herring*, the correct singular pronoun **it** to refer to *swimming*, and the correct plural possessive **their** to refer to *herring*. This answer is correct.

(C) they depend on it for *its* survival
   - The singular possessive *its* does not agree with the plural noun *herring*, to which it refers.

(D) *it* depends on *them* for *its* survival
   - The singular pronoun *it* does not agree with the plural noun *herring*, to which it refers.
   - The plural pronoun *them* does not agree with the singular noun *swimming*, to which it refers.
   - The singular possessive *its* does not agree with the plural noun *herring*, to which it refers.

(E) *it* depends on it for their survival
   - The singular pronoun *it* does not agree with the plural noun *herring*, to which it refers

2. This question tests **agreement**.

A bat's wings are a membrane of skin that link their enormously long fingers with the hind legs.

(A) A *bat*'s *wings* are a *membrane* of skin that link *their* enormously long fingers with the hind legs.
  - The singular noun *membrane* does not make sense when used with the plural noun *wings*.
  - The plural possessive *their* does not agree with the singular noun *bat*, to which it refers.

(B) A *bat*'s *wings* are membranes of skin that *links* its enormously long *finger* with the hind *leg*.
  - The singular verb *links* does not agree with the subject *that*, which refers to the plural noun *membranes*.
  - The singular nouns *finger* and *leg* do not make sense when used with the noun *bat* because a bat would logically have more than one finger and more than one leg.

(C) Bats' wings are *membranes* of skin *that links* its enormously long fingers with the hind legs.
  - The singular verb *links* does not agree with the subject *that*, which refers to the plural noun *membranes*.

(D) Bats' *wings* are a *membrane* of skin that link their enormously long *finger* with the hind *leg*.
  - The singular noun *membrane* does not make sense when used with the plural noun *wings*.
  - The singular nouns *finger* and *leg* do not make sense when used with the noun *bats* because a bat would logically have more than one finger and more than one leg.

(E) Bats' *wings* are membranes of skin *that* link their enormously long fingers with the hind legs.
  - This answer has the logical plural noun **membranes** to accompany *wings*, the correct plural verb **link** to agree with the subject *that*, which refers to *membranes*, and the logical plural nouns **fingers** and **legs**, which refer to the noun *bats*. This answer is correct.

3. This question tests **agreement**.

The extra *blood* in those who live at high altitudes consist primarily of red corpuscles, which carry the hemoglobin needed to absorb oxygen.

(A) those who live at high altitudes *consist* primarily of red corpuscles, which carry
  • The plural verb *consist* does not agree with the singular subject *blood*.

(B) *those who lives* at high altitudes *consist* primarily of red corpuscles, which carry
  • The singular verb *lives* does not agree with the subject *who*, which refers to the plural pronoun *those*.
  • The plural verb *consist* does not agree with the singular subject *blood*.

(C) *those who* live at high altitudes consists primarily of red *corpuscles, which* carry
  • This answer contains the correct plural verb **live** to agree with the subject *who*, which refers to the plural pronoun *those*, the correct singular verb **consists** to agree with the singular subject *blood*, and the correct plural verb **carry** to agree with the subject *which*, which refers to the plural noun *corpuscles*. This answer is correct.

(D) *those who lives* at high altitudes consists primarily of red *corpuscles, which carries*
  • The singular verb *lives* does not agree with the subject *who*, which refers to the plural pronoun *those*.
  • The singular verb *carries* does not agree with the subject *which*, which refers to the plural noun *corpuscles*.

(E) those who live at high altitudes consists primarily of red *corpuscles, which carries*
  • The singular verb *carries* does not agree with the subject *which*, which refers to the plural noun *corpuscles*.

4. This question tests **agreement**.

   Instead of using <u>bats or rackets, ancient Chinese of the Han Dynasty played a version of badminton using their feet</u> to kick the shuttlecock.

   (A) bats or rackets, ancient *Chinese* of the Han Dynasty played a version of badminton using their feet
   - This answer contains the logical plural nouns **bats** or **rackets** to accompany the plural noun *Chinese,* the correct plural possessive **their** to refer to the plural noun *Chinese,* and the logical plural noun **feet** to accompany the plural noun *Chinese*. This answer is correct.

   (B) bats or rackets, ancient *Chinese* of the Han Dynasty played a version of badminton using *his* feet
   - The singular possessive *his* does not agree with the plural noun *Chinese*, to which it refers.

   (C) bats or rackets, ancient *Chinese* of the Han Dynasty played a version of badminton using *his* *foot*
   - The singular possessive *his* does not agree with the plural noun *Chinese*, to which it refers.
   - The singular noun *foot* does not make sense when used with the plural noun *Chinese*.

   (D) *a bat or racket*, ancient *Chinese* of the Han Dynasty played a version of badminton using their feet
   - The singular nouns *a bat or racket* do not make sense when used with the plural noun *Chinese*.

   (E) *a bat or racket*, ancient *Chinese* of the Han Dynasty played a version of badminton using *his* *foot*
   - The singular nouns *a bat or racket* do not make sense when used with the plural noun *Chinese*.
   - The singular possessive *his* does not agree with the plural noun *Chinese*, to which it refers.
   - The singular noun *foot* does not make sense when used with the plural noun *Chinese*.

5. This question tests **agreement**.

    Patronymics, or last names derived from the father's first name, was widely employed in Scandinavian countries for centuries; fathers would pass his first name on to his sons, to which *-sen* in Denmark and Norway and *-son* in Sweden were added.

(A) last *names* derived from |the father's first name|, |was| widely employed in Scandinavian countries for centuries; fathers would pass their first names on to their sons
- The singular nouns in the expression |the father's first name| do not make sense when used with the plural nouns *Patronymics* and *names*.
- The singular verb |was| does not agree with the plural subject *Patronymics*.

(B) |a last name| derived from |the father's first name|, were widely employed in Scandinavian countries for centuries; fathers would pass their first names on to their sons
- The singular nouns in the expressions |a last name| and |the father's first name| do not make sense when used with the plural noun *Patronymics*.

(C) last names derived from fathers' first names, |was| widely employed in Scandinavian countries for centuries; fathers would pass |his| first |name| on to |his| sons
- The singular verb |was| does not agree with the plural subject *Patronymics*.
- The singular possessives |his| and |his| do not agree with the plural noun *fathers*, which they refer to.
- The singular noun |name| does not make sense when used with the plural noun *fathers*.

(D) last names derived from fathers' first names, were widely employed in Scandinavian countries for centuries; fathers would pass their first names on to their sons
- This answer contains the correct plural nouns in the expressions **last names** and **fathers' first names** to agree with the plural noun *Patronymics*, the correct plural verb **were** to agree with the plural subject *Patronymics*, the correct singular possessives *their* and *their* to agree with the plural noun *fathers*, and the correct plural noun *names* to agree with the plural noun *fathers*. This answer is correct.

(E) |a last name| derived from |the father's first name|, were widely employed in Scandinavian countries for centuries; fathers would pass |his| first |name| on to |his| sons
- The singular nouns in the expressions |a last name| and |the father's first name| do not make sense when used with the plural noun *Patronymics*.
- The singular possessives |his| and |his| do not agree with the plural noun *fathers*, which they refer to.
- The singular noun |name| does not make sense when used with the plural noun *fathers*.

6. This question tests **agreement**.

An individual's personal *values and morals* and the social context in which it occurs determine whether a particular behavior is seen as ethical or unethical.

(A) it occurs determine
- The singular pronoun *it* does not agree with the plural nouns in the expression *values and morals*. If *it* is changed to *they*, then the singular verb *occurs* is also incorrect.

(B) they occur determine
- This answer contains the correct plural pronoun **they** to refer to *values and morals*, the correct plural verb **occur** to agree with the subject *they*, and the correct plural verb **determine** to agree with the plural subject *values and morals*. This answer is correct.

(C) it occurs determines
- The singular pronoun *it* does not agree with the plural nouns in the expression *values and morals*. If *it* is changed to *they*, then the singular verb *occurs* is also incorrect.
- The singular verb *determines* does not agree with the plural subject *values and morals*.

(D) they occur determines
- The singular verb *determines* does not agree with the plural subject *values and morals*.

(E) it occur determine
- The singular pronoun *it* does not agree with the plural nouns *values and morals*.
- The plural verb *occur* does not agree with the singular subject *it*.

Lesson 3: Problems with PARALLELISM

> **Parallelism** involves making expressions as similar in structure as possible whenever these expressions are found in situations that require the expressions to be parallel. Expressions must be parallel -- as similar in structure as possible -- in the following situations:
> 1. when two expressions are joined with a coordinate conjunction such as *and, but, or*
> 2. when a series of expressions are in a list with commas and *and* (__, __, and __) or a list with comas and *or* (__, __, or __)
> 3. when expressions follow paired conjunctions such as *both...and (also), either...or, neither...nor, not only...but (also)*

EXAMPLE 1: This example shows two expressions joined with a coordinate conjunction.

INCORRECT: The senator prefers *to meet* with his constituents *and* then *spending* time with journalists.
CORRECT: The senator prefers *to meet* with his constituents *and* then **to spend** time with journalists.

In the incorrect example, the gerund *spending* is not parallel to the infinitive *to meet*, which means that these two expressions are not as similar in structure as possible. The coordinate conjunction *and* indicates that these two expression s should be parallel. In the correct example, the infinitive **to spend** is parallel to *to meet*, and the conjunction *and* indicates that they should be parallel.

- -

EXAMPLE 2: This example shows a series of expressions in a list.

INCORRECT: The passengers can travel to Venice *by plane, by train, or they can choose to travel by boat*.
CORRECT: The passengers can travel to Venice *by plane, by train, or* by boat.

In the incorrect example, the clause *they can choose to travel by boat* is not parallel to the two prepositional phrases *by plane* and *by train*, which means that these expressions are not as similar in structure as possible. The list joined with commas and the coordinate conjunction *or* (__, __, or __) indicates that they should be parallel. In the correct example, **by boat** is parallel to *by plane* and *by train*, and the conjunction *or* and the commas indicates that these three expressions should be parallel.

EXAMPLE 3: This example shows expressions following a paired conjunction.

INCORRECT: The newspaper article was *not only ridiculously biased but also* it was surprisingly inaccurate.
CORRECT: The newspaper article was *not only ridiculously biased but also* surprisingly inaccurate.

In the incorrect example, the clause *it was surprisingly inaccurate* is not parallel to the adjective phrase *ridiculously biased*, which means that these two expressions are not as similar in structure as possible. The paired conjunction *not only...but also* indicates that they should be parallel. In the correct example, the parallel expressions **surprisingly inaccurate** is parallel to *ridiculously biased,* and the paired conjunction *not only...but also* indicates that these two expressions should be parallel.

SKILLS PRACTICE: Find the problems with **parallelism** in the following sentences. (The number in parentheses indicates the number of problems you should find.) Then, study the explanations on the pages that follow.

1. Effective vision not only descends from above in an organization but also it comes from a considerable amount of exploring, analyzing, and to root around in the territory of the problem. *(2)*

2. The Eskimo not only make but they also use wooden "eyeglasses" with only narrow slits for eyepieces both to protect their eyes from glare reflected by ice and snow and also from harsh Arctic winds. *(2)*

3. The Hundred Years' War was neither a continuous, unbroken war nor did it last for only a hundred years; instead, it started in 1337 and ending in 1453, culminating with the expulsion of the English from France. *(2)*

4. The Minuet, originally a beloved peasant dance of Poitou but later a dance that was renowned at the court, was introduced to Paris in 1650, set to music by Jean-Baptiste Lully, and King Louis XIV danced it in full view of the court. *(2)*

5. The best periods of time for allergy sufferers to go outside are either right after it rains or after sunset on hotter, drier, and windy days. *(2)*

6. Environmental scanning as it is used in business is a process of gathering, analyze, and dispense information not only to improve strategic understanding and to maximize tactical effectiveness. *(2)*

7. Prince Henry the Navigator was given this moniker not because of his voyages of exploration but the institute for captains, navigators, builders of ships, and geographers that he ran in in Portugal. *(2)*

8. The magnitude of a tornado's rotation, its complexity, and how severe its effect is on atmospheric pressure account for not only the destructiveness of tornadoes and also the pranks they play. *(2)*

EXPLANATIONS (I = incorrect, C = correct)

1. Effective vision *not only descends from above* in an organization *but also it comes from* a considerable amount of *exploring, analyzing, and to root* around in the territory of the problem.

   - The expression *it comes from* is not parallel to *descends from above*. The structure *not only...but also* indicates that these expressions should be parallel.
     - I: *it comes from*
     - C: **comes from**

   - The expression *to root* is not parallel to *exploring* and *analyzing*. The structure with commas and *and* (___, ___, and ___) indicates that these expressions should be parallel.
     - I: *to root*
     - C: **rooting**

   -

2. The Eskimo *not only make but they also use* wooden "eyeglasses" with only narrow slits for eyepieces *both to protect their eyes* from glare reflected by ice and snow *and also from harsh Arctic winds*.

   - The expression *they...use* is not parallel to *make*. The structure *not only...but...also* indicates that these expressions should be parallel.
     - I: *but they also use*
     - C: **but also use**

   - The expression *from harsh Arctic winds* is not parallel to *to protect their eyes*. The structure *both...and also* indicates that these expressions should be parallel.
     - I: *from harsh Arctic winds*
     - C: **to protect their eyes from harsh Arctic winds**

   -

3. The Hundred Years' War was *neither a continuous, unbroken war* nor *did it last for only a hundred years*; instead, it *started* in 1337 and *ending* in 1453, culminating with the expulsion of the English from France.

   - The expression *did it last for only a hundred years* is not parallel to *a continuous, unbroken war*. The structure *neither...nor* indicates that these expressions should be parallel.
     - I: *did it last for only a hundred years*
     - C: **only a century-long war**

- The expression *ending* is not parallel to *started*. The structure *and* indicates that these expressions should be parallel.
    - I: *ending*
    - C: **ended**

- -

4. The Minuet, *originally a beloved peasant dance* of Poitou but *later a dance that was renowned* at the court, was *introduced to Paris* in 1650, *set to music* by Jean-Baptiste Lully, and *King Louis XIV danced it* in full view of the court.

    - The expression *later a dance that was renowned* is not parallel to *originally a beloved peasant dance*. The structure *but* indicates that these expressions should be parallel.
        - I: *later a dance that was renowned*
        - C: **later a renowned dance**

    - The expression *King Louis XIV danced it* is not parallel to *introduced to Paris* and *set to music*. The structure with commas and *and* (___, ___, and ___) indicates that these expressions should be parallel.
        - I: *King Louis IV danced it*
        - C: **danced by King Louis XIV**

- -

5. The best periods of time for allergy sufferers to go outside are *either right after it rains or* *after sunset* on *hotter, drier, and* *windy* days.

    - The expression *after sunset* is not parallel to *right after it rains*. The structure *either...or* indicates that these expressions should be parallel.
        - I: *after sunset*
        - C: **after the sun sets**

    - The expression *windy* is not parallel to *hotter* and *drier*. The structure ___, ___, and ___ indicates that these expressions should be parallel.
        - I: *windy*
        - C: **windier**

- -

6. Environmental scanning as it is used in business is a process of *gathering,* *analyze*, *and* *dispense* information *not only* to improve strategic understanding *and* to maximize tactical effectiveness.

- The expressions *analyze* and *dispense* are not parallel to *gathering*. The structure with commas and *and* (___, ___, and ___) indicates that these expressions should be parallel.
    - I: *analyze, and dispense*
    - C: **analyzing, and dispensing**

- *Not only...and* is an incorrect paired conjunction. *But (also)* and not *and*, must be used with *not only*.
    - I: *and*
    - C: **but (also)**

- -

7. Prince Henry the Navigator was given this moniker *not because of his voyages* of exploration *but* *the institute* for captains, navigators, *builders of ships*, *and* geographers that he ran in in Portugal.

- The expression *the institute* is not parallel to *because of his voyages*. The structure *not...but* indicates that these expressions should be parallel.
    - I: *the institute*
    - C: **because of the institute**

- The expression *builders of ships* is not parallel to *captains, navigators,* and *geographers*. The structure with commas and *and* (___, ___, ___, and ___) indicates that these expressions should be parallel.
    - I: *builders of ships*
    - C: **shipbuilders**

- -

8. The magnitude of *a tornado's rotation, its complexity, and* *how severe its effect is* on atmospheric pressure account for *not only* the destructiveness of tornadoes *and* *also* the pranks they play.

- The expression *how severe its effect is* is not parallel to *a tornado's rotation* and *its complexity*. The structure with commas and *and* (___, ___, and ___) indicates that these expressions should be parallel.
    - I: *how severe its effect is*
    - C: **its severe effect**

- *Not only...and also* is an incorrect paired conjunction. *But (also)*, and not *and*, must be used with *not only*.
    - I: *and also*
    - C: **but (also)**

GMAT-STYLE SKILLS PRACTICE: Choose the letter of the answer to each question that best reflects the style and accuracy of standard written English. Then, study the explanations on the pages that follow.

1. Regression analysis is useful not only for explaining relationships among variables of interest but also for predicting desired results.

    (A) for explaining relationships among variables
    (B) to explain the relationships among variables
    (C) for the explaining of the relationships among variables
    (D) the explanation of variable relationships
    (E) for the explanation of the variability of relationships

2. Marketing is the process of planning and executing the conception, pricing, promoting, and distribution of ideas, goods, and services to satisfy both individual as well as organizational objectives.

    (A) planning and executing the conception, pricing, promoting, and distribution of ideas, goods, and services to satisfy both individual as well as organizational objectives
    (B) planning and executing the conception, price, promotion, and distribution of ideas, goods, and services to satisfy both individual and organizational objectives
    (C) planning and executing the conceiving, pricing, promotion, and distribution of ideas, goods, and services to satisfy both individual and organization pricing
    (D) planning and execute the conception, price, promotion, and distribution of ideas, goods, and services in order to satisfy both individual objectives and organizational objectives
    (E) planning and executing the conception, price, promoting, and distributing of ideas, goods, and services to satisfy both individual or organizational objectives

Lesson 3: Problems with PARALLELISM

3. Starbucks was started in Seattle in 1971, not as a coffee house where prepared drinks could be purchased but as a shop for purchasing premium roasted coffee beans by the pound.

   (A) as a coffee house where prepared coffee drinks could be purchased
   (B) to be used as a coffee house for purchasing prepared coffee drinks
   (C) with the intent to use it as a coffee house where one could purchase prepared coffee drinks
   (D) to be used as a coffee house where the company could sell prepared coffee drinks
   (E) as a coffee house for purchasing prepared coffee drinks

4. The largest components of holding costs for most companies are the cost of space to store the inventory and the cost of tying up capital in inventory, capital that could be useful either in obtaining additional assets or in paying off debt.

   (A) the cost of space to store the inventory and the cost of tying up capital in inventory, capital that could be useful either in obtaining additional assets or in paying off debt
   (B) the cost of space for storing the inventory and that of using capital to finance the inventory, capital that could be used either to obtain additional assets or to pay off debt
   (C) the cost of space for storing the inventory and the cost of capital for financing the inventory, capital that could be used either in obtaining additional assets or paying off debt
   (D) the cost of space to store the inventory and the cost of capital to finance the inventory, capital that could be used either in obtaining additional assets or to pay off debts
   (E) the cost of space to store the inventory and the cost of capital to finance the inventory, capital that could be used either to obtain additional assets or to pay off debt

Lesson 3: Problems with PARALLELISM

5. Vowel sounds differ from consonant sounds in that they are produced not by blocking air in its passage from the lungs but by passing air through different shapes of the mouth and positions of the tongue and lips that are different.

   (A) by passing air through different shapes of the mouth and positions of the tongue and lips that are different
   (B) they pass air through different shapes of the mouth and different positions of the tongue and lips
   (C) by passing air through different shapes of the mouth and different positions of the tongue and lips
   (D) passing air through different shapes of the mouth and different positions of the tongue and lips
   (E) by passing air through different shapes of the mouth and with the tongue and lips in different positions

6. Written by Chinese general Sun Tzu in the 6th century BC, *The Art of War* is a military strategy book that, for managerial purposes, recommends awareness of and acting on strengths and weaknesses of both a manager's organization and a foe's.

   (A) awareness of and acting on strengths and weaknesses of both a manager's organization or a foe's
   (B) being aware of and acting on the strengths and weaknesses both of a manager's organization and a foe's
   (C) being aware and taking action on strengths and the weaknesses of both the organization of a manager and a foe's
   (D) being aware of and acting on strengths and weaknesses of both a manager's organization and a foe's
   (E) awareness of and action on the strengths and weaknesses of both a manager's organization and that of a foe's

EXPLANATIONS

1. This question tests **parallelism**.

   Regression analysis is useful *not only* for explaining relationships among variables of interest *but also for predicting desired results.*

   (A) for explaining relationships among variables
   - This answer contains the expression **for explaining relationships**, which is parallel to the expression *for predicting desired results*. The paired conjunction *not only...but also* indicates that these two expressions should be parallel. This answer is correct.

   (B) to explain the relationships among variables
   - The expression *to explain* is not parallel to *for predicting*. The structure *not only...but also* indicates that these expressions should be parallel.

   (C) for the explaining of the relationships among variables
   - The expression *for the explaining of* is not parallel to *for predicting*. The structure *not only...but also* indicates that these expressions should be parallel.

   (D) the explanation of variable relationships
   - The expression *the explanation of* is not parallel to *for predicting*. The structure *not only...but also* indicates that these expressions should be parallel.

   (E) for the explanation of the variability of relationships
   - The expression *for the explanation of* is not parallel to *for predicting*. The structure *not just...but also* indicates that these expressions should be parallel.

2. This question tests **parallelism**.

Marketing is the process of <u>planning and executing the conception, pricing, promoting, and distribution of ideas, goods, and services to satisfy both individual as well as organizational objectives.</u>

(A) planning and executing the *conception, pricing, promoting, and distribution* of ideas, goods, and services to satisfy *both* individual *as well as* organizational objectives
- The expressions *pricing* and *promoting* are not parallel to *conception* and *distribution*. The structure with commas and *and* (___, ___, ___, and ___) indicates that these expressions should be parallel.
- *Both...and* is a paired conjunction. *And*, and not *as well as*, must be used with *both*.

(B) planning and executing the conception, price, promotion, and distribution of ideas, goods, and services to satisfy *both* individual *and* organizational objectives
- This answer has the parallel expressions **conception, price, promotion**, and **distribution** in the structure with commas and *and* (___, ___, ___, and ___) and the parallel expressions **individual** and **organizational** following *both* and *and*. This answer is correct.

(C) planning and executing the *conceiving, pricing,* promotion, and distribution of ideas, goods, and services to satisfy both *individual* and *organization* pricing
- The expressions *conceiving* and *pricing* are not parallel to *promotion* and *distribution*. The structure with commas and *and* (___, ___, ___, and ___) indicates that these expressions should be parallel.
- The expression *organization* is not parallel to *individual*. The structure *both...and* indicates that these expressions should be parallel.

(D) *planning and execute* the conception, price, promotion, and distribution of ideas, goods, and services in order to satisfy both individual objectives and organizational objectives
- The expression *execute* is not parallel to *planning*. The structure *and* indicates that these expressions should be parallel.

(E) planning and executing the *conception, price, promoting, and distributing* of ideas, goods, and services to satisfy *both* individual *or* organizational objectives
- The expressions *promoting* and *distributing* are not parallel to *conception* and *price*. The structure with commas and *and* (___, ___, ___, and ___) indicates that these expressions should be parallel.
- *Both...and* is a paired conjunction. *And*, and not *or*, must be used with *both*.

3. This question tests **parallelism**.

Starbucks was started in Seattle in 1971, *not as a coffee house where prepared drinks could be purchased but as a shop for purchasing premium roasted coffee beans* by the pound.

(A) as a coffee house *where prepared coffee drinks could be purchased*
- The expression *where prepared coffee drinks could be purchased* is not parallel to *for purchasing premium roasted coffee beans*. The structure *not...but* indicates that these expressions should be parallel.

(B) *to be used as a coffee house* for purchasing prepared coffee drinks
- The expression *to be used as a coffee house* is not parallel to *as a shop*. The structure *not...but* indicates that these expressions should be parallel.

(C) *with the intent to use it as a coffee house where one could purchase prepared coffee drinks*
- The expression *with the intent to use it as a coffee house* is not parallel to *as a shop*. The structure *not...but* indicates that these expressions should be parallel.
- The expression *where one could purchase prepared coffee drinks* is not parallel to *for purchasing premium roasted coffee beans*. The structure *not...but* indicates that these expressions should be parallel.

(D) *to be used as a coffee house where the company could sell prepared coffee drinks*
- The expression *to be used as a coffee house* is not parallel to *as a shop*. The structure *not...but* indicates that these expressions should be parallel.
- The expression *where the company could sell prepared coffee drinks* is not parallel to *for purchasing premium roasted coffee beans*. The structure *not...but* indicates that these expressions should be parallel.

(E) as a coffee house for purchasing prepared coffee drinks
- This answer contains the expression **as a coffee house for purchasing prepared coffee drinks**, which is parallel to *as a shop for purchasing premium roasted coffee beans*. The structure *not...but* indicates that these expressions should be parallel. This answer is correct.

4. This question tests **parallelism**.

The largest components of holding costs for most companies are <u>the cost of space to store the inventory and the cost of tying up capital in inventory, capital that could be useful either in obtaining additional assets or in paying off debt</u>.

(A) *the cost of space to store the inventory and the cost of tying up capital in inventory, capital that could be useful either in obtaining additional assets or in paying off debt*
- The expression *the cost of tying up capital in inventory* is not parallel to *the cost of space to store the inventory*. The structure *and* indicates that these expressions should be parallel.

(B) *the cost of space for storing the inventory and that of using capital to finance the inventory, capital that could be used either to obtain additional assets or to pay off debt*
- The expression *that of using capital to finance the inventory* is not parallel to *the cost of space for storing the inventory*. The structure *and* indicates that these expressions should be parallel.

(C) the cost of space for storing the inventory and the cost of capital for financing the inventory, capital that could be used *either* in obtaining additional assets *or* paying off debt
- The expression *paying off debt* is not parallel to *in obtaining additional assets*. The structure *either...or* indicates that these expressions should be parallel.

(D) the cost of space to store the inventory and the cost of capital to finance the inventory, capital that could be used *either in obtaining additional assets or* to pay off debts
- The expression *to pay off debts* is not parallel to *in obtaining additional assets*. The structure *either...or* indicates that these expressions should be parallel.

(E) the cost of space to store the inventory *and* the cost of capital to finance the inventory, capital that could be used *either* to obtain additional assets *or* to pay off debt
- This answer contains the parallel expressions **the cost of space to store** and **the cost of capital to finance** connected with *and*. It also contains the parallel expressions **to obtain** and **to pay off** following *either* and *or*. This answer is correct.

5. This question tests **parallelism**.

Vowel sounds differ from consonant sounds in that they are produced *not by blocking air* in its passage from the lungs *but* by passing air through different shapes of the mouth and positions of the tongue and lips that are different.

(A) by passing air through *different shapes of the mouth and positions of the tongue and lips that are different*
- The expression *positions of the tongue and lips that are different* is not parallel to *different shapes of the mouth*. The structure *and* indicates that these expressions should be parallel.

(B) *they pass air* through different shapes of the mouth and different positions of the tongue and lips
- The expression *they pass air* is not parallel to *by blocking air*. The structure *not...but* indicates that these expressions should be parallel.

(C) by passing air through different shapes of the mouth and different positions of the tongue and lips
- This answer contains **by passing air**, which is parallel to *by blocking air*. The structure *not...but* indicates that they should be parallel. This answer also contains the parallel expressions **different shapes of the mouth** and **different positions of the tongue and lips** connected with *and*. This answer is correct.

(D) *passing air* through different shapes of the mouth and different positions of the tongue and lips
- The expression *passing air* is not parallel to *by blocking air*. The structure *not...but* indicates that these expressions should be parallel.

(E) by passing air through *different shapes of the mouth and* with the tongue and lips in different positions
- The expression *with the tongue and lips in different positions* is not parallel to *different shapes of the mouth*. The structure *and* indicates that these expressions should be parallel.

6. This question tests **parallelism**.

   Written by Chinese general Sun Tzu in the 6th century BC, *The Art of War* is a military strategy book that, for managerial purposes, recommends awareness of and acting on strengths and weaknesses of both a manager's organization and *a foe's*.

(A) *awareness of and* acting on *strengths and weaknesses of both* a manager's organization or *a foe's*
   - The expression acting on is not parallel to *awareness of*. The structure *and* indicates that these expressions should be parallel.
   - *Both...and* is a paired conjunction. *And*, and not or, must be used with *both*.

(B) being aware of and acting on the strengths and weaknesses both of a manager's organization and *a foe's*
   - The expression of a manager's organization is not parallel to *a foe's* because of the preposition *of* preceding *manager's*. The structure *both...and* indicates that these expressions should be parallel.

(C) being aware and taking action on strengths and the weaknesses of both the organization of a manager and *a foe's*
   - The expression being aware is not parallel to *taking action on* because of the missing preposition *of* following *aware*. The structure *and* indicates that these expressions should be parallel.
   - The word strengths is not parallel to *the weaknesses*. The structure *and* indicates that these expressions should be parallel.
   - The expression the organization of a manager is not parallel to *a foe's*. The structure *both...and* indicates that these expressions should be parallel.

(D) being aware of and acting on strengths and weaknesses of both a manager's organization and a foe's
   - This answer contains the parallel expressions **being aware of** and **acting on** connected with *and*, the parallel expressions **strengths** and **weaknesses** connected with *and*, and the parallel expressions *a manager's organization* and *a foe's* following *both* and *and*. This answer is correct.

(E) awareness of and action on the strengths and weaknesses of both a manager's organization and that of a foe's
   - The expression a manager's organization is not parallel to *that of a foe's*. The structure *both...and* indicates that these expressions should be parallel.

Lesson 4: Problems with COMPARISONS

Comparisons involve showing how two or more things are similar or dissimilar. Problems with comparisons generally occur in the following situations on the GMAT:
1. when incorrect forms of comparatives are used
2. when comparative adjectives and adverbs are confused
3. when comparative pairs *(as...as, more...than, -er...than)* are used incorrectly
4. when comparative pairs lack parallelism
5. when expressions following *like* or *unlike* lack parallelism
6. when *different* is used to make a comparison

EXAMPLE 1: This example shows two incorrectly formed comparatives.

INCORRECT: This house is *more big* than the last one, but its location is *worser*.
CORRECT: This house is **bigger** than the last one, but its location is **worse**.

In the incorrect example, the comparatives *more big* and *worser* are formed incorrectly. *Big* is a one-syllable adjective that forms its comparative with *-er* rather than *more*, and *worse* is an irregularly formed comparative of *bad*. In the correct example, the correctly formed comparatives **bigger** and **worse** are used.

- -

EXAMPLE 2: This example shows confusion between a comparative adjective and a comparative adverb.

INCORRECT: The athlete *completed* the race five seconds *quicker* this time than last time.
CORRECT: The athlete *completed* the race five seconds **more quickly** this time than last time.

In the incorrect example, the comparative adjective *quicker* is used to describe the verb *completed*, and a comparative adverb is needed in this situation. In the correct example, the comparative adverb **more quickly** is used to describe the verb *completed*.

- -

EXAMPLE 3: This example shows an incorrectly used comparative pair.

INCORRECT: Your house is not *as* expensive *than* mine.
CORRECT: Your house is not as expensive as mine.

In the incorrect example, the incorrect comparative pair *as...than* is used. In the correct example, the comparative pair **as...as** is correctly used.

- -

EXAMPLE 4: This example shows a comparative pair that lacks parallelism.

INCORRECT: *Your actions* are *more* important *than what you say*.
CORRECT: *Your actions* are *more* important *than* your words.

In the incorrect example, the expression *what you say* is not parallel to the expression *Your actions*. The comparative pair *more...than* indicates that they should be parallel. In the correct example, the expressions **your words** is parallel to *your actions*.

- -

EXAMPLE 5: This example shows expressions following *like* that lack parallelism.

INCORRECT: *Like some of the other students*, *an extra assignment* must be completed by Sally.
CORRECT: *Like some of the other students*, Sally is required to complete an extra assignment.

In the incorrect example, the expression *an extra assignment* is not parallel to the expression *some of the other students*. The word *Like* indicates that they should be parallel. In the correct example, the expressions **Sally** and *some of the other students* are parallel.

- -

EXAMPLE 6: This example shows *different* used incorrectly in a comparison.

INCORRECT: The conclusions in their report were *different than* those in mine.
CORRECT: The conclusions in their report were different from those in mine.

In the incorrect example, the expression *different than* is used in a comparison. While the expression *different than* is commonly used in comparisons, the stylistic preference on GMAT is for the expression *different from*. In the correct example, the stylistically preferred expression **different from** is used.

SKILLS PRACTICE: Find the problems with **comparisons** in the following sentences. (The number in parentheses indicates the number of problems you should find.) Then, study the explanations on the pages that follow.

1. Many species of animals have communication systems that are much more complex as one might imagine but still appear to be very different than human language. *(2)*

2. Unlike a negative balance of trade, economists generally view a positive balance of trade favorably since the value of a country's exports is greater than that of its imports and new money flows into the country from the greater value of its exports. *(1)*

3. At the beginning of the sixteenth century the Incan Empire extended more than 2,600 miles along western South America and was one of the largest states in the world, only slightly smaller than the size of China. *(1)*

4. One of the unresolved puzzles of prehistory is why people in Europe did not produce pottery vessels much earlier that they did; they understood how to make clay figures hard as stone by firing them in ovens as early as 32,000BCE, yet it was not until 7,000BCE that they began making vessels using the same technique. *(2)*

5. The hedge fund manager explained to her protégé that he was not as confident as he needed to be and that he needed to act bolder if he wanted to be taken more seriously then he currently was. *(2)*

6. A more recent study done by researchers at Duke University was just as newsworthy as, if not more newsworthy as the previous study. *(1)*

7. As people become more and more old, strokes are usually associated with advanced atherosclerosis or prolonged high blood pressure, while in young people stokes are more likely to result from defects present at birth as from the diseases that generally cause them in the elderly. *(2)*

8. Crack cocaine is created through a different chemical process than powdered cocaine, one that causes the high from crack cocaine to be more strong, immediate, and short than powdered cocaine. *(3)*

EXPLANATIONS (I = incorrect, C = correct)

1. Many species of animals have communication systems that are much *more* complex *as* one might imagine but still appear to be very *different than* human language.

    - The comparative *more* should be completed with *than* rather than *as*.
        - I: *much more complex*
        - C: **much more complex than**

    - The comparative expression *different than* is considered stylistically unacceptable. The stylistic preference is for *different from*.
        - I: *different than*
        - C: **different from**

    -

2. *Unlike a negative balance of trade, economists* generally view a positive balance of trade favorably since the value of a country's exports is greater than that of its imports and new money flows into the country from the greater value of its exports.

    - The word *economists* is not parallel to the expression *a negative balance of trade*. The comparative *Unlike* indicates that they should be parallel.
        - I: *economists generally view a positive balance of trade favorably*
        - C: **a positive balance of trade is generally viewed favorably by economists**

    -

3. At the beginning of the sixteenth century *the Incan Empire* extended more than 2,600 miles along western South America and was one of the largest states in the world, *only slightly smaller than the size of China*.

    - The expression *the size of China* is not parallel to the expression *the Incan Empire*. The comparison *only slightly smaller than* indicates that they should be parallel.
        - I: *the size of China*
        - C: **the Chinese Empire**

    -

4. One of the unresolved puzzles of prehistory is why people in Europe did not produce pottery vessels *much earlier that* they did; they understood how to make clay figures *hard as* stone by firing them in ovens as early as 32,000BCE, yet it was not until 7,000BCE that they began making vessels using the same technique.

- The comparative *much earlier* should be completed with *than* rather than *that*.
    - I: *much earlier that*
    - C: **much earlier than**

- *As...as* is a comparative pair. *As* is required preceding *hard as*.
    - I: *hard as*
    - C: **as hard as**

- -

5. The hedge fund manager explained to her protégé that he was not as confident as he needed to be and that he needed *to act bolder* if he wanted to be taken *more seriously then* he currently was.

- The comparative adjective *bolder* cannot be used to modify the verb *to act*. A comparative adverb is needed to modify a verb.
    - I: *bolder*
    - C: **more boldly**

- The comparative *more seriously* should be completed with *than* rather than *then*.
    - I: *more seriously then*
    - C: **more seriously than**

- -

6. A more recent study done by researchers at Duke University was just as newsworthy as, if not *more newsworthy as* the previous study.

- The comparative *more newsworthy* should be completed with *than* rather than *as*.
    - I: *more newsworthy as*
    - C: **more newsworthy than**

- -

7. As people become *more and more old*, strokes are usually associated with advanced atherosclerosis or prolonged high blood pressure, while in young people stokes are *more likely* to result from defects present at birth *as* from the diseases that generally cause them in the elderly.

- The comparative *more and more old* is incorrectly formed. The comparative of a one-syllable word should be formed with *-er* rather than *more*.
    - I: *more and more old*
    - C: **older and older**

- The comparative *more likely* should be completed with *than* rather than *as*.
    - I: *more likely...as*
    - C: **more likely...than**

- -

8. Crack cocaine is created through a *different* chemical process *than* powdered cocaine, one that causes *the high from crack cocaine* to be *more strong, immediate, and short* than *powdered cocaine*.

- The comparative expression *different...than* is considered stylistically unacceptable. The stylistic preference is for *different...from*.
    - I: *a different chemical process than*
    - C: **a different chemical process from**

- The comparatives *more strong* and *more...short* are incorrectly formed. Comparative forms of one-syllable words should be formed with *-er* rather than *more*.
    - I: *more strong, immediate, and short*
    - C: **stronger, more immediate, and shorter**

- The expression *powdered cocaine* is not parallel to the expression *the high from crack cocaine*. The comparisons *more strong, immediate, and short* (corrected to *stronger, more immediate, and shorter*) indicate that they should be parallel.
    - I: *powdered cocaine*
    - C: **the high from powdered cocaine**

GMAT-STYLE SKILLS PRACTICE: Choose the letter of the answer that best reflects the style and accuracy of standard written English. Then, study the explanations on the pages that follow.

1. More of Mozart's compositions are in active use today <u>than any other composer</u> in history, with the possible exception of J.S. Bach.

    (A) than any other composer
    (B) as of any other composer's works
    (C) than of any other composer's works
    (D) as the works of any other composer
    (E) than is any other composer

2. Unlike adjectives in Modern English, <u>adjectives in Old English were inflected</u> for gender, number, and case to agree with their head noun.

    (A) adjectives in Old English were inflected
    (B) an adjective in Old English was inflected
    (C) Old English had adjectives that were inflected
    (D) an Old English adjective with inflection
    (E) the inflection of Old English adjectives was

3. In an average year more people are killed by falling coconuts than are killed when sharks bite.

    (A) than are killed when sharks bite
    (B) as are killed when sharks bite
    (C) as are killed by sharks when they bite
    (D) than are killed by shark bites
    (E) as are killed by shark bites

4. In order to lift the upper arm away from the trunk quicker, the anterior and posterior sections of the deltoid muscle balance each other out, while the middle sector works harder and harder to carry out the work.

    (A) quicker, the anterior and posterior sections of the deltoid muscle balance each other out, while the middle sector works harder and harder
    (B) quicker, the anterior and posterior sections of the deltoid muscle balance each other out, while the middle sector works more and more hard
    (C) more quickly, the anterior and posterior sections of the deltoid muscle balance each other out, while the middle sector works more and more harder
    (D) more quickly, the anterior and posterior sections of the deltoid muscle balance each other out, while the middle sector works more and more hard
    (E) more quickly, the anterior and posterior sections of the deltoid muscle balance each other out, while the middle sector works harder and harder

5. Although the distinction between inns and taverns was sometimes blurred in the Middle Ages, inns were different than taverns in that inns offered lodging to their customers and inns were generally larger in size and served customers of a more elite class as taverns.

    (A) than taverns in that inns offered lodging to their customers and inns were generally larger in size and served customers of a more elite class as
    (B) than taverns in that inns offered lodging to their customers and inns were generally larger in size and served customers of a more elite class than
    (C) from taverns in that inns offered lodging to their customers and inns were generally larger in size and served customers of a more elite class than
    (D) from taverns in that inns offered lodging to their customers and inns were generally more large in size and served customers of a more elite class as
    (E) from taverns in that inns offered lodging to their customers and inns were generally more large in size and served customers of a more elite class than

6. Like many other entrepreneurs, when war with England came in 1812, the conflict was seen by eighteen-year-old Cornelius Vanderbilt as a giant opportunity, one that allowed him to do quite well transporting army supplies along the Hudson River and ferrying food to a blockaded New York City.

    (A) when war with England came in 1812, the conflict was seen by eighteen-year-old Cornelius Vanderbilt as a giant opportunity,
    (B) the conflict with England that started in 1812 was viewed by eighteen-year-old Cornelius Vanderbilt as a giant opportunity,
    (C) the giant opportunity provided to eighteen-year-old Cornelius Vanderbilt when war with England came in 1812 was
    (D) the conflict with England that started in 1812 provided an opportunity to eighteen-year-old Cornelius Vanderbilt,
    (E) eighteen-year-old Cornelius Vanderbilt viewed the 1812 war with England as a giant opportunity,

EXPLANATIONS

1. This question tests **comparisons**.

    More of Mozart's compositions are in active use today <u>than any other composer</u> in history, with the possible exception of J.S. Bach.

(A) than *any other composer*
   - The expression *any other composer* is not parallel to *of Mozart's compositions*. The comparative structure *More...than* indicates that these expressions should be parallel.

(B) *as* of any other composer's works
   - The comparative *More* should be completed with *than* rather than *as*.

(C) than of any other composer's works
   - This answer contains **than** to complete the comparative pair *more...than*, and *than* is followed by the expression **of any other composer's works**, which is parallel to the expression *of Mozart's compositions* that follows *More*. This answer is correct.

(D) *as the works of any other composer*
   - The comparative *more* should be completed with *than* rather than *as*.
   - The expression *the works of any other composer* is not parallel to *of Mozart's compositions*. The comparative structure *More...as* (should be *than*) indicates that these expressions should be parallel.

(E) than *is any other composer*
   - The expression *is any other composer* is not parallel to *of Mozart's compositions*. The comparative structure *More...than* indicates that these expressions should be parallel.

2. This question tests **comparisons**.

Unlike adjectives in Modern English, adjectives in Old English were inflected for gender, number, and case to agree with their head noun.

(A) adjectives in Old English were inflected
- This answer contains the expression **adjectives in Old English**, which is parallel to the expression *adjectives in Modern English*. The comparative structure *Unlike* indicates that these expressions should be parallel. This answer is correct.

(B) an adjective in Old English was inflected
- The expression *an adjective in Old English* is not parallel to *adjectives in Modern English*. The comparative structure *Unlike* indicates that these expressions should be parallel.

(C) Old English had adjectives that were inflected
- The expression *Old English had adjectives* is not parallel to *adjectives in Modern English*. The comparative structure *Unlike* indicates that these expressions should be parallel.

(D) an Old English adjective with inflection
- The expression *an Old English adjective* is not parallel to *adjectives in Modern English*. The comparative structure *Unlike* indicates that these expressions should be parallel.

(E) the inflection of Old English adjectives was
- The expression *the inflection of Old English adjectives* is not parallel to *adjectives in Modern English*. The comparative structure *Unlike* indicates that these expressions should be parallel.

3. This question tests **comparisons**.

In an average year *more people are killed by falling coconuts* than are killed when sharks bite.

(A) than *are killed when sharks bite*
- The expression *are killed when sharks bite* is not parallel to *are killed by falling coconuts*. The comparative structure *more...than* indicates that these expressions should be parallel.

(B) as *are killed when sharks bite*
- The comparative *more people* should be completed with *than* rather than *as*.
- The expression *are killed when sharks bite* is not parallel to *are killed by falling coconuts*. The comparative structure *more...as* (should be *than*) indicates that these expressions should be parallel.

(C) as *are killed by sharks when they bite*
- The comparative *more people* should be completed with *than* rather than *as*.
- The expression *are killed by sharks when they bite* is not parallel to *are killed by falling coconuts*. The comparative structure *more...as* (should be *than*) indicates that these expressions should be parallel.

(D) than *are killed by shark bites*
- This answer contains **than** to complete the comparative pair *more...than*, and *than* is followed by the expression **are killed by shark bites**, which is parallel to the expression *are killed by falling coconuts* that follows *more*. This answer is correct.

(E) as are killed by shark bites
- The comparative *more people* should be completed with *than* rather than *as*.

4. This question tests **comparisons**.

In order *to lift* the upper arm away from the trunk quicker, the anterior and posterior sections of the deltoid muscle balance each other out, while the middle sector works harder and harder to carry out the work.

(A) quicker, the anterior and posterior sections of the deltoid muscle balance each other out, while the middle sector works harder and harder
  - The comparative adjective quicker cannot be used to modify the verb *to lift*. A comparative adverb *more quickly* is needed to modify a verb.

(B) quicker, the anterior and posterior sections of the deltoid muscle balance each other out, while the middle sector works more and more hard
  - The comparative adjective quicker cannot be used to modify the verb *to lift*. A comparative adverb *more quickly* is needed to modify a verb.
  - The comparative form of a one-syllable word such as *hard* in the expression more and more hard should be formed with -er (harder) rather than more to create the expression *harder and harder*.

(C) more quickly, the anterior and posterior sections of the deltoid muscle balance each other out, while the middle sector works more and more harder
  - The comparative form of a one-syllable word such as *hard* in the expression more and more harder should be formed with -er (harder) rather than both *more* and -er to create the expression *harder and harder*.

(D) more quickly, the anterior and posterior sections of the deltoid muscle balance each other out, while the middle sector works more and more hard
  - The comparative form of a one-syllable word such as *hard* in the expression more and more hard should be formed with -er (harder) rather than more to create the expression *harder and harder*.

(E) more quickly, the anterior and posterior sections of the deltoid muscle balance each other out, while the middle sector works harder and harder
  - This answer contains the correct comparative adverb **more quickly** and the correctly formed comparative **harder and harder**. This answer is correct.

5. This question tests **comparisons**.

Although the distinction between inns and taverns was sometimes blurred in the Middle Ages, inns were *different than taverns in that inns offered lodging to their customers and inns were generally larger in size and served customers of a more elite class as* taverns.

(A) *than* taverns in that inns offered lodging to their customers and inns were generally *larger* in size and served customers of a more elite class *as*
- The comparative expression *different than* is considered stylistically unacceptable. The stylistic preference is for *different from*.
- The comparative *larger* should be completed with *than* rather than *as*.

(B) *than* taverns in that inns offered lodging to their customers and inns were generally larger in size and served customers of a more elite class than
- The comparative expression *different than* is considered stylistically unacceptable. The stylistic preference is for *different from*.

(C) *from* taverns in that inns offered lodging to their customers and inns were generally *larger* in size and served customers of a more elite class *than*
- This answer has the stylistically preferred *different from* and the correct comparative form *larger* completed correctly with *than*. This answer is correct.

(D) from taverns in that inns offered lodging to their customers and inns were generally *more large* in size and served customers of a more elite class *as*
- The comparative form of a one-syllable word such as *large* should be formed with *-er (larger)* rather than *more*.
- The comparative *more large (larger)* should be completed with *than* rather than *as*.

(E) from taverns in that inns offered lodging to their customers and inns were generally *more large* in size and served customers of a more elite class than
- The comparative form of a one-syllable word such as *large* should be formed with *-er (larger)* rather than *more*.

6. This question tests **comparisons**.

    Like many other entrepreneurs, <u>when war with England came in 1812, the conflict was seen by eighteen-year-old Cornelius Vanderbilt as a giant opportunity,</u> one that allowed him to do quite well transporting army supplies along the Hudson River and ferrying food to a blockaded New York City.

(A) when war with England came in 1812, *the conflict* was seen by eighteen-year-old Cornelius Vanderbilt as a giant opportunity,
  - The expression *the conflict* is not parallel to the expression *many other entrepreneurs*. The comparison *Like* indicates that they should be parallel.

(B) *the conflict* with England that started in 1812 was viewed by eighteen-year-old Cornelius Vanderbilt as a giant opportunity,
  - The expression *the conflict* is not parallel to the expression *many other entrepreneurs*. The comparison *Like* indicates that they should be parallel.

(C) *the giant opportunity* provided to eighteen-year-old Cornelius Vanderbilt when war with England came in 1812 was
  - The expression *the giant opportunity* is not parallel to the expression *many other entrepreneurs*. The comparison *Like* indicates that they should be parallel.

(D) *the conflict* with England that started in 1812 provided an opportunity to eighteen-year-old Cornelius Vanderbilt,
  - The expression *the conflict* is not parallel to the expression *many other entrepreneurs*. The comparison *Like* indicates that they should be parallel.

(E) eighteen-year-old Cornelius Vanderbilt viewed the 1812 war with England as a giant opportunity,
  - This answer contains the expression **eighteen-year-old Cornelius Vanderbilt**, which is parallel to the expression *many other entrepreneurs*. The comparison *Like* indicates that they should be parallel. This answer is correct.

Lesson 5: Problems with VERBS

> **Verbs** are words that show action or state of being. There are numerous verb tenses in English and therefore many, many potential problems with verbs. The problems with verbs that occur most often on the GMAT are the following:
> 1. the switch from the past to the present for no logical reason
> 2. the misuse of the present perfect tense (*have* + the past participle or *has* + the past participle)
> 3. the misuse of the past perfect tense (*had* + the past participle)
> 4. the incorrect use of simple past and past participle forms
> 5. the misuse of verb tenses in *if* sentences
> 6. the misuse of verb tenses with the expression *so that*

EXAMPLE 1: This example shows an illogical switch from the past to the present.

INCORRECT: I *knew* exactly what you are doing.
CORRECT: I *knew* exactly what you were doing.

In the incorrect example, the sentence switches illogically from the past *knew* to the present are doing. It is possible to use the past and the present together if the meaning is logical (i.e. *I know what you did*). However, the switch in tenses here is not logical. In the correct example, the present *knew* is logically used with the past **were doing**.

- -

EXAMPLE 2: This example shows a misused present perfect tense.

INCORRECT: The researcher has completely finished the economic report *yesterday*.
CORRECT: The researcher completely finished the economic report *yesterday*.

In the incorrect example, the present perfect tense has...finished is used incorrectly with the time word *yesterday*. The present perfect tense is often used to show an action that occurred sometime between the past and the present and cannot be used correctly with a time word such as *yesterday* that indicates the past only. In the correct example, the simple past tense **finished** is used correctly with *yesterday*.

- -

EXAMPLE 3: This example shows a misused past perfect tense.

INCORRECT: By the time the curtain *had fallen*, the entire audience *had left*.
CORRECT: By the time the curtain **fell**, the entire audience *had left*.

In the incorrect example, the past perfect tense *had fallen* is used incorrectly. The past perfect tense is used when one past action occurs prior to another, and in this case the audience *had left* prior to when the curtain *fell*. In the correct example, the simple past tense **fell** and is used correctly with the past perfect tense *had left* to show that the audience *had left* prior to the when the curtain *fell*.

- -

EXAMPLE 4: This example shows confusion between the past participle and the simple past tense.

INCORRECT: After the tanker hit a large iceberg, it *sunk*.
CORRECT: After the tanker hit a large iceberg, it **sank**.

In the incorrect example, the past participle *sunk* is used where the simple past tense is needed. In the correct example, the simple past tense **sank** is correctly used.

- -

EXAMPLE 5: This example shows a misused verb tense in an *if* sentence.

INCORRECT: *If* the man *would have remembered* the location, he would not have been late.
CORRECT: *If* the man **had remembered** the location, he would not have been late.

In the incorrect example, the conditional perfect tense *would have remembered* is used as the verb in the clause directly following *if*. A conditional tense with *would* is never used in a clause directly following *if*. In the correct example, the conditional perfect tense *would have remembered* has been replaced with the past perfect tense **had remembered**.

- -

EXAMPLE 6: This example shows misused verb tenses with the expression *so that*.

INCORRECT: The group needs to work harder on the project *so that* it *is coming* out on top.
CORRECT: The group needs to work harder on the project *so that* it **will come** out on top.

In the incorrect example, the incorrect verb tense *is coming* is used following *so that*. The verb following *so that* should indicate a desired result rather than an actual result, but the verb *is coming* indicates an actual result. In the correct example, the desired result **will come** out on top follows *so that*.

SKILLS PRACTICE: Find the problems with **verbs** in the following sentences. (The number in parentheses indicates the number of problems you should find.) Then, study the explanations on the pages that follow.

1. Scholars disagree about where Odysseus went on his voyages and which locations in Homer's tome on Odysseus are mythical rather than real. *(1)*

2. The most successful of the seabed fish, such as the monkfish, are flat and camouflaged so that they are not seen by predators or prey. *(1)*

3. As soon as the circus clown sprung out of his hiding place, the frightened children shrunk against their parents in fear; had the clown knew the effect of his actions, he would never have did what he done. *(5)*

4. According to the mythology of the Aborigines of Australia, the stars and constellations are ancestors who had ascended into the sky and are spending their afterlives sitting around campfires, some of which burn more brightly than others. *(1)*

5. The Ashanti War in 1824 would have turned out better for the British forces if the British military would have actually packed boxes of reserve ammunition instead of what turned out to be boxes of biscuits. *(1)*

6. Educators who formerly had to instruct students in the use of technological equipment so that their students will be proficient in its use now find that their students are "digital natives," who were using computers from the time they were toddlers and had little need for instruction in the use of technology today. *(3)*

7. Founded in 1325 and lain out on islands in the middle of a vast lake, Tenochtitlan evolved into a metropolis of some 200,000 people, far bigger than the largest European city of its day, by the time Spanish conquistadors had first laid eyes on it in 1519. *(3)*

8. The belief that all natural phenomena are explainable by physical laws became fashionable among scientists in the 17th century; as a result, since then mystical ideas lost much of their importance in natural philosophy, and chemistry has became an accepted scientific discipline. *(2)*

EXPLANATIONS (I = incorrect, C = correct)

1. Scholars *disagree* about where Odysseus *went* on his voyages and which locations in Homer's tome on Odysseus *are* mythical rather than real.

   - The simple present tense *are* is used incorrectly. The sentence contains the present tense *disagree*, the simple past tense *went*, and the simple present tense *are*. It is possible to use the past and present tenses together in a sentence if the meaning is logical, but the meaning here is not logical.
     - I: are
     - C: **were**

   -

2. The most successful of the seabed fish, such as the monkfish, *are* flat and camouflaged *so that* they *are not seen* by predators or prey.

   - The present tense *are not seen* is used incorrectly. Because the verb *are* preceding *so that* is in the present tense, the verb following *so that*, *are not seen*, should be in the future *(will)* tense to indicate a desired result.
     - I: are not seen
     - C: **will not be seen**

   -

3. As soon as the circus clown *sprung* out of his hiding place, the frightened children *shrunk* against their parents in fear; had the clown *knew* the effect of his actions, he would never have *did* what he *done*.

   - The form of the verb *sprung* is incorrect. *Sprung* is a past participle and is not the simple past tense.
     - I: sprung
     - C: **sprang**

   - The form of the verb *shrunk* is incorrect. *Shrunk* is a past participle and is not the simple past tense.
     - I: shrunk
     - C: **shrank**

   - The form of the verb *knew* is incorrect. *Knew* is the simple past tense and is not the past participle.
     - I: knew
     - C: **known**

   - The form of the verb *did* is incorrect. *Did* is the simple past tense and is not the past participle.
     - I: did
     - C: **done**

   - The form of the verb *done* is incorrect. *Done* is a past participle and is not the simple past tense.

I: *done*
C: **did**

---

4. According to the mythology of the Aborigines of Australia, the stars and constellations *are* ancestors who *had ascended* into the sky and are spending their afterlives sitting around campfires, some of which burn more brightly than others.

    - The past perfect tense *had ascended* is used incorrectly. The past perfect tense should be used when one past action is completed prior to another. The present tense *are* indicates that this past action was not prior to another past action.
        I: *had ascended*
        C: **have ascended**

---

5. The Ashanti War in 1824 would have turned out better for the British forces *if* the British military *would have* actually *packed* boxes of reserve ammunition instead of what turned out to be boxes of biscuits.

    - The conditional perfect tense *would have...packed* following *if* is used incorrectly. A conditional tense with *would* is never used in a clause directly following *if*.
        I: *would have...packed*
        C: **had...packed**

---

6. Educators who formerly *had* to instruct students in the use of technological equipment *so that* their students *will be* proficient in its use now *find* that their students are "digital natives," who *were using* computers *from the time they were toddlers* and *have* little need for instruction in the use of technology.

    - The future tense *will be* is used incorrectly. Because the verb *had* preceding *so that* is in the simple past tense, the verb following *so that*, *will be*, should be in the conditional *(would)* tense to indicate a desired result.
        I: *will be*
        C: **would be**

    - The past progressive tense *were using* is used incorrectly. Because the expression *from the time they were toddlers* indicates a period of time from the past to the present, the verb associated with this expression, *were using*, should be in the present perfect tense and not the simple past tense.
        I: *were using*
        C: **have been using**

    - The simple past tense *had* is used incorrectly. The sentence contains the present tense verb *find* and the simple past tense *had*. It is possible to use the past and present tenses together in a sentence if the meaning is logical, but the meaning here is not logical.

I: had
C: **has**

---

7. Founded in 1325 and *lain* out on islands in the middle of a vast lake, Tenochtitlan *evolved* into a metropolis of some 200,000 people, far bigger than the largest European city of its day, *by the time* Spanish conquistadors *had* first *laid* eyes on it in 1519.

    - The form of the verb *lain* is incorrect. *Lain* is the past participle of the verb *lie*, and the past participle of the verb *lay* is required.
        I: *lain*
        C: **laid**

    - The simple past tense *evolved* is incorrect. The time expression *by the time* indicates that this past action was completed prior to another past action and that the past perfect tense is required.
        I: *evolved*
        C: **had evolved**

    - The past perfect tense *had...laid* is used incorrectly. The past perfect tense should be used when one past action is completed prior to another. The time expression *by the time* indicates that this past action was not prior to another action.
        I: *had...laid*
        C: **laid**

---

8. The belief that all natural phenomena are explainable by physical laws became fashionable among scientists in the 17th century; as a result, *since* then mystical ideas *lost* much of their importance in natural philosophy, and chemistry *has* *became* an accepted scientific discipline.

    - The simple past tense *lost* is used incorrectly. Because the time expression *since* indicates a period of time from the past to the present, the main verb *lost* should be in the present perfect tense and not the simple past tense.
        I: *lost*
        C: **have lost**

    - The form of the verb *became* is incorrect. *Became* is the simple past tense and is not the past participle, which is required following *has*.
        I: *became*
        C: **become**

It Works! GMAT Sentence Correction

GMAT-STYLE SKILLS PRACTICE: Choose the letter of the answer to each question that best reflects the style and accuracy of standard written English. Then, study the explanations on the pages that follow.

1. Since people had begun to write some 5,000 years ago, they have kept records on a variety of materials, including clay or wax tablets, pieces of broken pottery, papyrus, animals skins, and finally paper.

    (A) had begun to write some 5,000 years ago, they have kept
    (B) begun to write some 5,000 years ago, they kept
    (C) began to write some 5,000 years ago, they have kept
    (D) began to write some 5,000 years ago, they kept
    (E) had begun to write some 5,000 years ago, they kept

2. When Harvard College was constructed in 1636, it was surrounded by a tall stockade so that its inhabitants would be protected from wolves and hostile natives, an edifice that, not surprisingly, no longer exists.

    (A) was constructed in 1636, it was surrounded by a tall stockade so that its inhabitants would be protected from wolves and hostile natives, an edifice that, not surprisingly, no longer exists
    (B) was constructed in 1636, it was surrounded by a tall stockade so that its inhabitants were protected from wolves and hostile natives, an edifice that, not surprisingly, no longer exists
    (C) was constructed in 1636, it was surrounded by a tall stockade so that its inhabitants would be protected from wolves and hostile natives, an edifice that, not surprisingly, no longer existed
    (D) had been constructed in 1636, it was surrounded by a tall stockade so that its inhabitants were protected from wolves and hostile natives, an edifice that, not surprisingly, no longer exists
    (E) had been constructed in 1636, it was surrounded by a tall stockade so that its inhabitants would be protected from wolves and hostile natives, an edifice that, not surprisingly, no longer existed

3. The presidential campaign of 1920 was the first in which women could vote, and the results might have been different if candidate Warren Harding had not been so welcoming to female voters and his wife Florence would have taken a less prominent role in the campaign.

    (A) had not been so welcoming to female voters and his wife Florence would have taken
    (B) would not have been so welcoming to female voters and his wife Florence would have had
    (C) would not have been so welcoming to female voters and his wife Florence had taken
    (D) had not been so welcoming to female voters and his wife Florence would have had
    (E) had not been so welcoming to female voters and his wife Florence had taken

4. As the Great Influenza pandemic made its way around the world in 1918, millions of people were struck with a debilitating form of the disease; by the time the pandemic ran its course, somewhere between twenty and forty million people died worldwide.

    (A) struck with a debilitating form of the disease; by the time the pandemic ran its course, somewhere between twenty and forty million people died
    (B) struck with a debilitating form of the disease; by the time the pandemic had run its course, somewhere between twenty and forty million people had died
    (C) stricken with a debilitating form of the disease; by the time the pandemic had run its course, somewhere between twenty and forty million people had died
    (D) stricken with a debilitating form of the disease; by the time the pandemic ran its course, somewhere between twenty and forty million people died
    (E) stricken with a debilitating form of the disease; by the time the pandemic ran its course, somewhere between twenty and forty million people had died

5. In Szechwan province thousands of years ago, the Chinese were using natural gas for lighting by bringing gas that has formed in rock salt 1600 feet underground to the surface through bamboo pipes so that they illuminated their homes.

   (A) were using natural gas for lighting by bringing gas that has formed in rock salt 1600 feet underground to the surface through bamboo pipes so that they illuminated
   (B) were using natural gas for lighting by bringing gas that formed in rock salt 1600 feet underground to the surface through bamboo pipes so that they illuminated
   (C) have been using natural gas for lighting by bringing gas that formed in rock salt 1600 feet underground to the surface through bamboo pipes so that they could illuminate
   (D) were using natural gas for lighting by bringing gas that formed in rock salt 1600 feet underground to the surface through bamboo pipes so that they could illuminate
   (E) have been using natural gas for lighting by bringing gas that has formed in rock salt 1600 feet underground to the surface through bamboo pipes so that they could illuminate

6. Nearly two thousand years after the curative waters in the town of Baden-Baden brang Roman forces to the area, Mark Twain took the waters there in the 1870s and swore that he has, quite literally, left his rheumatism in the waters.

   (A) brang Roman forces to the area, Mark Twain took the waters there in the 1870s and swore that he has, quite literally, left
   (B) brought Roman forces to the area, Mark Twain took the waters there in the 1870s and swore that he had, quite literally, left
   (C) brang Roman forces to the area, Mark Twain has taken the waters there in the 1870s and swore that he had, quite literally, left
   (D) brought Roman forces to the area, Mark Twain had taken the waters there in the 1870s and swore that he had, quite literally, left
   (E) brought Roman forces to the area, Mark Twain has taken the waters there in the 1870s and swore that he has, quite literally, left

EXPLANATIONS

1. This question tests **verbs**.

   Since people <u>had begun to write some 5,000 years ago, they have kept</u> records on a variety of materials, including clay or wax tablets, pieces of broken pottery, papyrus, animals skins, and finally paper.

(A) *had begun* to write some 5,000 years ago, they have kept
   - The past perfect tense *had begun* is used incorrectly. The past perfect tense should be used when one past action is completed prior to another. The time expression *since* indicates that this past action was not prior to another action.

(B) *begun* to write some 5,000 years ago, they *kept*
   - The form of the verb *begun* is incorrect. *Begun* is a past participle and is not the simple past tense *began*.
   - The simple past tense *kept* is used incorrectly. Because the time expression *Since* indicates a period of time from the past to the present, the main verb *kept* should be in the present perfect tense *have kept* and not the simple past.

(C) **began** to write some 5,000 years ago, they **have kept**
   - This answer contains the correct simple past form **began** and the correctly used present perfect tense **have kept**. This answer is correct.

(D) began to write some 5,000 years ago, they *kept*
   - The simple past tense *kept* is used incorrectly. Because the time expression *Since* indicates a period of time from the past to the present, the main verb *kept* should be in the present perfect tense *have kept* and not the simple past.

(E) *had begun* to write some 5,000 years ago, they *kept*
   - The past perfect tense *had begun* is used incorrectly. The past perfect tense should be used when one past action is completed prior to another. The time expression *since* indicates that this past action was not prior to another action.
   - The simple past tense *kept* is used incorrectly. Because the time expression *Since* indicates a period of time from the past to the present, the main verb *kept* should be in the present perfect tense *have kept* and not the simple past.

It Works! GMAT Sentence Correction

2. This question tests **verbs**.

    When Harvard College was constructed in 1636, it was surrounded by a tall stockade so that its inhabitants would be protected from wolves and hostile natives, an edifice that, not surprisingly, no longer exists.

(A) **was constructed** in 1636, it was surrounded by a tall stockade so that its inhabitants **would be protected** from wolves and hostile natives, an edifice that, not surprisingly, no longer **exists**
   - This answer contains the correctly used past tense **was constructed**, the correctly used conditional tense **would be protected**, and the correctly used present tense **exists**. This answer is correct.

(B) was constructed in 1636, it was surrounded by a tall stockade so that its inhabitants *were protected* from wolves and hostile natives, an edifice that, not surprisingly, no longer exists
   - The past verb *were protected* is used incorrectly. Because the verb *was surrounded* preceding *so that* is in the simple past tense, the verb following *so that, were protected*, should be in the conditional *(would)* tense to indicate a desired result.

(C) was constructed in 1636, it was surrounded by a tall stockade so that its inhabitants would be protected from wolves and hostile natives, an edifice that, not surprisingly, no longer *existed*
   - The simple past tense *existed* is used incorrectly. Although *was constructed* and *was surrounded* are in the past, *existed* should be in the present because of the time expression *no longer*. The present and past can be used in one sentence if the meaning is logical.

(D) *had been constructed* in 1636, it was surrounded by a tall stockade so that its inhabitants *were protected* from wolves and hostile natives, an edifice that, not surprisingly, no longer exists
   - The past perfect tense *had been constructed* is used incorrectly. The past perfect tense should be used when one past action is completed prior to another. The time expression *when* indicates that this past action was not prior to another action.
   - The past tense verb *were protected* is used incorrectly. Because the verb *was surrounded* preceding *so that* is in the past tense, the verb following *so that, were protected*, should be in the conditional *(would)* tense to indicate a desired result.

(E) *had been constructed* in 1636, it was surrounded by a tall stockade so that its inhabitants would be protected from wolves and hostile natives, an edifice that, not surprisingly, no longer *existed*
   - The past perfect tense *had been constructed* is used incorrectly. The past perfect tense should be used when one past action is completed prior to another. The time expression *when* indicates that this past action was not prior to another action.
   - The simple past tense *existed* is used incorrectly. Although *was constructed* and *was surrounded* are in the past, *existed* should be in the present because of the time expression *no longer*. The present and past can be used in one sentence if the meaning is logical.

It Works! GMAT Sentence Correction

3. This question tests **verbs**.

   The presidential campaign of 1920 was the first in which women could vote, and the results might have been different *if* candidate Warren Harding had not been so welcoming to female voters and his wife Florence would have taken a less prominent role in the campaign.

(A) had not been so welcoming to female voters and his wife Florence would have taken
   - The conditional perfect tense *would have taken* following *if* is used incorrectly. A conditional tense with *would* is never used in a clause directly following *if*.

(B) would not have been so welcoming to female voters and his wife Florence would have had
   - The conditional perfect tenses *would not have been* and *would have had* following *if* are used incorrectly. A conditional tense with *would* is never used in a clause directly following *if*.

(C) would not have been so welcoming to female voters and his wife Florence had taken
   - The conditional perfect tense *would not have been* following *if* is used incorrectly. A conditional tense with *would* is never used in a clause directly following *if*.

(D) had not been so welcoming to female voters and his wife Florence would have had
   - The conditional perfect tense *would have had* following *if* is used incorrectly. A conditional tense with *would* is never used in a clause directly following *if*.

(E) had not been so welcoming to female voters and his wife Florence had taken
   - This answer contains correctly used past perfect tenses **had not been** and **had taken** following *if*. This answer is correct.

4. This question tests **verbs**.

As the Great Influenza pandemic made its way around the world in 1918, millions of people were struck with a debilitating form of the disease; by the time the pandemic ran its course, somewhere between twenty and forty million people died worldwide.

(A) struck with a debilitating form of the disease; by the time the pandemic ran its course, somewhere between twenty and forty million people died
   - The form of the verb *struck* is incorrect. The verb *strike* has two past participle, *struck* (which refers to sudden physical force) and *stricken* (which refers to less sudden or less physical actions), and *stricken* is preferable here.
   - The simple past tense *died* is used incorrectly. The time expression *by the time* indicated that this past action was completed before another past action and that the past perfect tense *had died* is required.

(B) struck with a debilitating form of the disease; by the time the pandemic had run its course, somewhere between twenty and forty million people had died
   - The form of the verb *struck* is incorrect. The verb *strike* has two past participle, *struck* (which refers to sudden physical force) and *stricken* (which refers to less sudden or less physical actions) and *stricken* is preferable here.
   - The past perfect tense *had run* is used incorrectly. The past perfect tense should be used when one past action is completed prior to another. The time expression *by the time* indicates that this past action was not prior to another past action.

(C) stricken with a debilitating form of the disease; by the time the pandemic had run its course, somewhere between twenty and forty million people had died
   - The past perfect tense *had run* is used incorrectly. The past perfect tense should be used when one past action is completed prior to another. The time expression *by the time* indicates that this past action was not prior to another past action.

(D) stricken with a debilitating form of the disease; by the time the pandemic ran its course, somewhere between twenty and forty million people died
   - The simple past tense *died* is used incorrectly. The time expression *by the time* indicated that this past action was completed before another past action and that the past perfect tense *had died* is required.

(E) stricken with a debilitating form of the disease; by the time the pandemic ran its course, somewhere between twenty and forty million people had died
   - This answer contains the correct past participle form **stricken**, the correctly used simple past tense **ran**, and the correctly used past perfect tense **had died**. This answer is correct.

5. This question tests **verbs**.

In Szechwan province thousands of years ago, the Chinese <u>were using natural gas for lighting by bringing gas that has formed in rock salt 1600 feet underground to the surface through bamboo pipes so that they illuminated</u> their homes.

(A) were using natural gas for lighting by bringing gas that has formed in rock salt 1600 feet underground to the surface through bamboo pipes so that they illuminated
- The present perfect tense *has formed* is used incorrectly. The present perfect tense should be used when an action occurs in the period from the past to the present. The time expression *thousands of years ago* indicates that this is not the case.
- The simple past tense *illuminated* is used incorrectly. The verb *formed* preceding *so that* is in the simple past tense, the verb following *so that, illuminated* should be in the conditional *(would* or *could)* tense to indicate a desired result.

(B) were using natural gas for lighting by bringing gas that formed in rock salt 1600 feet underground to the surface through bamboo pipes so that they illuminated
- The simple past tense *illuminated* is used incorrectly. The verb *formed* preceding *so that* is in the simple past tense, the verb following *so that, illuminated* should be in the conditional *(would* or *could)* tense to indicate a desired result.

(C) have been using natural gas for lighting by bringing gas that formed in rock salt 1600 feet underground to the surface through bamboo pipes so that they could illuminate
- The present perfect tense *have been using* is used incorrectly. The present perfect tense should be used when an action occurs in the period from the past to the present. The time expression *thousands of years ago* indicates that this is not the case.

(D) were using natural gas for lighting by bringing gas that formed in rock salt 1600 feet underground to the surface through bamboo pipes so that they could illuminate
- This answer contains the correctly used past tense **were using**, the correctly used simple past tense **formed**, and the correctly used conditional tense **could illuminate**. This answer is correct.

(E) have been using natural gas for lighting by bringing gas that has formed in rock salt 1600 feet underground to the surface through bamboo pipes so that they could illuminate
- The present perfect tense *have been using* is used incorrectly. The present perfect tense should be used when an action occurs in the period from the past to the present. The time expression *thousands of years ago* indicates that this is not the case.
- The present perfect tense *has formed* is used incorrectly. The present perfect tense should be used when an action occurs in the period from the past to the present. The time expression *thousands of years ago* indicates that this is not the case.

6. This question tests **verbs**.

Nearly two thousand years after the curative waters in the town of Baden-Baden <u>brang Roman forces to the area, Mark Twain took the waters there in the 1870s and swore that he has, quite literally, left</u> his rheumatism in the waters.

(A) *brang* Roman forces to the area, Mark Twain took the waters there in the 1870s and swore that he *has*, quite literally, *left*
  - The form of the verb *brang* is incorrect. The correct past of the verb *bring* is *brought*.
  - The present perfect tense *has...left* is used incorrectly. The present perfect tense should be used when an action occurs in the period from the past to the present. The time expression *in the 1870s* indicates that this is not the case.

[(B)] **brought** Roman forces to the area, Mark Twain **took** the waters there in the 1870s and swore that he **had**, quite literally, **left**
  - This answer contains the correct past form **brought**, the correctly used simple past tense **took**, and the correctly used past perfect tense **had...left**. This answer is correct.

(C) *brang* Roman forces to the area, Mark Twain *has taken* the waters there in the 1870s and swore that he had, quite literally, left
  - The form of the verb *brang* is incorrect. The correct past of the verb *bring* is *brought*.
  - The present perfect tense *has taken* is used incorrectly. The present perfect tense should be used when an action occurs in the period from the past to the present. The time expression *in the 1870s* indicates that this is not the case.

(D) brought Roman forces to the area, Mark Twain *had taken* the waters there in the 1870s and swore that he had, quite literally, left
  - The past perfect tense *had taken* is used incorrectly. The past perfect tense should be used when one past action is completed prior to another. The time expression *Nearly two thousand years after* indicates that this past action was not prior to another past action.

(E) brought Roman forces to the area, Mark Twain *has taken* the waters there in the 1870s and swore that he *has*, quite literally, *left*
  - The present perfect tense *has taken* is used incorrectly. The present perfect tense should be used when an action occurs in the period from the past to the present. The time expression *in the 1870s* indicates that this is not the case.
  - The present perfect tense *has...left* is used incorrectly. The present perfect tense should be used when an action occurs in the period from the past to the present. The time expression *in the 1870s* indicates that this is not the case.

Lesson 6: Problems with MODIFIERS

> **Modifiers** are words that describe other words. Adjectives -- which describe nouns or pronouns -- and adverbs -- which describe verbs, adjectives, or other adverbs -- are the two types of modifiers. The following kinds of problems with modifiers appear commonly on the GMAT:
> 1. an adverb used between a verb and its object
> 2. an adverb used between the two parts of an infinitive (a split infinitive)
> 3. an introductory adjective phrase that does not modify the subject (a dangling modifier)
> 4. two consecutive adjectives that are confused with an adverb modifying an adjective
> 5. the modifier *only* when it is not used directly in front of the expression it modifies

EXAMPLE 1: This example shows the problem of an adverb used between a verb and its object.

INCORRECT: The company *has posted* *recently* its less than stellar quarterly *report*.
CORRECT: The company *has posted* its less than stellar quarterly *report* recently.

In the incorrect example, the adverb *recently* is positioned incorrectly between the verb *has posted* and its object *report*. In the correct example, the adverb **recently** has been moved so that it is not positioned between the verb *has posted* and its object *report*.

- -

EXAMPLE 2: This example shows the problem of an adverb used between the two parts of an infinitive (a split infinitive).

INCORRECT: The new tax is expected *to* *dramatically* *increase* the revenue collected next quarter.
CORRECT: The new tax is expected *to increase* the revenue collected next quarter dramatically.

In the incorrect example, the adverb *dramatically* is incorrectly positioned between *to* and *increase*, the two parts of an infinitive. In the correct example, the adverb **dramatically** has been moved so that it is not in the middle of the infinitive *to increase*.

- -

EXAMPLE 3: This example shows the problem of an introductory adjective phrase that does not modify the subject (a dangling modifier).

INCORRECT: *Running only on fumes in the gas tank*, the *driver* somehow managed to get the car to the gas station.
CORRECT: Running only on fumes in the gas tank, the *car* somehow made it to the gas station.

In the incorrect example, the introductory adjective phrase *Running only on fumes in the gas tank* does not describe the subject *driver;* it was not the *driver* that was running only on fumes in the gas tank. In the correct example, the sentence has been changed so that the introductory adjective phrase **Running only on fumes in the gas tank** does describe the subject *car*.

- -

EXAMPLE 4: This example shows the problem of two consecutive adjectives confused with an adverb modifying an adjective

INCORRECT: He told me a *true* remarkable story from his past.
CORRECT: He told me a **truly** remarkable story from his past.

In the incorrect example, the modifiers *true* and *remarkable* could be adjectives modifying the noun *story,* but the meaning is not logical because *true* should modify the adjective *remarkable* and not the noun *story.* In the correct example, the adverb **truly** modifies the adjective *remarkable,* which in turn modifies the noun *story.*

- -

EXAMPLE 5: This example shows the problem of *only* when it is not used directly in front of the expression it modifies.

INCORRECT: The man could not pay cash for the meal because he *only* had *five dollars* in his wallet.
CORRECT: The man could not pay cash for the meal because he had **only** *five dollars* in his wallet.

In the incorrect example, the modifier *only* actually modifies the expression *five dollars,* but it is incorrectly placed because it is not directly in front of *five dollars.* In the correct example, **only** is directly in front of the expression *five dollars* that it modifies.

SKILLS PRACTICE: Find the problems with **modifiers** in the following sentences. (The number in parentheses indicates the number of problems you should find.) Then, study the explanations on the pages that follow.

1. The teachers can only start the meeting after the first class has ended, and then they will only have twenty minutes to complete the entire meeting. *(2)*

2. In the years after the Great Famine began in Ireland in 1845, experts determined that the shocking detrimental failure of the potato crop there was most likely caused when a ship from North America introduced accidentally a fungus there. *(2)*

3. The ability to rapidly make decisions at all levels of the organization enables management to effectively respond to issues that occur in the marketplace. *(2)*

4. Credited with having the longest continuously cultural history in the world, the cultural history of the Aboriginal people of Australia goes back to the last ice age. *(2)*

5. Only using prefixes and suffixes in its word formation, English differs from many other languages that use also infixes. *(2)*

6. Initially rejected as forgeries, archeologists later validated the Upper Paleolithic cave paintings discovered in Altamira Spain in 1879 only after similar paintings discovered in France were proven to not be counterfeit because of a layer of mineral deposits that had built up on them. *(2)*

7. Captured by merchantmen on a rival Genoese ship in 1298, Marco Polo was imprisoned in the port city of Genoa, where he recounted at length the story of his travels to a writer named Rusticello, a historic accurate account that was published in early Italian and is still available today. *(2)*

8. So called because the ideas of innovative artists from outside London influenced greatly artistic development in London rather than the other way around, eighteenth century British art was captivated by the remarkable phenomenon of the Provincial Enlightenment. *(2)*

EXPLANATIONS (I = incorrect, C = correct)

1. The teachers can *only* start the meeting *after the first class has ended*, and then they will *only* have *twenty minutes* to complete the entire meeting.

    - The modifier *only* is positioned incorrectly because it is not directly in front of the idea *after the first class has ended* that it modifies.
        - I: *only start the meeting after*
        - C: **start the meeting only after**

    - The modifier *only* is positioned incorrectly because it is not directly in front of the idea *twenty minutes* that it modifies.
        - I: *only have twenty minutes*
        - C: **have only twenty minutes**

    -

2. In the years after the Great Famine began in Ireland in 1845, experts determined that the *shocking detrimental failure* of the potato crop there was most likely caused when a ship from North America *introduced accidentally* a *fungus* there.

    - The modifiers *shocking* and *detrimental* could be adjectives modifying the noun *failure*, but the meaning is not logical. The adverb *shockingly* is needed to modify the adjective *detrimental*.
        - I: *shocking detrimental failure*
        - C: **shockingly detrimental failure**

    - The modifier *accidentally* is positioned incorrectly because an adverb cannot be positioned between a verb *introduced* and its direct object *fungus*.
        - I: *introduced accidentally a fungus*
        - C: **accidentally introduced a fungus**

    -

3. The ability *to rapidly make* decisions at all levels of the organization enables management *to effectively respond* to issues that occur in the marketplace.

    - The modifier *rapidly* is positioned incorrectly because an adverb cannot be used between the two parts of an infinitive (*to* and *make*). This is called a split infinitive.
        - I: *to rapidly make decisions*
        - C: **to make decisions rapidly**

    - The modifier *effectively* is positioned incorrectly because an adverb cannot be used between the two parts of an infinitive (*to* and *respond*). This is called a split infinitive.
        - I: *to effectively respond*
        - C: **to respond effectively**

4. *Credited with having* the longest *continuously* *cultural* history in the world, *the cultural history* of the Aboriginal people of Australia goes back to the last ice age.

    - The expression *Credited with having...* is a dangling modifier because an introductory adjective should modify the subject of main clause directly following the comma. In this sentence, this expression modifies the subject *the cultural history*, and this is not logical.
        - I: *the cultural history of the Aboriginal people of Australia*
        - C: **the Aboriginal people of Australia have a cultural history that**

    - The modifier *continuously* could be an adverb modifying *cultural*, but the meaning is not logical. The adjective *continuous* is needed to modify the noun *history*.
        - I: *continuously cultural history*
        - C: **continuous cultural history**

---

5. *Only* using *prefixes and suffixes* in its word formation, English differs from many other languages that *use* *also* *infixes*.

    - The modifier *Only* is positioned incorrectly because it is not directly in front of the idea *prefixes and suffixes* that it modifies.
        - I: *Only using prefixes and suffixes*
        - C: **Using only prefixes and suffixes**

    - The modifier *also* is positioned incorrectly because an adverb cannot be positioned between a verb *use* and its direct object *infixes*.
        - I: *use also infixes*
        - C: **also use infixes**

---

6. *Initially rejected as forgeries*, *archeologists* later validated the Upper Paleolithic cave paintings discovered in Altamira Spain in 1879 only after similar paintings discovered in France were proven *to* *not* *be* counterfeit because of a layer of mineral deposits that had built up on them.

    - The expression *Initially rejected as forgeries* is a dangling modifier because an introductory adjective should modify the subject of main clause directly following the comma. In this sentence, this expression modifies the subject *archeologists*, and this is not logical.
        - I: *archeologists later validated the Upper Paleolithic cave paintings discovered in Altamira Spain in 1879*
        - C: **the Upper Paleolithic cave paintings discovered in Altamira Spain in 1879 were later validated by archeologists**

    - The modifier *not* is positioned incorrectly because an adverb cannot be used between the two parts of an infinitive (*to* and *be*). This is called a split infinitive.

>   I: *to not be*
>   C: **not to be**

- -

7. Captured by merchantmen on a rival Genoese ship in 1298, Marco Polo was imprisoned in the port city of Genoa, where he *recounted* *at length* the *story* of his travels to a writer named Rusticello, a *historic accurate account* that was published in early Italian and is still available today.

    - The modifier *at length* is positioned incorrectly because an adverb phrase cannot be positioned between a verb *recounted* and its direct object *story*.
        >   I: *recounted at length the story*
        >   C: **recounted the story at length**

    - The modifiers *historic* and *accurate* could be adjectives modifying the noun *account*, but the meaning is not logical. The adverb *historically* is needed to modify the adjective *accurate*.
        >   I: *historic accurate account*
        >   C: **historically accurate account**

- -

8. *So called* because the ideas of innovative artists from outside London *influenced* *greatly* artistic *development* in London rather than the other way around, *eighteenth century British art* was captivated by the remarkable phenomenon of the Provincial Enlightenment.

    - The expression *So called...* is a dangling modifier because an introductory adjective should modify the subject of main clause directly following the comma. In this sentence, this expression modifies the subject *eighteenth century British art*, and this is not logical.
        >   I: *eighteenth century British art was captivated by the remarkable phenomenon of the Provincial Enlightenment*
        >   C: **the remarkable phenomenon of the provincial Enlightenment captivated eighteenth century British art**

    - The modifier *greatly* is positioned incorrectly because an adverb cannot be positioned between a verb *influenced* and its direct object *development*.
        >   I: *influenced greatly artistic development*
        >   C: **greatly influenced artistic development**

GMAT-STYLE SKILLS PRACTICE: Choose the letter of the answer to each question that best reflects the style and accuracy of standard written English. Then, study the explanations on the pages that follow.

1. Adverse selection shows that private markets cannot <u>provide economically insurance to all when only those most likely to need the insurance are willing to voluntarily buy it</u>.

    (A) provide economically insurance to all when only those most likely to need the insurance are willing to voluntarily buy it
    (B) provide economically to all insurance only when those most likely to need the insurance are willing to buy it voluntarily
    (C) provide insurance to all economically when only those most likely to need the insurance are willing to buy it voluntarily
    (D) provide to all insurance economically only when those most likely to need the insurance are willing to buy it voluntarily
    (E) provide insurance to all economically when only those most likely to need the insurance are willing to voluntarily buy it

2. Not having the benefit of a formal education as a scientist, <u>Mary Anning nevertheless used to the fullest extent her keen eyesight and powers of observation to become</u> one of the most successful fossil hunters of the early 1800s.

    (A) Mary Anning nevertheless used to the fullest extent her keen eyesight and powers of observation to become
    (B) Mary Anning nevertheless used her keen eyesight and powers of observation to the fullest extent to become
    (C) Mary Anning's keen eyesight and powers of observation were nevertheless used to the fullest extent to make her
    (D) keen eyesight and powers of observation were nevertheless used to the fullest extent by Mary Anning to make her
    (E) Mary Anning's use of her keen eyesight and powers of observation nevertheless made her

3. Rheumatoid arthritis, an autoimmune form of the disease, develops when the immune system, usually triggered by an antigen in <u>a genetically predisposed person, begins to attack body tissue surreptitiously</u>.

   (A) a genetically predisposed person, begins to attack body tissue surreptitiously
   (B) a genetic predisposed person, begins to surreptitiously attack body tissue
   (C) a genetically predisposed person, begins to surreptitiously attack body tissue
   (D) a genetic predisposed person, begins to attack surreptitiously body tissue
   (E) a genetically predisposed person, begins to attack surreptitiously body tissue

4. Long linked to revolutionary movements, <u>Mexican artist Diego Rivera's paintings reflect clearly the political and industrial reality of his times</u>.

   (A) Mexican artist Diego Rivera's paintings reflect clearly the political and industrial reality of his times
   (B) Mexican artist Diego Rivera reflects clearly the politically industrial reality of his times in his paintings
   (C) Mexican artist Diego Rivera clearly reflects the politically industrial reality of his times in his paintings
   (D) Mexican artist Diego Rivera's paintings clearly reflect the political and industrial reality of his times
   (E) Mexican artist Diego Rivera clearly reflects the political and industrial reality of his times in his paintings

5. In 1928, Seattle passed an ordinance prohibiting dance marathons, an ordinance which was prompted by the attempted suicide of a Seattle woman who had <u>completed from start to finish a 19-day marathon in the Seattle Armory and only placed fifth</u>.

    (A) completed from start to finish a 19-day marathon in the Seattle Armory and only placed fifth
    (B) completed a 19-day marathon from start to finish in the Seattle Armory and only placed fifth
    (C) completed in the Seattle Armory a 19-day marathon from start to finish and placed only fifth
    (D) completed a 19-day marathon from start to finish in the Seattle Armory and placed only fifth
    (E) completed from start to finish in the Seattle Armory a 19-day marathon and only placed fifth

6. In the later stages of aging, the elderly commonly cease <u>to regularly recognize familiar places, objects, and family members from their current lives while maintaining remarkably vivid memories</u> from their earlier lives.

    (A) to regularly recognize familiar places, objects, and family members from their current lives while maintaining remarkably vivid memories
    (B) to regularly recognize familiar places, objects, and family members from their current lives while maintaining remarkable vivid memories
    (C) to recognize regularly familiar places, objects, and family members from their current lives while maintaining remarkably vivid memories
    (D) to recognize familiar places, objects, and family members regularly from their current lives while maintaining remarkable vivid memories
    (E) to regularly recognize familiar places, objects, and family members regularly from their current lives while maintaining remarkably vivid memories

Lesson 6: Problems with MODIFIERS | 93

EXPLANATIONS

1. This question tests **modifiers**.

   Adverse selection shows that private markets cannot <u>provide economically insurance to all when only those most likely to need the insurance are willing to voluntarily buy it</u>.

(A)   *provide* economically *insurance* to all when only those most likely to need the insurance are willing *to* voluntarily *buy it*
   - The modifier *economically* is positioned incorrectly because an adverb cannot be positioned between a verb *provide* and its direct object *insurance*.
   - The modifier *voluntarily* is positioned incorrectly because an adverb cannot be used between the two parts of an infinitive, *to* and *buy*. This is called a split infinitive.

(B)   *provide* economically to all *insurance* only when *those* most likely to need the insurance are willing to buy it voluntarily
   - The modifiers *economically* and *to all* are positioned incorrectly because an adverb or adverb phrase cannot be positioned between a verb *provide* and its direct object *insurance*.
   - The modifier *only* is positioned incorrectly because it is not directly in front of the idea *those* that it modifies.

(C)   **provide insurance to all economically** when only those most likely to need the insurance are willing to buy it **voluntarily**
   - In this answer, the modifiers **to all, economically**, and **voluntarily** are all positioned correctly. This answer is correct.

(D)   *provide* to all *insurance* economically only when *those* most likely to need the insurance are willing to buy it voluntarily
   - The modifier *to all* is positioned incorrectly because an adverb phrase cannot be positioned between a verb *provide* and its direct object *insurance*.
   - The modifier *only* is positioned incorrectly because it is not directly in front of the idea *those* that it modifies.

(E)   provide insurance to all economically when only those most likely to need the insurance are willing *to* voluntarily *buy it*
   - The modifier *voluntarily* is positioned incorrectly because an adverb cannot be used between the two parts of an infinitive, *to* and *buy*. This is called a split infinitive.

2. This question tests **modifiers**.

Not having the benefit of a formal education as a scientist, Mary Anning nevertheless used to the fullest extent her keen eyesight and powers of observation to become one of the most successful fossil hunters of the early 1800s.

(A) Mary Anning nevertheless *used to the fullest extent* her keen *eyesight* and powers of observation to become
   • The modifier *to the fullest extent* is positioned incorrectly because an adverb phrase cannot be positioned between a verb *used* and its direct object *eyesight*.

(B) Mary Anning nevertheless used her keen eyesight and powers of observation to the fullest extent to become
   • This answer lacks the dangling modifier of several of the other answers because it uses the subject **Mary Anning** following the introductory modifier *Not having the benefit of a formal education as a scientist,* which modifies *Mary Anning*. In addition, the adverb phrase **to the fullest extent** is positioned correctly. This answer is correct.

(C) Mary Anning's keen eyesight and powers of observation were nevertheless used to the fullest extent to make her
   • The expression *Not having the benefit of a formal education as a scientist* is a dangling modifier because an introductory adjective should modify the subject of main clause directly following the comma. In this sentence, this expression modifies the subject *Mary Anning's keen eyesight and excellent powers of observation*, and this is not logical.

(D) keen eyesight and powers of observation were nevertheless used to the fullest extent by Mary Anning to make her
   • The expression *Not having the benefit of a formal education as a scientist* is a dangling modifier because an introductory adjective should modify the subject of main clause directly following the comma. In this sentence, this expression modifies the subject *keen eyesight and excellent powers of observation*, and this is not logical.

(E) Mary Anning's use of her keen eyesight and powers of observation nevertheless made her
   • The expression *Not having the benefit of a formal education as a scientist* is a dangling modifier because an introductory adjective should modify the subject of main clause directly following the comma. This expression modifies the subject *Mary Anning's use of her keen eyesight and excellent powers of observation*, and this is not logical.

3. This question tests **modifiers**.

   Rheumatoid arthritis, an autoimmune form of the disease, develops when the immune system, usually triggered by an antigen in a genetically predisposed person, begins to attack body tissue surreptitiously.

   (A) a genetically *predisposed* person, begins to attack body tissue **surreptitiously**
   - This answer has the correct adverb **genetically** modifying the adjective *predisposed* and the correctly positioned modifier **surreptitiously**. This answer is correct.

   (B) a genetic *predisposed person*, begins *to surreptitiously attack* body tissue
   - The modifiers genetic and *predisposed* could be adjectives modifying the noun *person*, but the meaning is not logical because genetic should be an adverb modifying *predisposed*.
   - The modifier surreptitiously is positioned incorrectly because an adverb cannot be used between the two parts of an infinitive, *to* and *attack*. This is called a split infinitive.

   (C) a genetically predisposed person, begins *to* surreptitiously *attack* body tissue
   - The modifier surreptitiously is positioned incorrectly because an adverb cannot be used between the two parts of an infinitive, *to* and *attack*. This is called a split infinitive.

   (D) a genetic *predisposed person*, begins to *attack* surreptitiously body *tissue*
   - The modifiers *genetic* and *predisposed* could be adjectives modifying the noun *person*, but the meaning is not logical because genetic should be an adverb modifying *predisposed*.
   - The modifier surreptitiously is positioned incorrectly because an adverb cannot be positioned between a verb *attack* and its direct object *tissue*.

   (E) a genetically predisposed person, begins to *attack* surreptitiously body *tissue*
   - The modifier surreptitiously is positioned incorrectly because an adverb cannot be positioned between a verb *attack* and its direct object *tissue*.

4. This question tests **modifiers**.

   Long linked to revolutionary movements, Mexican artist Diego Rivera's paintings reflect clearly the political and industrial reality of his times.

(A) Mexican artist Diego Rivera's paintings reflect clearly the political and industrial *reality* of his times
   - The expression *Long linked to revolutionary movements* is a dangling modifier because an introductory adjective should modify the subject of main clause directly following the comma. In this sentence, this expression modifies *Mexican artist Diego Rivera's paintings*, and this is not logical.
   - The modifier *clearly* is positioned incorrectly because an adverb cannot be positioned between a verb *reflect* and its direct object *reality*.

(B) Mexican artist Diego Rivera *reflects* *clearly* the *politically* industrial reality of his times in his paintings
   - The modifier *clearly* is positioned incorrectly because an adverb cannot be positioned between a verb *reflects* and its direct object *reality*.
   - The modifier *politically* could be an adverb modifying the adjective *industrial*, but the meaning is not logical. The adjective *political* is needed to modify the noun *reality*.

(C) Mexican artist Diego Rivera clearly reflects the *politically* industrial reality of his times in his paintings
   - The modifier *politically* could be an adverb modifying the adjective *industrial*, but the meaning is not logical. The adjective *political* is needed to modify the noun *reality*.

(D) Mexican artist Diego Rivera's paintings clearly reflect the political and industrial reality of his times
   - The expression *Long linked to revolutionary movements* is a dangling modifier because an introductory adjective should modify the subject of main clause directly following the comma. In this sentence, this expression modifies the subject *Mexican artist Diego Rivera's paintings*, and this is not logical.

(E) Mexican artist Diego Rivera clearly reflects the political and industrial reality of his times in his paintings
   - This answer lacks the dangling modifier of some of the other answers because it uses the subject **Mexican artist Diego Rivera** following the introductory modifier *Long linked to revolutionary movements*, which modifies *Mexican artist Diego Rivera*. The adverb **clearly** is positioned correctly, and the logical adjective **political** is used in place of the illogical adverb *politically* found in some of the other responses. This answer is correct.

5. This question tests **modifiers**.

In 1928, Seattle passed an ordinance prohibiting dance marathons, an ordinance which was prompted by the attempted suicide of a Seattle woman who had completed from start to finish a 19-day marathon in the Seattle Armory and only placed fifth.

(A) completed *from start to finish* a 19-day *marathon* in the Seattle Armory and *only* placed *fifth*
- The modifier *from start to finish* is positioned incorrectly because an adverb phrase cannot be positioned between a verb *completed* and its direct object *marathon*.
- The modifier *only* is positioned incorrectly because it is not directly in front of the idea *fifth* that it modifies.

(B) completed a 19-day marathon from start to finish in the Seattle Armory and *only* placed *fifth*
- The modifier *only* is positioned incorrectly because it is not directly in front of the idea *fifth* that it modifies.

(C) completed *in the Seattle Armory* a 19-day *marathon* from start to finish and placed only fifth
- The modifier *in the Seattle Armory* is positioned incorrectly because an adverb phrase cannot be positioned between a verb *completed* and its direct object *marathon*.

(D) completed a 19-day marathon from start to finish in the Seattle Armory and placed only fifth
- This answer contains the correctly placed modifiers **from start to finish, in the Seattle Armory,** and **only**. This answer is correct.

(E) completed *from start to finish* *in the Seattle Armory* a 19-day *marathon* and *only* placed *fifth*
- The modifiers *from start to finish* and *in the Seattle Armory* are positioned incorrectly because adverb phrases cannot be positioned between a verb *completed* and its direct object *marathon*.
- The modifier *only* is positioned incorrectly because it is not directly in front of the idea *fifth* that it modifies.

6. This question tests **modifiers**.

In the later stages of aging, the elderly commonly cease to regularly recognize familiar places, objects, and family members from their current lives while maintaining remarkably vivid memories from their earlier lives.

(A) to *regularly* recognize familiar places, objects, and family members from their current lives while maintaining remarkably vivid memories
- The modifier *regularly* is positioned incorrectly because an adverb cannot be used between the two parts of an infinitive, *to* and *recognize*. This is called a split infinitive.

(B) to *regularly* recognize familiar places, objects, and family members from their current lives while maintaining *remarkable* vivid memories
- The modifier *regularly* is positioned incorrectly because an adverb cannot be used between the two parts of an infinitive, *to* and *recognize*. This is called a split infinitive.
- The modifiers *remarkable* and *vivid* could be adjectives modifying the noun *memories*, but the meaning is not logical because the adjective *remarkable* should modify the adjective *vivid*. An adverb is needed to modify the adjective *vivid*.

(C) to recognize *regularly* familiar places, objects, and family members from their current lives while maintaining remarkably vivid memories
- The modifier *regularly* is positioned incorrectly because an adverb cannot be positioned between a verb *recognize* and its direct objects *places*, *objects*, and *members*.

(D) to recognize familiar places, objects, and family members regularly from their current lives while maintaining *remarkable* vivid memories
- The modifiers *remarkable* and *vivid* could be adjectives modifying the noun *memories*, but the meaning is not logical because the adjective *remarkable* should modify the adjective *vivid*. An adverb is needed to modify the adjective *vivid*.

(E) to recognize familiar places, objects, and family members **regularly** from their current lives while maintaining **remarkably** *vivid* memories
- This answer contains the correctly positioned modifier **regularly** and the logical adverb **remarkably**, which modifies the adjective *vivid*. This answer is correct.

Lesson 7: Problems with SENTENCES

Sentences involve making sure that the structure of each sentence is accurate: each sentence must contain at least one subject and verb; in addition, in a sentence containing more than one subject and verb, the subjects and verbs much be connected with either appropriate conjunctions or appropriate punctuation. The following problems with sentences are the most common on the GMAT:
1. a fragment in a simple sentence (a sentence that should have one subject and verb but is lacking either a subject or a verb)
2. a fragment in a compound sentence (a sentence that has more than one subject and verb joined by a comma and *and, but, or, so* but is lacking either a subject or a verb)
3. a subordinate clause fragment (a sentence consisting of only a subject and verb introduced by a subordinate clause conjunction)
4. a sentence with an extra subject
5. a run-on sentence (two subjects and verbs that are connected incorrectly)
6. the incorrect use of a semi-colon

EXAMPLE 1: This example shows a main clause fragment in a simple sentence.

INCORRECT: The *document* with all the necessary signatures and stamps [lying] on the desk unmailed.
CORRECT: The *document* with all the necessary signatures and stamps is lying on the desk unmailed.

In the incorrect example, this is a fragment in a simple sentence because the one subject *document* lacks a verb. [*Lying*] is a participle and is not a verb. In the correct example, the sentence has both a subject *document* and a verb **is lying**.

- -

EXAMPLE 2: This example shows a fragment in a compound sentence.

INCORRECT: Two *researchers arrived* on time for the meeting, *but* [no one] else.
CORRECT: Two *researchers arrived* on time for the meeting, *but* no one else did.

In the incorrect example, this is a fragment in a compound sentence because the comma (,) and *but* should be joining two subjects and verbs, but they are joining the subject and verb *researchers arrived* and a subject without a verb [no one]. In the correct example, the comma (,) and *but* are joining the subject and verb *researchers arrived* and the subject and verb **no one...did**.

EXAMPLE 3: This example shows a subordinate clause fragment.

INCORRECT: *Because* no one in the department *knew* anything about the new management team.
CORRECT: *No one* in the department *knew* anything about the new management team.

In the incorrect example, this is a subordinate clause fragment because the only subject and verb *no one...knew* are introduced with the subordinate conjunction *Because*. A sentence introduced with a subordinate conjunction such as *Because* must have more than one subject and verb. In the correct example, the subordinate conjunction has been removed, leaving a complete sentence with the subject *No one* and the verb *knew*.

EXAMPLE 4: This example shows an incorrect sentence with an extra subject.

INCORRECT: The *results* of the investigation undertaken by the detective squad *they* *will be announced* at the press conference.
CORRECT: The *results* of the investigation undertaken by the detective squad *will be announced* at the press conference.

In the incorrect example, *results* is the subject of the verb *will be announced,* and *they* is an extra subject. In the correct example, the extra subject *they* has been removed, leaving a correct sentence with the subject *results* and the verb *will be announced.*

EXAMPLE 5: This example shows an example of a run-on sentence.

INCORRECT: The *contest was announced* on the radio , however few *people participated*.
CORRECT: The *contest was announced* on the radio ; however, few *people participated*.

In the incorrect example, this is a run-on sentence because the two subjects and verbs *contest was announced* and *people participated* are connected with a comma , . A comma cannot be used to connect two subjects and verbs without a conjunction, and *however* is an adverb and is not a conjunction. In the correct example, the two subjects and verbs *contest was announced* and *people participated* are correctly connected with a semi-colon ; .

- -

EXAMPLE 6: This example shows the incorrect use of a semi-colon.

INCORRECT: Many *people voted* for the candidate; *though not with much excitement*.
CORRECT: Many *people voted* for the candidate; however, **they felt** little excitement.

In the incorrect example, there is a complete subject and verb *people voted* preceding the semi-colon (;), but there is no subject and verb in the idea *though not with much excitement* that follows the semi-colon. There must be a complete subject and verb on either side of a semi-colon. In the correct example, there is a complete subject and verb *people voted* preceding the semi-colon (;) and a complete subject and verb **they felt** following the semi-colon.

SKILLS PRACTICE: Find the problems with **sentences** in the following sentences. (The number in parentheses indicates the number of problems you should find.) Then, study the explanations on the pages that follow.

1. Organizations requiring integration as well as specialization and synthesis as well as analysis. *(1)*

2. The highway patrol made numerous public comments about conducting drunk-driving check points over the holidays; with numerous motorists caught at the checkpoints and arrested anyway. *(1)*

3. Alexander the Great's remains were preserved in a giant crock of honey, interestingly this was a practice that was not uncommon at the time for personages of great importance. *(1)*

4. Most western folk music it can be classified as isometric. Since a single meter predominates throughout the song. *(2)*

5. The tentacles of the saucer-shaped compass jellyfish with millions of stinging cells, but juvenile fish still hide among them to protect themselves from predators. *(1)*

6. The Epstein-Barr virus was once thought to be the cause of chronic fatigue syndrome, however, more recent research points to an immune system dysfunction originating in the central nervous system. *(1)*

7. James Garfield, the first president to use a phone in the White House, he responded when Alexander Graham Bell called; his words: "Please speak a little more slowly. *(2)*

8. Because many programmers were developing different computer languages in the 1950s. Computer experts formed a panel in1959 to develop a language for business programming, as a result, the language that emerged, COBOL, it became the standard for business and government for some time to come. *(3)*

EXPLANATIONS (I = incorrect, C = correct)

1. *Organizations requiring* integration as well as specialization and synthesis as well as analysis.

   - This sentence is a simple sentence fragment. The subject in this simple sentence *Organizations* lacks a verb. *Requiring* is a participle and is not a complete verb.
     - I: *Requiring*
     - C: **Require**

   -

2. The highway patrol made numerous public comments about conducting drunk-driving check points over the holidays ; with numerous *motorists caught* at the checkpoints and arrested anyway.

   - This sentence has an incorrectly used semi-colon ;. The subject *motorists* following the semi-colon lacks a verb because *caught* is a past participle and is not a verb. There must be a complete subject and verb on either side of a semi-colon.
     - I: *; with numerous motorists caught*
     - C: **, with numerous motorists caught**

   -

3. Alexander the Great's *remains were preserved* in a giant crock of honey , *interestingly this was* a practice that was not uncommon at the time for personages of great importance.

   - This is a run-on sentence because the two subjects and verbs *remains were preserved* and *this was* are connected with a comma ,. A comma cannot be used to connect two subjects and verbs without a conjunction, and *interestingly* is an adverb and is not a conjunction.
     - I: *honey, interestingly*
     - C: **honey; interestingly,**

   -

4. Most western *folk music it can be classified* as isometric. *Since* a single *meter predominates* throughout the song.

   - The first sentence has an extra subject because *folk music* is the subject of the verb *can be classified* and *it* is an extra subject.
     - I: *folk music it can be classified*
     - **C: folk music can be classified**

   - This second sentence is a subordinate clause fragment because the subject and verb *meter predominates* are introduced by the subordinate conjunction *Since*. A sentence introduced by a subordinate conjunction such as *Since* must have more than one subject and verb.
     - I: *isometric. Since*
     - **C: isometric since**

---

5. The *tentacles* of the saucer-shaped compass jellyfish *with* millions of stinging cells, *but* juvenile fish still hide among them to protect themselves from predators.

   - This sentence is a compound sentence fragment because the part of this sentence preceding the comma *(,)* and *but* is a has a subject *tentacles* but lacks a verb. *With* is a preposition and is not a verb.
     - I: *with*
     - **C: have**

---

6. The Epstein-Barr *virus was* once thought to be the cause of chronic fatigue syndrome , *however*, more recent *research points* to an immune system dysfunction originating in the central nervous system.

   - This is a run-on sentence because the two subjects and verbs *virus was* and *research points* are connected with a comma *,*. A comma cannot be used to connect two subjects and verbs without a conjunction, and *however* is an adverb and is not a conjunction.
     - I: *syndrome, however*
     - **C: syndrome; however**

It Works! GMAT Sentence Correction

7. *James Garfield*, the first president to use a phone in the White House, *he responded* when Alexander Graham Bell called; his *words*: "Please speak a little more slowly.

   - This sentence has an extra subject because *James Garfield* is the subject of the verb *responded* and *he* is an extra subject.
     I: *James Garfield...he responded*
     C: James Garfield...responded

   - This sentence has an incorrectly used semi-colon (;). The subject *words* following the semi-colon lacks a verb, and there must be a complete subject and verb on either side of a semi-colon.
     I: *his words*
     C: his words were

   -

8. *Because* many *programmers were developing* different computer languages in the 1950s. Computer *experts formed* a panel in 1959 to develop a language for business programming, *as a result*, the *language* that emerged, COBOL, *it became* the standard for business and government for some time to come.

   - This first sentence is a subordinate clause fragment because the subject and verb *programmers were developing* are introduced by the subordinate conjunction *Because*. A sentence introduced by a subordinate conjunction such as *Because* must have more than one subject and verb.
     I: *Because many programmers were developing*
     C: Many programmers were developing

   - This is a run-on sentence because the two subjects and verbs *experts formed* and *language...became* are connected with a comma. A comma cannot be used to connect two subjects and verbs without a conjunction, and *as a result* is an adverb phrase and is not a conjunction.
     I: *programming, as a result*
     C: programming; as a result

   - This sentence has an extra subject because *language* is the subject of the verb *became* and *it* is an extra subject.
     I: *language...it became*
     C: language...became

It Works! GMAT Sentence Correction

GMAT-STYLE SKILLS PRACTICE: Choose the letter of the answer to each question that best reflects the style and accuracy of standard written English. Then, study the explanations on the pages that follow.

1. Computer projections <u>will be plotting the plates' locations</u> along the San Andreas fault in fifty million years place Los Angeles somewhere in the vicinity of the current location of Anchorage, Alaska.

    (A) will be plotting the plates' locations
    (B) plotting the location of the plates
    (C) are plotting the location of the plates
    (D) have been plotting the plates and their locations
    (E) plot the plates' locations

2. In the AD400s, Hawaii-Loa, a Polynesian chief, sailed some 2,400 miles of open water in the Pacific Ocean from the Marquesas Islands <u>near Tahiti, he landed</u> in what are today called the Hawaiian Islands.

    (A) near Tahiti, he landed
    (B) near Tahiti; landing
    (C) near Tahiti, then he landed
    (D) near Tahiti, landing
    (E) near Tahiti; his landing

108 | Lesson 7: Problems with SENTENCES

3. The Sun's color is most likely closer to white than to yellow, but it has such a bright yellow color when it viewed from Earth because it is being viewed through Earth's atmosphere.

   (A) yellow, but it has such a bright yellow color when it is viewed from Earth because it is being viewed
   (B) yellow, but it has such a bright yellow color when it is viewed from Earth; because it is being viewed
   (C) yellow, but it has such a bright yellow color when it is viewed from Earth, this is because it is being viewed
   (D) yellow, but has such a bright yellow color when it is viewed from Earth; because it is being viewed
   (E) yellow, but has such a bright yellow color when it is viewed from Earth; this is because it is being viewed

4. Taking preemptive action during Prohibition, police raided the home of Philo Richard Farnsworth in the mistaken belief that he was making illegal alcohol, at the time he was in reality working on the invention of the television.

   (A) alcohol, at the time he was in reality working
   (B) alcohol when in reality was working
   (C) alcohol; when he was in reality working
   (D) alcohol, in reality he was working
   (E) alcohol; at the time, he was in reality working

5. It is possible to tell a great deal about how a bird lives from the shape of its wings, for example, an albatross has long, slender wings for flying in strong winds on the open ocean.

    (A) its wings, for example, an albatross has
    (B) its wings; for example, an albatross using
    (C) its wings; an albatross, for example, has
    (D) its wings; an albatross, for example, with
    (E) its wings, an albatross for example has

6. In 1927, 26-year-old J. Willard Marriott and his bride Allie started in business by opening a root beer stand in Washington, D.C., and today has grown into Marriott International, Inc., a leading worldwide hospitality company.

    (A) started in business by opening a root beer stand in Washington, D.C., and today has grown
    (B) got their start in business by opening a root beer stand in Washington, D.C., today this has grown
    (C) started in business by opening a root beer stand in Washington, D.C., and today this has grown
    (D) starting in business by opening a root beer stand in Washington, D.C., and today this has grown
    (E) their start in business by opening a root beer stand in Washington, D.C., today this has grown

EXPLANATIONS

1. This question tests **sentences**.

   Computer *projections* will be plotting the plates' locations along the San Andreas fault in fifty million years *place* Los Angeles somewhere in the vicinity of the current location of Anchorage, Alaska.

   (A) will be plotting the plates' locations
   - This is an incorrect sentence because the subject *projections* already has a verb *place* and does not need the extra verb *will be plotting*.

   (B) plotting the location of the plates
   - This answer has a participle **plotting**, which is not a verb, providing a correct sentence with a subject *projections* and verb *place*. This answer is correct.

   (C) are plotting the location of the plates
   - This is an incorrect sentence because the subject *projections* already has a verb *place* and does not need the extra verb *are plotting*.

   (D) have been plotting the plates and their locations
   - This is an incorrect sentence because the subject *projections* already has a verb *place* and does not need the extra verb *have been plotting*.

   (E) plot the plates' locations
   - This is an incorrect sentence because the subject *projections* already has a verb *place* and does not need the extra verb *plot*.

2. This question tests **sentences**.

In the AD400s, Hawaii-Loa, a Polynesian chief, sailed some 2,400 miles of open water in the Pacific Ocean from the Marquesas Islands near Tahiti, he landed in what are today called the Hawaiian Islands.

(A) near Tahiti [,] he landed
   - This answer creates a run-on sentence because the two subjects and verbs *Hawaii-Loa...sailed* and *he landed* are connected with a comma [,]. A comma cannot be used to connect two subjects and verbs without a conjunction.

(B) near Tahiti [;] *landing*
   - This sentence contains a fragment following the semi-colon [;]. There must be a complete subject and verb on either side of a semi-colon, and this sentence has only the participle *landing* following the semi-colon.

(C) near Tahiti [,] then he landed
   - This answer creates a run-on sentence because the two subjects and verbs *Hawaii-Loa...sailed* and *he landed* are connected with a comma [,]. A comma cannot be used to connect two subjects and verbs without a conjunction, and *then* is an adverb and is not a conjunction.

[(D)] near Tahiti, **landing**
   - This answer has only the participle **landing** following a comma (,). This answer is correct.

(E) near Tahiti [;] his *landing*
   - This sentence contains a fragment following the semi-colon [;]. There must be a complete subject and verb on either side of a semi-colon, and this sentence has a subject *landing* but lacks a verb following the semi-colon.

It Works! GMAT Sentence Correction

3. **This question tests sentences.**

   The Sun's color is most likely closer to white than to yellow, *but* it has such a bright yellow color when it viewed from Earth because it is being viewed through Earth's atmosphere.

(A) yellow, but **it has** such a bright yellow color when it is viewed from Earth **because** it is being viewed
   - This answer correctly has a subject and verb **it has** following the comma (,) and *but* and no punctuation preceding **because it is**. This answer is correct.

(B) yellow, but it has such a bright yellow color when it is viewed from Earth ⟦;⟧ ⟦because it is being viewed⟧
   - This sentence contains a subordinate fragment *because it is being viewed* following the semi-colon ⟦;⟧. There must be a complete main clause subject and verb on either side of a semi-colon.

(C) yellow, but *it has* such a bright yellow color when it is viewed from Earth ⟦,⟧ *this is* because it is being viewed
   - This answer creates a run-on sentence because the two subjects and verbs *it has* and *this is* are connected with a comma ⟦,⟧. A comma cannot be used to connect two subjects and verbs without a conjunction.

(D) yellow, *but has* such a bright yellow color when it is viewed from Earth ⟦;⟧ ⟦because it is being viewed⟧
   - The part of this sentence ⟦, *but has*⟧ is a fragment because a subject and a verb are required following a comma (,) and *but*. This answer has a verb *has* but no subject following the comma (,) and *but*.
   - This sentence contains a subordinate fragment *because it is being viewed* following the semi-colon ⟦;⟧. There must be a complete main clause subject and verb on either side of a semi-colon.

(E) yellow, *but has* such a bright yellow color when it is viewed from Earth; this is because it is being viewed
   - The part of this sentence ⟦, *but has*⟧ is a fragment because a subject and a verb are required following a comma (,) and *but*. This answer has a verb *has* but no subject following the comma (,) and *but*.

Lesson 7: Problems with SENTENCES

4. This question tests **sentences**.

Taking preemptive action during Prohibition, *police raided* the home of Philo Richard Farnsworth in the mistaken belief that he was making illegal alcohol, at the time he was in reality working on the invention of the television.

(A) alcohol [,] at the time *he was* in reality *working*
  - This answer creates a run-on sentence because the two subjects and verbs *police raided* and *he was* are connected with a comma [,]. A comma cannot be used to connect two subjects and verbs without a conjunction, and *at the time* is an adverb phrase and is not a conjunction.

(B) alcohol *when* in reality [was working]
  - This sentence is a subordinate clause fragment because subordinate conjunction *when* should be followed by both a subject and a verb but here is followed by only the verb [was working].

(C) alcohol [;] [when he was] in reality [working]
  - This sentence contains a subordinate fragment [when he was...working] following the semi-colon [;]. There must be a complete main clause subject and verb on either side of a semi-colon.

(D) alcohol [,] in reality *he was working*
  - This answer creates a run-on sentence because the two subjects and verbs *police raided* and *he was working* are connected with a comma [,]. A comma cannot be used to connect two subjects and verbs without a conjunction, and *in reality* is an adverb phrase and is not a conjunction.

(E) alcohol; at the time, he was in reality working
  - This answer has a complete subject and verb **he was...working** following the semi-colon (;). This creates a sentence with two subjects and verbs joined with a semi-colon (;). This answer is correct.

5. This question tests **sentences**.

It is possible to tell a great deal about how a bird lives from the shape of its wings, for example, an albatross has long, slender wings for flying in strong winds on the open ocean.

(A) its wings [,] for example, an *albatross has*
   • This answer creates a run-on sentence because the two subjects and verbs *It is* and *albatross has* are connected with a comma [,]. *For example* is an adverb phrase and is not a conjunction.

(B) its wings [;] for example, an *albatross using*
   • This sentence is a fragment because a complete subject and verb must follow a semi-colon and there is only the subject *albatross* and no verb following the semi-colon [;]. *Using* is a participle and not a complete verb.

[(C)] its wings; an *albatross*, for example, has
   • This answer contains a subject and verb **albatross...has** following the semicolon (;), creating an answer with two subjects and verbs *(It is* and *albatross...has)* connected with a semi-colon. This answer is correct.

(D) its wings [;] an *albatross*, for example, with
   • This sentence is a fragment because a complete subject and verb must follow a semi-colon and there is only the subject *albatross* and no verb following the semi-colon [;].

(E) its wings [,] an *albatross* for example *has*
   • This answer creates a run-on sentence because the two subjects and verbs *it is* and *albatross...has* are connected with a comma [,]. *For example* is an adverb phrase and is not a conjunction.

6. This question tests **sentences**.

In 1927, 26-year-old *J. Willard Marriott and his bride Allie* started in business by opening a root beer stand in Washington, D.C., and today has grown into Marriott International, Inc., a leading worldwide hospitality company.

(A) started in business by opening a root beer stand in Washington, D.C., *and* today *has grown*
  • The part of this sentence following the comma *(,)* and *and* is a fragment because a subject and a verb are required following a comma *(,)* and *and*. This answer has a verb *has grown* but no subject. *Today* is an adverb and is not a subject.

(B) *got their start* in business by opening a root beer stand in Washington, D.C. *,* today *this has grown*
  • This answer creates a run-on sentence because the two subjects and verbs *J. Willard Marriott and his bride Allie started* and *this has grown* are connected with only a comma *,* . A comma cannot be used to connect two subjects and verbs without a conjunction, and *today* is an adverb and is not a conjunction.

[(C)] *started* in business by opening a root beer stand in Washington, D.C., and today *this has grown*
  • This answer creates a sentence containing two subjects and verbs *J. Willard Marriott and his bride Allie started* and *this has grown* correctly connected with a comma (**,**) and **and**. This answer is correct.

(D) *starting* in business by opening a root beer stand in Washington, D.C., *and* today this has grown
  • The first part of this sentence is a fragment because this answer creates a sentence with a subject *Willard Marriott and his bride Allie* and without a verb since *starting* is a participle and is not a verb.

(E) *their start* in business by opening a root beer stand in Washington, D.C. *,* today *this has grown*
  • The first part of this sentence is a fragment because this answer creates a sentence with a subject *Willard Marriott and his bride Allie* and without a verb since *their start* is not a verb.
  • The part of this sentence following the comma *,* is run-on because a subject and verb such as *this has grown* cannot be connect to a main sentence with a comma and no conjunction. *Today* is an adverb and is not a conjunction.

Lesson 8: Problems with WORDINESS

> **Wordiness** is a stylistic problem involving language that, while it may not actually be grammatically incorrect, is not expressed in the most concise way possible. The following kinds of problems with wordiness are common on the GMAT:
> 1. ideas expressed in a long way when a shorter (and more natural-sounding) way is possible
> 2. ideas expressed in a complex structure when a simpler (and more natural-sounding) structure is possible
> 3. ideas that are redundant (that is, ideas that are repeated elsewhere in the sentence)

EXAMPLE 1: This example shows ideas expressed in a long way when a shorter way is possible.

INCORRECT: *Should no other witnesses come forward, in addition to all the witnesses who have already come forward*, then the prosecutors are prepared to *bring the case to a close*.

CORRECT: If there are no more witnesses, then the prosecutors are prepared to close the case.

In the incorrect example, the ideas *Should no other witnesses come forward, in addition to all the witnesses who have already come forward* and *bring the case to a close* are too wordy. The stylistic preference is for more concise language. In the correct example, the wordy ideas have been replaced with the more concise ideas **If there are no more witnesses** and **close the case**.

- -

EXAMPLE 2: This example shows ideas expressed in complex structures when simpler structures are possible.

INCORRECT: What the message meant was that what she had done was a mistake.
CORRECT: The message meant that she had made a mistake.

In the incorrect example, the ideas *What the message meant* and *what she had done was a mistake* are complex. The stylistic preference is for simpler language. In the correct example, the complex ideas have been replaced with the simpler ideas **The message meant** and **she had made a mistake**.

- -

EXAMPLE 3: This example shows ideas that are redundant.

INCORRECT: The *first initial* phase of this project *may possibly* be completed soon.
CORRECT: The initial phase of this project may be completed soon.

In the incorrect example, *first* is redundant because its meaning is included within the word *initial,* and *possibly* is redundant because its meaning is included within the word *may.* In the correct example, the redundant ideas have been omitted and only the non-redundant **initial** and **may** remain.

SKILLS PRACTICE: Find the problems with **wordiness** in the following sentences. (The number in parentheses indicates the number of problems you should find.) Then, study the explanations on the pages that follow.

1. A huge throng headed for the exits after someone caught a brief glimpse of an armed gunman taking actions that appeared potentially dangerous to the person who saw them occurring. *(4)*

2. In a situation in which a tidal wave is almost on the verge of hitting a coastline, the water first recedes all the way back to the horizon before crashing into the coast. *(3)*

3. Snowfalls that are heavy and winds that are strong both of which occurring in urban environments can result in the effect of chaos as hazardous conditions and disruptions in transportation, in both its public form and its private form, cause problems for anyone who dares to venture outside. *(5)*

4. If the situation were such that an individual were to wake up completely during a nightmare, he or she would generally remember without forgetting the entirety of the nightmare as a whole. *(3)*

5. What today is known as the Charleston is a dance that originally developed in African-American communities which were in the United States; it became a popular dance craze both within the United States and also in countries outside the United States during the era in the 1920s called the Roaring Twenties. *(6)*

6. If a moving car is traveling at a speed of 55 miles per hour, it will travel 56 feet before an average driver can shift his or her foot from where it is on the accelerator to where it needs to be on the brake. *(3)*

7. The board of directors reached the general consensus that management's reaction to the serious crisis was not adequate enough and that the reason why this happened was a lack of advanced planning, one of the important essentials of success in business. *(6)*

8. An objective that could be deemed to be fundamental to many e-commerce websites is increasing sales while at the same time reducing the need for person-to-person human interaction, thereby resulting in increased profits. *(4)*

It Works! GMAT Sentence Correction

EXPLANATIONS (I = incorrect, C = correct)

1. A *huge throng* headed for the exits after someone caught a *brief glimpse* of an *armed gunman* taking actions that appeared potentially dangerous *to the person who saw them occurring*.

    - The word *huge* is redundant because its meaning is included within the word *throng*.
        - I: *a huge throng*
        - C: **a throng**

    - The word *brief* is redundant because its meaning is included within the word *glimpse*.
        - I: *a brief glimpse*
        - C: **a glimpse**

    - The word *armed* is redundant because its meaning is included within the word *gunman*.
        - I: *an armed gunman*
        - C: **a gunman**

    - The idea *to the person who saw them occurring* is overly wordy. The stylistic preference is for more concise language.
        - I: *to the person who saw them occurring*
        - C: **to the witness**

    -

2. *In a situation in which a tidal wave* is *almost* on the verge of hitting a coastline, the water first *recedes* all the way *back* to the horizon before crashing into the coast.

    - The idea *In a situation in which a tidal wave* is overly complex. The stylistic preference is for simpler language.
        - I: *In a situation in which a tidal wave*
        - C: **If a tidal wave**

    - The word *almost* is redundant because its meaning is included within the expression *on the verge*.
        - I: *almost on the verge*
        - C: **on the verge**

    - The word *back* is redundant because its meaning is included within the word *recedes*.
        - I: *recedes all the way back*
        - C: **recedes all the way**

    -

3. Snowfalls that are heavy and winds that are strong both of which occurring in urban environments can result in the effect of chaos as hazardous conditions and disruptions in transportation, in both its public form and its private form, cause problems for anyone who dares to venture outside.

- The idea *Snowfalls that are heavy and winds that are strong* is overly complex. The stylistic preference is for simpler language.
  - I: *Snowfalls that are heavy and winds that are strong*
  - C: **Heavy snowfalls and strong winds**

- The idea *both of which occurring in urban environments* is overly wordy and complex. The stylistic preference is for more concise and simpler language.
  - I: *both of which occurring in urban environments*
  - C: **in urban environments**

- The idea *the effect of* is redundant because its meaning is included within the idea *result in*.
  - I: *result in the effect of*
  - C: **result in**

- The idea *transportation, in both its public form and its private form*, is overly wordy and complex. The stylistic preference is for more concise and simpler language.
  - I: *transportation, in both its public form and its private form*
  - C: **public and private transportation**

- The word *dares* is redundant because its meaning is included within the word *venture*.
  - I: *anyone who dares to venture*
  - C: **anyone who ventures**

---

4. If the situation were such that an individual were to wake up completely during a nightmare, he or she would generally *remember* without forgetting the *entirety* of the nightmare as a whole.

- The idea *If the situation were such that an individual were to wake up completely* is overly wordy. The stylistic preference is for more concise language.
  - I: *If the situation were such that an individual were to wake up completely*
  - C: **If an individual woke up completely**

- The idea *without forgetting* is redundant because its meaning is included within the word *remember*.
  - I: *remember without forgetting*
  - C: **remember**

- The idea *as a whole* is redundant because its meaning is included within the word *entirety*.
  - I: *the entirety of the nightmare as a whole*
  - C: **the entire nightmare**

5. ~~What today is known as the Charleston is a dance~~ that ~~originally~~ developed in African-American communities ~~which were in the United States~~; it became a ~~popular~~ dance craze ~~both within the United States and also in countries outside the United States~~ ~~during the era in the 1920s called the Roaring Twenties~~.

- The idea *What today is known as the Charleston is a dance* is overly complex. The stylistic preference is for simpler language.
    - I: *What today is known as the Charleston is a dance*
    - C: **The Charleston is a dance**

- The word *originally* is redundant because its meaning is included within the word *developed*.
    - I: *originally developed*
    - C: **developed**

- The idea *which were in the United States* is overly complex. The stylistic preference is for simpler language.
    - I: *which were in the United States*
    - C: **in the United States**

- The word *popular* is redundant because its meaning is included within the word *craze*.
    - I: *a popular dance craze*
    - C: **a dance craze**

- The idea *both within the United States and also in countries outside the United States* is overly wordy. The stylistic preference is for more concise language.
    - I: *both within the United States and also in countries outside the United States*
    - C: **both in the United States and outside the country**

- The idea *during the era in the 1920s called the Roaring Twenties* is overly wordy. The stylistic preference is for more concise language.
    - I: *during the era in the 1920s called the Roaring Twenties*
    - C: **during the Roaring Twenties**

6. If a *moving* car is *traveling* at a *speed* of *55 miles per hour*, it will travel 56 feet before an average driver can shift his or her foot *from where it is on the accelerator to where it needs to be on the brake*.

- The word *moving* is redundant because its meaning is included within the word *traveling*.
    - I: *a moving car is traveling*
    - C: **a car is traveling**

- The word *speed* is redundant because its meaning is included within the idea *55 miles per hour*.
    - I: *at a speed of 55 miles per hour*
    - C: **at 55 miles per hour**

- The idea *from where it is on the accelerator to where it needs to be on the brake* is overly complex. The stylistic preference is for simpler language.
    - I: *from where it is on the accelerator to where it needs to be on the brake*
    - C: **from the accelerator to the brake**

- -

7. The board of directors reached the *general* consensus that management's reaction to the *serious* crisis was not adequate *enough* and that the reason *why* this happened was a lack of *advanced* planning, one of the *important* essentials of success in business.

- The word *general* is redundant because its meaning is included within the word *consensus*.
    - I: *the general consensus*
    - C: **the consensus**

- The word *serious* is redundant because its meaning is included within the word *crisis*.
    - I: *the serious crisis*
    - C: **the crisis**

- The word *enough* is redundant because its meaning is included within the word *adequate*.
    - I: *not adequate enough*
    - C: **not adequate**

- The word *why* is redundant because its meaning is included within the word *reason*.
    - I: *the reason why*
    - C: **the reason that**

- The word *advanced* is redundant because its meaning is included within the word *planning*.
    - I: *advanced planning*
    - C: **planning**

- The word *important* is redundant because its meaning is included within the word *essentials*.
    - I: *the important essentials*
    - C: **the essentials**

8. *An objective that could be deemed to be fundamental to many e-commerce websites* is increasing sales *while at the same time* reducing the need for *person-to-person* human interaction, *thereby* resulting in increased profits.

- The idea *An objective that could be deemed to be fundamental to many e-commerce websites* is overly wordy and complex. The stylistic preference is for more concise and simpler language.
    - I: *An objective that could be deemed to be fundamental to many e-commerce websites*
    - C: **A fundamental objective of many e-commerce websites**

- The idea *at the same time* is redundant because its meaning is included within the word *while*.
    - I: *while at the same time*
    - C: **while**

- The idea *person-to-person* is redundant because its meaning is included within the word *human*.
    - I: *person-to-person human interaction*
    - C: **human interaction**

- The word *thereby* is redundant because its meaning is included within the word *resulting*.
    - I: *thereby resulting*
    - C: **resulting**

It Works! GMAT Sentence Correction

GMAT-STYLE SKILLS PRACTICE: Choose the letter of the answer to each question that best reflects the style and accuracy of standard written English. Then, study the explanations on the pages that follow.

1. Amphetamines operate by stimulating the production of neurotransmitters, which are chemicals that transmit messages between nerve endings.

    (A) Amphetamines operate by stimulating
    (B) The way that amphetamines operate is by stimulating
    (C) The way that amphetamine drugs are able to operate is that they stimulate
    (D) The way that amphetamines are able to operate is that they stimulate
    (E) Amphetamine drugs operate by stimulating

2. An astoundingly prolific and productive fieldworker as well as theorist, Edward Sapir recorded for the posterity of future generations thirty-nine Amerindian languages, often working with the last living speaker.

    (A) prolific and productive fieldworker as well as theorist, Edward Sapir recorded for the posterity of future generations thirty-nine Amerindian languages, often working with the last living speaker
    (B) prolific and productive fieldworker as well as theorist, Edward Sapir recorded for future generations thirty-nine Amerindian languages, often working with the last living speaker still on Earth
    (C) prolific fieldworker as well as theorist, Edward Sapir recorded for posterity thirty-nine Amerindian languages, often working with the last speaker still on Earth
    (D) productive fieldworker as well as theorist, Edward Sapir recorded for the posterity of future generations thirty-nine Amerindian languages, often working with the last speaker still on Earth
    (E) prolific fieldworker as well as theorist, Edward Sapir recorded for posterity thirty-nine Amerindian languages, often working with the last living speaker still on Earth

Lesson 8: Problems with WORDINESS | 125

3. It has been estimated that within the entire universe as a whole there are more than a trillion galaxies and that a galaxy comparable to size to the Milky Way contains roughly 100 billion stars.

   (A) within the entire universe as a whole there are more than a trillion galaxies and that a galaxy comparable in size to the Milky Way contains roughly100 billion stars
   (B) within the entire universe there are more than a trillion galaxies and that a galaxy of a size comparable to size of the Milky Way contains 100 billion stars or so
   (C) within the entire universe as a whole there are more than a trillion galaxies and that a galaxy of a size comparable to size of the Milky Way contains roughly 100 billion stars or so
   (D) within the entire universe there are more than a trillion galaxies and that a galaxy comparable in size to the Milky Way contains roughly 100 billion stars
   (E) within the entire universe there are more than a trillion galaxies and that a galaxy comparable in size to the Milky Way contains roughly 100 billion stars or so

4. A disease known as Huntington's disease is a disorder of the central nervous system that causes degeneration of cells in the brain, slowly impairing a person's ability to walk, think, talk and reason.

   (A) A disease known as Huntington's disease is a disorder of the central nervous system that causes degeneration of cells in the brain, slowly impairing a person's ability to walk, think, talk and reason.
   (B) Huntington's disease is a disorder of the central nervous system that causes degeneration of cells in the brain, impairing a person's ability to walk, think, talk and reason over time.
   (C) Huntington's disease is a disorder of the central nervous system that causes progressive degeneration of cells in the brain, slowly impairing a person's ability to walk, think, talk and reason.
   (D) Huntington's disease is a disorder of the central nervous system that is responsible for causing degeneration of cells in the brain, slowly impairing a person's ability to walk, think, talk and reason.
   (E) Huntington's disease is a disorder of the central nervous system, one that is responsible for causing degeneration of cells in the brain, impairing a person's ability to walk, think, talk and reason over time.

5. Under conditions that could be consider optimal, intense low pressure systems outside the tropics can deepen to become so dangerous that they can be considered as dangerous as midlevel tropical hurricanes.

    (A) Under conditions that could be consider optimal, intense low pressure systems outside the tropics can deepen to become so dangerous that they can be considered as dangerous as
    (B) Under conditions that could be consider optimal, low pressure systems that are intense and are outside the tropics can deepen to become as dangerous as
    (C) Under optimal conditions, low pressure systems that are intense and are outside the tropics can deepen to become as dangerous as
    (D) Under optimal conditions, intense low pressure systems outside the tropics can deepen to become as dangerous as
    (E) Under optimal conditions, intense low pressure systems outside the tropics can deepen to become so dangerous that they can be considered as dangerous as

6. When psychologists provide test subjects with an ordered list of items, the subjects tend to exhibit the serial position effect, which in overly simplistic terms is that subjects tend to remember items positioned earlier and later in the list better than those positioned in the middle.

    (A) which in overly simplistic terms is that subjects tend to remember items positioned earlier and later in the list better than those positioned
    (B) which in simplistic terms is that subjects tend to remember items that psychologists have positioned earlier and later in the list better than those that have been positioned
    (C) which is to say in simplistic terms is that subjects tend to remember items that psychologists have positioned earlier and later in the list better than those that have been positioned
    (D) which is to say in overly simplistic terms is that subjects tend to remember items positioned earlier and later in the list better than those positioned
    (E) which in simplistic terms is that subjects tend to remember items positioned earlier and later in the list better than those positioned

EXPLANATIONS

1. This question tests **wordiness**.

   <u>Amphetamines operate by stimulating</u> the production of neurotransmitters, which are chemicals that transmit messages between nerve endings.

   (A) Amphetamines operate by stimulating
   - This answer avoids the overly complex idea *The way that* found in some of the other answers, uses the non-redundant **Amphetamines** in place of the redundant idea *amphetamine drugs* found in some of the other responses, and uses the less wordy idea **operate by stimulating** in place of the overly wordy idea *are able to operate is that they stimulate* found in some of the other answers. This answer is correct.

   (B) *The way that* amphetamines operate is by stimulating
   - The idea *The way that* is overly complex. The stylistic preference is for simpler language.

   (C) *The way that* amphetamine *drugs* *are able to operate is that they stimulate*
   - The idea *The way that* is overly complex. The stylistic preference is for simpler language.
   - The word *drugs* is redundant because its meaning is included within the word *amphetamine*.
   - The idea *are able to operate is that they stimulate* is overly wordy. The stylistic preference is for more concise language.

   (D) *The way that* amphetamines *are able to operate is that they stimulate*
   - The idea *The way that* is overly complex. The stylistic preference is for simpler language.
   - The idea *are able to operate is that they stimulate* is overly wordy. The stylistic preference is for more concise language.

   (E) Amphetamine *drugs* operate by stimulating
   - The word *drugs* is redundant because its meaning is included within the word *amphetamine*.

2. This question tests **wordiness**.

An astoundingly prolific and productive fieldworker as well as theorist, Edward Sapir recorded for the posterity of future generations thirty-nine Amerindian languages, often working with the last living speaker.

(A) *prolific* and *productive* fieldworker as well as theorist, Edward Sapir recorded for the *posterity* of *future generations* thirty-nine Amerindian languages, often working with the last living speaker
- The word *productive* is redundant because its meaning is included within the word *prolific*.
- The idea *future generations* is redundant because its meaning is included within the word *posterity*.

(B) *prolific* and *productive* fieldworker as well as theorist, Edward Sapir recorded for future generations thirty-nine Amerindian languages, often working with the last *living* speaker *still on Earth*
- The word *productive* is redundant because its meaning is included within the word *prolific*.
- The idea *still on Earth* is redundant because its meaning is included within the word *living*.

(C) prolific fieldworker as well as theorist, Edward Sapir recorded for posterity thirty-nine Amerindian languages, often working with the last speaker still on Earth
- This answer uses the non-redundant ideas **prolific, posterity,** and **still on Earth** in place of the redundant ideas *prolific and productive, the posterity of future generations,* and *the last living speaker still on Earth* found in some of the other answers. This answer is correct.

(D) productive fieldworker as well as theorist, Edward Sapir recorded for the *posterity* of *future generations* thirty-nine Amerindian languages, often working with the last speaker still on Earth
- The idea *future generations* is redundant because its meaning is included within the word *posterity*.

(E) prolific fieldworker as well as theorist, Edward Sapir recorded for posterity thirty-nine Amerindian languages, often working with the last *living* speaker *still on Earth*
- The idea *still on Earth* is redundant because its meaning is included within the word *living*.

3. This question tests **wordiness**.

It has been estimated that within the entire universe as a whole there are more than a trillion galaxies and that a galaxy comparable to size to the Milky Way contains roughly 100 billion stars.

(A) within the *entire* universe as a whole there are more than a trillion galaxies and that a galaxy comparable in size to the Milky Way contains roughly 100 billion stars
- The idea *as a whole* is redundant because its meaning is included within the word *entire*.

(B) within the entire universe there are more than a trillion galaxies and that a galaxy of a size comparable to size of the Milky Way contains 100 billion stars or so
- The idea *a galaxy of a size comparable to the size of the Milky Way* is overly wordy. The stylistic preference is for more concise language.

(C) within the *entire* universe as a whole there are more than a trillion galaxies and that a galaxy of a size comparable to size of the Milky Way contains *roughly* 100 billion stars or so
- The idea *as a whole* is redundant because its meaning is included within the word *entire*.
- The idea *a galaxy of a size comparable to the size of the Milky Way* is overly wordy. The stylistic preference is for more concise language.
- The idea *or so* is redundant because its meaning is included within the word *roughly*.

(D) within the entire universe there are more than a trillion galaxies and that **a galaxy comparable in size to the Milky Way contains roughly 100 billion stars**
- This answer contains the non-redundant idea **entire** in place of the redundant idea *entire...as a whole* found in some of the other answers, contains the less wordy idea **a galaxy comparable in size to the Milky Way** in place of the overly word idea *a galaxy of a size comparable to the size of he Milky Way* found in some of the other answers, and contains the non-redundant idea **roughly** in place of the redundant idea *roughly...or so* found in some of the other answers. This answer is correct.

(E) within the entire universe there are more than a trillion galaxies and that a galaxy comparable in size to the Milky Way contains *roughly* 100 billion stars or so
- The idea *or so* is redundant because its meaning is included within the word *roughly*.

4. This question tests **wordiness**.

A disease known as Huntington's disease is a disorder of the central nervous system that causes degeneration of cells in the brain, slowly impairing a person's ability to walk, think, talk and reason.

(A) *A disease known as Huntington's disease* is a disorder of the central nervous system that causes degeneration of cells in the brain, slowly impairing a person's ability to walk, think, talk and reason.
- The idea *A disease known as Huntington's disease* is overly wordy. The stylistic preference is for more concise language.

(B) Huntington's disease is a disorder of the central nervous system that causes degeneration of cells in the brain, impairing a person's ability to walk, think, talk and reason over time.
- This answer contains the less wordy idea **Huntington's disease** in place of the overly wordy idea *A disease known as Huntington's disease* found in some of the other answers, contains the simpler idea **a disorder of the central nervous system that** in place of the overly complex idea *a disorder of the central nervous system, one that* found in some of the other answers, and contains and the non-redundant ideas **causes** and **degeneration** in place of the redundant ideas *is responsible for causing* and *progressive degeneration* found in some of the other answers. This answer is correct.

(C) Huntington's disease is a disorder of the central nervous system that causes *progressive degeneration* of cells in the brain, slowly impairing a person's ability to walk, think, talk and reason.
- The word *progressive* is redundant because its meaning is included within the word *degeneration*.

(D) Huntington's disease is a disorder of the central nervous system that *is responsible for* causing degeneration of cells in the brain, slowly impairing a person's ability to walk, think, talk and reason.
- The idea *is responsible for* is redundant because its meaning is included within the word *causing*.

(E) Huntington's disease is *a disorder of the central nervous system, one that* *is responsible for* causing degeneration of cells in the brain, impairing a person's ability to walk, think, talk and reason over time.
- The idea *a disorder of the central nervous system, one that* is overly wordy and complex. The stylistic preference is for more concise and simpler language.
- The idea *is responsible for* is redundant because its meaning is included within the word *causing*.

5. This question tests **wordiness**.

Under conditions that could be consider optimal, intense low pressure systems outside the tropics can deepen to become so dangerous that they can be considered as dangerous as midlevel tropical hurricanes.

(A) Under conditions that could be consider optimal, intense low pressure systems outside the tropics can deepen to become so dangerous that they can be considered as dangerous as
  - The idea *Under conditions that could be considered optimal* is overly wordy and complex. The stylistic preference is for more concise and simpler language.
  - The idea *so dangerous that they can be considered as dangerous as* is overly wordy and complex. The stylistic preference is for more concise and simpler language.

(B) Under conditions that could be consider optimal, low pressure systems that are intense and are outside the tropics can deepen to become as dangerous as
  - The idea *Under conditions that could be considered optimal* is overly wordy and complex. The stylistic preference is for more concise and simpler language.
  - The idea *low pressure systems that are intense and are outside the tropics* is overly wordy and complex. The stylistic preference is for more concise and simpler language.

(C) Under optimal conditions, low pressure systems that are intense and are outside the tropics can deepen to become as dangerous as
  - The idea *low pressure systems that are intense and are outside the tropics* is overly wordy and complex. The stylistic preference is for more concise and simpler language.

(D) Under optimal conditions, intense low pressure systems outside the tropics can deepen to become as dangerous as
  - This answer contains the less wordy and simpler ideas **Under optimal conditions, intense low pressure systems outside the tropics**, and **as dangerous as** in place of the overly wordy and complex ideas *under conditions that could be considered optimal, low pressure systems that are intense and are outside the tropics,* and *so dangerous that they can be considered as dangerous as* found in some of the other answers. This answer is correct.

(E) Under optimal conditions, intense low pressure systems outside the tropics can deepen to become so dangerous that they can be considered as dangerous as
  - The idea *so dangerous that they can be considered as dangerous as* is overly wordy and complex. The stylistic preference is for more concise and simpler language.

6. This question tests **wordiness**.

When psychologists provide test subjects with an ordered list of items, the subjects tend to exhibit the serial position effect, which in overly simplistic terms is that subjects tend to remember items positioned earlier and later in the list better than those positioned in the middle.

(A) which in overly simplistic terms is that subjects tend to remember items positioned earlier and later in the list better than those positioned
- The word *overly* is redundant because its meaning is included within the word *simplistic*.

(B) which in simplistic terms is that subjects tend to remember items that psychologists have positioned earlier and later in the list better than those that have been positioned
- The idea *items that psychologists have positioned earlier and later in the list better than those that have been positioned* is overly wordy. The stylistic preference is for more concise language.

(C) which is to say in simplistic terms is that subjects tend to remember items that psychologists have positioned earlier and later in the list better than those that have been positioned
- The idea *which is to say* is overly complex. The stylistic preference is for simpler language.
- The idea *items that psychologists have positioned early and later in the list better than those that have been positioned* is overly wordy. The stylistic preference is for more concise language.

(D) which is to say in overly simplistic terms is that subjects tend to remember items positioned earlier and later in the list better than those positioned
- The idea *which is to say* is overly complex. The stylistic preference is for simpler language.
- The word *overly* is redundant because its meaning is included within the word *simplistic*.

(E) which in simplistic terms is that subjects tend to remember items positioned earlier and later in the list better than those positioned
- This answer contains the simpler idea **which** in place of the overly complex idea *which is to say* found in some of the other answers, contains the non-redundant idea **simplistic** in place of the redundant idea *overly simplistic* found in some of the other responses, and contains the less wordy idea **items positioned earlier and later in the list better than those positioned** in place of the overly wordy idea *items that psychologists have positioned earlier and later in the list better than those that have been positioned* found in some of the other answers. This answer is correct.

Lesson 9: Problems with AWKWARDNESS

> **Awkwardness** is a stylistic problem involving language that, while it may not actually be grammatically incorrect, is not expressed in the most graceful and natural way possible. The following kinds of problems with awkwardness are common on the GMAT:
> 1. language that sounds unnatural to a native speaker
> 2. the unnecessary use of the gerund (a verbal noun ending in *-ing*)
> 3. the unnecessary use of the passive voice
> 4. the omission of the conjunction *that*
> 5. the use of *in that*

EXAMPLE 1: This example shows language that sounds unnatural to a native speaker.

INCORRECT: The manager has decided that, *with the exception of no one but himself*, everyone must submit time cards daily.
CORRECT: The manager has decided that everyone except him must submit time cards daily.

In the incorrect example, the idea *with the exception of no one but himself* sounds unnatural to a native speaker. The stylistic preference is for more a more natural-sounding way of expressing this idea. In the correct example, this idea is expressed using the more natural-sounding **everyone except him**.

- -

EXAMPLE 2: This example shows the unnecessary use of a gerund (a verbal noun ending in *-ing*).

INCORRECT: The *starting* of construction is scheduled to begin on Tuesday.
CORRECT: The start of construction is scheduled to begin on Tuesday.

In the incorrect example, the gerund *starting* is unnecessary here because a regular noun with an appropriate meaning *(start)* exists in English. The stylistic preference is to avoid unnecessary gerunds. In the correct example, this idea *starting* is expressed using the more natural-sounding **start**.

- -

EXAMPLE 3: This example shows the unnecessary use of the passive voice.

INCORRECT: The speech was delivered by the congressman, and the audience reacted negatively to it.
CORRECT: The congressman delivered the speech, and the audience reacted negatively to it.

In the incorrect example, the passive voice *The speech was delivered by the congressman* is unnecessary. The more direct active voice would be stylistically preferable here. In the correct example, this idea is expressed using the more direct active voice **The congressman delivered the speech**.

- -

EXAMPLE 4: This example shows the omission of the conjunction *that*.

INCORRECT: The forecaster said the next few days would be stormy.
CORRECT: The forecaster said that the next few days would be stormy.

In the incorrect example, the conjunction *that* has been omitted in front of the subject and verb *the next few days would be*. The stylistic preference is to include the conjunction **that**. In the correct example, the conjunction **that** has been included in front of the subject and verb *the next few days would be stormy*.

- -

EXAMPLE 5: This example shows the awkward use of *in that*.

INCORRECT: A new accounting firm needs to be hired in that there are so many problems with the current firm.
CORRECT: A new accounting firm needs to be hired because there are so many problems with the current firm.

In the incorrect example, the expression *in that* is considered stylistically awkward and overly formal by GMAT. The stylistic preference is for more a more natural-sounding way of expressing this. In the correct example, *in that* has been replaced by **because**.

SKILLS PRACTICE: Find the problems with **awkwardness** in the following sentences. (The number in parentheses indicates the number of problems you should find.) Then, study the explanations on the pages that follow.

1. Someone who has lost his or her consciousness may be suffering from some kind of thing as minor as a fainting spell or as serious as a stroke. *(2)*

2. Some archaeologists who have claimed Neanderthals did not die out but instead interbred with later arrivals believe a fossil from Lagar Velho represents a hybrid between Neanderthals and modern humans. *(2)*

3. Edward Jenner's developing of a vaccine for the killer disease smallpox during the 18th century was a scientific breakthrough, but interestingly how the vaccine worked was not completely understood by Jenner. *(2)*

4. Alzheimer's disease in a predominant way affects the parts of the brain that have a controlling ability over thought, memory, and language ability, such that the result is a loss of cognitive ability known as dementia. *(3)*

5. When the Windy City was swept through by the Great Chicago Fire in 1873, the city's architects knew they had an opportunity lacking in precedence to build anew, with innovative materials, techniques, and inventions. *(3)*

6. In many regions, a buildup of snow on the ground is important for agriculture and water storage in that the percolating of meltwater into the soil and the reducing of water loss are helped by snow cover. *(4)*

7. It is the determination of scientists that the sun does not possess the perfection of a sphere because of a thin "cantaloupe skin" the sun develops during the years solar activity is high and the sun's oblateness has been increased. *(5)*

8. Lady Godiva's infamous riding through Coventry was provoked when, on behalf of the citizenry of Coventry, Godiva's husband Leofric was importuned by her to lower taxes, and he promised he would do her bidding only if she were to take the action considered untoward of riding naked through the town. *(4)*

Lesson 9: Problems with AWKWARDNESS

EXPLANATIONS (I = incorrect, C = correct)

1. Someone who *has lost his or her consciousness* may be suffering from *some kind of thing* as minor as a fainting spell or as serious as a stroke.

   - The idea *has lost his or her consciousness* is awkward. The stylistic preference is for a more natural-sounding way of expressing this idea.
     - I: *has lost his or her consciousness*
     - C: **has lost consciousness**

   - The idea *some kind of thing* is awkward. The stylistic preference is for a more natural-sounding way of expressing this idea.
     - I: *some kind of thing*
     - C: **something**

   -

2. Some archaeologists *who have claimed Neanderthals did not die out* but instead interbred with later arrivals believe *a fossil* from Lagar Velho *represents* a hybrid between Neanderthals and modern humans.

   - The conjunction *that* has been omitted in front of the subject and verb *Neanderthals did not die out*. The stylistic preference on GMAT is to include the conjunction **that**.
     - I: *Neanderthals did not die out*
     - C: **that Neanderthals did not die out**

   - The conjunction *that* has been omitted in front of the subject and verb *a fossil...represents*. The stylistic preference on GMAT is to include the conjunction **that**.
     - I: *a fossil...represents*
     - C: **that a fossil...represents**

   -

3. Edward Jenner's *developing* of a vaccine for the killer disease smallpox during the 18th century was a scientific breakthrough, but interestingly how the vaccine worked *was not completely understood by* Jenner.

   - The part of the answer *developing* is awkward. The stylistic preference is to avoid unnecessary gerunds (*-ing* verbal nouns).
     - I: *developing*
     - C: **development**

   - The passive voice *was not completely understood by* is unnecessary here. The more direct active voice would be stylistically preferable.
     - I: *how the vaccine worked was not completed understood by Jenner*
     - C: **Jenner did not completely understand how the vaccine worked**

   -

It Works! GMAT Sentence Correction

4. Alzheimer's disease *in a predominant way* affects the parts of the brain that *have a controlling ability over* thought, memory, and language ability, *such that the result is* a loss of cognitive ability known as dementia.

   - The idea *in a predominant way* is awkward. The stylistic preference is for a more natural-sounding way of expressing this idea.
     - I: *in a predominant way*
     - C: **predominantly**

   - The idea *have a controlling ability over* is awkward. The stylistic preference is for a more natural-sounding way of expressing this idea.
     - I: *have a controlling ability over*
     - C: **control**

   - The idea *such that the result is* is awkward. The stylistic preference is for a more natural-sounding way of expressing this idea.
     - I: *such that the result is*
     - C: **resulting in**

   -

5. When the Windy City *was swept through by* the Great Chicago Fire in 1873, the city's architects knew *they had an opportunity lacking in precedence* to build anew, with innovative materials, techniques, and inventions.

   - The passive voice *was swept through by* is unnecessary here. The more direct active voice would be stylistically preferable.
     - I: *the Windy City was swept through by the Great Chicago Fire*
     - C: **the Great Chicago Fire swept through the Windy City**

   - The conjunction *that* has been omitted in front of the subject and verb *they had*. The stylistic preference on GMAT is to include the conjunction **that**.
     - I: *they had*
     - C: **that they had**

   - The idea *an opportunity lacking in precedence* is awkward. The stylistic preference is for a more natural-sounding way of expressing this idea.
     - I: *an opportunity lacking in precedence*
     - C: **an unprecedented opportunity**

   -

Lesson 9: Problems with AWKWARDNESS | 139

6. In many regions, a buildup of snow on the ground is important for agriculture and water storage *in that the percolating* of meltwater into the soil and *the reducing* of water loss *are helped by* snow cover.

- The expression *in that* is considered stylistically awkward and overly formal by GMAT. The stylistic preference is for a more natural-sounding way of expressing this.
    - I: *in that*
    - C: **since**

- The idea *the percolating* is awkward. The stylistic preference is to avoid unnecessary gerunds (*-ing* verbal nouns).
    - I: *the percolating*
    - C: **the percolation**

- The idea *the reducing* is awkward. The stylistic preference is to avoid unnecessary gerunds (*-ing* verbal nouns).
    - I: *the reducing*
    - C: **the reduction**

- The passive voice *are helped by* is unnecessary here. The more direct active voice would be stylistically preferable.
    - I: *the percolating of meltwater into the soil and the reducing of water loss are helped by snow*
    - C: **snow helps the percolating (or the percolation) of meltwater into the soil and the reducing (or the reduction) of water loss**

- -

7. *It is the determination of scientists* that the sun *does not possess the perfection of a sphere* because of a thin "cantaloupe skin" *the sun develops* during the years *solar activity is* high and the sun's oblateness *has been increased*.

- The idea *It is the determination of scientists* is awkward. The stylistic preference is for a more natural-sounding way of expressing this idea.
    - I: *It is the determination of scientists*
    - C: **Scientists have determined**

- The idea *does not possess the perfection of a sphere* is awkward. The stylistic preference is for a more natural-sounding way of expressing this idea.
    - I: *does not possess the perfection of a sphere*
    - C: **is not perfectly spherical**

- The conjunction *that* has been omitted in front of the subject and verb *the sun develops*. The stylistic preference on GMAT is to include the conjunction **that**.
    - I: *the sun develops*
    - C: **that the sun develops**

- The conjunction *that* has been omitted in front of the subject and verb solar activity is. The stylistic preference on GMAT is to include the conjunction **that**.
    - I: *solar activity is*
    - C: **that solar activity is**

- The passive voice has been increased is unnecessary here. The more direct active voice would be stylistically preferable.
    - I: *the sun's oblateness has been increased*
    - C: **the sun's oblateness has increased**

- -

8. Lady Godiva's infamous riding through Coventry was provoked when, on behalf of the citizenry of Coventry, Godiva's husband Leofric was importuned by her to lower taxes, and he promised he would do her bidding only if she were to take the action considered untoward of riding naked through the town.

    - The part of the answer riding is awkward. The stylistic preference is to avoid unnecessary gerunds (*-ing* verbal nouns).
        - I: *riding*
        - C: **ride**

    - The passive voice was importuned by is unnecessary here. The more direct active voice would be stylistically preferable.
        - I: *Godiva's husband Leofric was importuned by her*
        - C: **Godiva importuned her husband Leofric**

    - The conjunction *that* has been omitted in front of the subject and verb he would do. The stylistic preference on GMAT is to include the conjunction **that**.
        - I: *he would do*
        - C: **that he would do**

    - The idea if she were to take the action considered untoward is awkward. The stylistic preference is for a more natural-sounding way of expressing this idea.
        - I: *if she were to take the action considered untoward*
        - C: **if she took the untoward action**

GMAT-STYLE SKILLS PRACTICE: Choose the letter of the answer to each question that best reflects the style and accuracy of standard written English. Then, study the explanations on the pages that follow.

1. In 1911, when the dissolving of Standard Oil Company was ordered by the U.S. Supreme Court given that the company was in contravention of the of the country's antirust laws, John D. Rockefeller stepped down as president.

   (A) the dissolving of Standard Oil Company was ordered by the U.S. Supreme Court given that
   (B) the U.S. Supreme Court ordered the dissolving of Standard Oil Company in that
   (C) the U.S. Supreme Court ordered the dissolution of Standard Oil Company given that
   (D) the U.S. Supreme Court ordered the dissolution of Standard Oil Company in that
   (E) the dissolution of Standard Oil Company was ordered by the U.S. Supreme Court given that

2. For a short time in the 1830s, a modicum of popularity was enjoyed by ketchup during the marketing of it as the patented medicine, *Dr. Miles's Compound Extract of Tomato*.

   (A) a modicum of popularity was enjoyed by ketchup during the marketing of it
   (B) ketchup enjoyed a modicum of popularity during the marketing of it
   (C) the enjoying of a modicum of popularity was experienced by ketchup during its marketing campaign
   (D) ketchup enjoyed a modicum of popularity during its marketing campaign
   (E) the enjoyment of a modicum of popularity was experieced by ketchup when because of its naming after Dr. Miles it was successfully marketed

3. Researchers are unsure about the roots of the myth that storks bring babies, but they believe that it may be related to the notion that storks resting on a house will ensure fertility in that household.

    (A) that it may be related to the notion that storks resting on a house will ensure fertility in that household
    (B) that it may be related to the notion that the resting of storks on a house will ensure fertility in that household
    (C) that it may be related to the notion that fertility in a household will be ensured by storks resting on the house
    (D) it may be related to the notion that storks resting on a house will ensure fertility in that household
    (E) it may be related to the notion that fertility in a household will be ensured by the resting of storks

4. Fin whales can empty followed by refilling their lungs in less than two seconds, half the time taken by humans in spite of the whales' breathing in 3,000 times more of the air.

    (A) Fin whales can empty followed by refilling their lungs in less than two seconds, half the time humans take in spite of the whales' breathing in 3,000 times more of the air.
    (B) Fin whales can empty and then refill their lungs in less than two seconds, half the time that humans take even though the whales breathe in 3,000 times more air.
    (C) Fin whales can empty and then refill their lungs in less than two seconds, half the time taken by humans even though the whales breathe in 3,000 times more of the air.
    (D) Fin whales can empty followed by refilling their lungs in less than two seconds, half the time that humans take in spite of the whales' breathing in 3,000 times more air.
    (E) Fin whales can empty and then refill their lungs in less than two seconds, half the time humans take even though the whales breathe in 3,000 times more air.

5.   It is without surprise that large areas of both the United States and Australia are extremely fire-prone since aridity and drought conditions prevail in large swaths of both countries.

   (A)   It is without surprise that large areas of both the United States and Australia are extremely fire-prone since
   (B)   Without surprise it is that large areas of both the United States and Australia are extremely fire-prone in that
   (C)   No surprise is it that large areas of both the United States and Australia have an extreme tending toward being fire-prone since
   (D)   It is no surprise that large areas of both the United States and Australia have an extreme fire-prone tendency in that
   (E)   It is no surprise that large areas of both the United States and Australia are extremely fire-prone since

6.   Genghis Khan is believed to have fathered hundreds if not thousands of children, and, as a result, his Y chromosome has been estimated to be carried by 0.5 percent of the world's male population today.

   (A)   Genghis Khan is believed to have fathered hundreds if not thousands of children, and, as a result, his Y chromosome has been estimated to be carried by 0.5 percent of the world's male population today.
   (B)   Genghis Khan is believed to have fathered hundreds if not thousands of children, and, as a result, an estimated .5 percent of the world's male population today carries his Y chromosome.
   (C)   Researchers believe Genghis Khan fathered hundreds if not thousands of children, and, as a result, his Y chromosome has been estimated to be carried by 0.5 percent of the world's male population today.
   (D)   Researchers believe that Genghis Khan fathered hundreds if not thousands of children and that, as a result, .5 percent of the world's male population today carries his Y chromosome.
   (E)   Researchers believe Genghis Khan fathered hundreds if not thousands of children and, as a result, his Y chromosome has been estimated to be carried by 0.5 percent of the world's male population today.

EXPLANATIONS

1. This question tests **awkwardness**.

   In 1911, when <u>the dissolving of Standard Oil Company was ordered by the U.S. Supreme Court given that</u> the company was in contravention of the of the country's antirust laws, John D. Rockefeller stepped down as president.

(A) *the dissolving* of Standard Oil Company *was ordered by* the U.S. Supreme Court given that
   - The part of the answer *the dissolving* is awkward. The stylistic preference is to avoid unnecessary gerunds (*-ing* verbal nouns) if possible.
   - The passive voice *was ordered by* is unnecessary here. The more direct active voice would be stylistically preferable.

(B) the U.S. Supreme Court ordered *the dissolving* of Standard Oil Company *in that*
   - The part of the answer *the dissolving* is awkward. The stylistic preference is to avoid unnecessary gerunds (*-ing* verbal nouns) if possible.
   - The expression *in that* is considered stylistically awkward and overly formal by GMAT. The stylistic preference is for a more natural-sounding way of expressing this.

(C) the U.S. Supreme Court **ordered the dissolution** of Standard Oil Company **given that**
   - This answer contains the stylistically preferable active verb **ordered** in place of the unnecessary passive *was ordered* found in some of the other answers, the regular noun **dissolution** in place of the unnecessary gerund (*-ing* verbal noun) *dissolving* found in some of the other answers, and the expression **given that** in place of the stylistically awkward expression *in that* found in some of the other answers. This answer is correct.

(D) the U.S. Supreme Court ordered the dissolution of Standard Oil Company *in that*
   - The expression *in that* is considered stylistically awkward and overly formal by GMAT. The stylistic preference is for a more natural-sounding way of expressing this.

(E) the dissolution of Standard Oil Company *was ordered by* the U.S. Supreme Court given that
   - The passive voice *was ordered by* is unnecessary here. The more direct active voice would be stylistically preferable.

2. This question tests **awkwardness**.

For a short time in the 1830s, a modicum of popularity was enjoyed by ketchup during the marketing of it as the patented medicine, *Dr. Miles's Compound Extract of Tomato*.

(A) a modicum of popularity *was enjoyed by* ketchup during *the marketing of it*
  - The passive voice *was enjoyed by* is unnecessary here. The more direct active voice would be stylistically preferable.
  - The part of the answer *the marketing of it* is awkward. The stylistic preference is to avoid unnecessary gerunds (*-ing* verbal nouns) if possible.

(B) ketchup enjoyed a modicum of popularity during *the marketing of it*
  - The part of the answer *the marketing of it* is awkward. The stylistic preference is to avoid unnecessary gerunds (*-ing* verbal nouns) if possible.

(C) *the enjoying* of a modicum of popularity *was experienced by* ketchup during its marketing campaign
  - The part of the answer *the enjoying* is awkward. The stylistic preference is to avoid unnecessary gerunds (*-ing* verbal nouns) if possible.
  - The passive voice *was experienced by* is unnecessary here. The more direct active voice would be stylistically preferable.

(D) ketchup **enjoyed** a modicum of popularity during its **marketing** campaign
  - This answer contains the stylistically preferable active voice verb **enjoyed** and the adjective **marketing** in place of the unnecessary gerunds (*-ing* verbal nouns) and passive voice verbs found in some of the other answers. This answer is correct.

(E) the enjoyment of a modicum of popularity *was experieced by* ketchup when because of *its naming* after Dr. Miles it *was successfully marketed*
  - The passive voice *was experienced by* is unnecessary here. The more direct active voice would be stylistically preferable.
  - The part of the answer *its naming* is awkward. The stylistic preference is to avoid unnecessary gerunds (*-ing* verbal nouns) if possible.
  - The passive voice *was successfully marketed* is unnecessary here. The more direct active voice would be stylistically preferable.

It Works! GMAT Sentence Correction

3. **This question tests awkwardness.**

   Researchers are unsure about the roots of the myth that storks bring babies, but they believe <u>that it may be related to the notion that storks resting on a house will ensure fertility in that household</u>.

   (A) **that** *it may be related* to the notion that storks **resting** on a house **will ensure** fertility in that household
   - This answer contains the stylistically preferable conjunction **that** in front of the subject and verb *it may be related* that is missing in some of the other answers, the adjective **resting** in place of the unnecessary gerund (*-ing* verbal noun) *the resting* found in some of the other answers, and the stylistically preferable active voice verb **will ensure** in place of the unnecessary passive *will be ensured* found in some of the other answers. This answer is correct.

   (B) that it may be related to the notion that *the resting* of storks on a house will ensure fertility in that household
   - The part of the answer *the resting* is awkward. The stylistic preference is to avoid unnecessary gerunds (*-ing* verbal nouns) if possible.

   (C) that it may be related to the notion that fertility in a household *will be ensured by* storks resting on the house
   - The passive voice *will be ensured by* is unnecessary here. The more direct active voice would be stylistically preferable.

   (D) *it may be related* to the notion that storks resting on a house will ensure fertility in that household
   - The conjunction *that* has been omitted in front of the subject and verb *it may be related*. The stylistic preference on GMAT is to include the conjunction **that**.

   (E) *it may be related* to the notion that fertility in a household *will be ensured by* *the resting* of storks
   - The conjunction *that* has been omitted in front of the subject and verb *it may be related*. The stylistic preference on GMAT is to include the conjunction **that**.
   - The passive voice *will be ensured by* is unnecessary here. The more direct active voice would be stylistically preferable.
   - The part of the answer *the resting* is awkward. The stylistic preference is to avoid unnecessary gerunds (*-ing* verbal nouns) if possible.

4. This question tests **awkwardness**.

Fin whales can empty followed by refilling their lungs in less than two seconds, half the time taken by humans in spite of the whales' breathing in 3,000 times more of the air.

(A) Fin whales can empty followed by refilling their lungs in less than two seconds, half the time humans take in spite of the whales' breathing in 3,000 times more of the air.
- The idea *can empty followed by refilling* is awkward. The stylistic preference is for a more natural-sounding way of expressing this idea.
- The conjunction *that* has been omitted in front of the subject and verb *humans take*. The stylistic preference on GMAT is to include the conjunction **that**.
- The idea *in spite of the whales' breathing in* is awkward. The stylistic preference is for a more natural-sounding way of expressing this idea.
- The idea *3,000 times more of the air* is awkward. The stylistic preference is for a more natural-sounding way of expressing this idea.

(B) Fin whales **can empty and then refill** their lungs in less than two seconds, half the time **that** *humans take* even though the whales breathe in 3,000 times more air.
- This answer contains the stylistically preferable expression **can empty and then refill** in place of the more awkward expressions found in some of the other answers, the stylistically preferable conjunction **that** followed by the active subject and verb *humans take*, and the stylistically preferable expressions **even though the whales breathe in** and **3,000 times more air** in place of the more awkward expressions found in some of the other responses. This answer is correct.

(C) Fin whales can empty and then refill their lungs in less than two seconds, half the time taken by humans even though the whales breathe in 3,000 times more of the air.
- The passive voice *taken by humans* is unnecessary here. The more direct active voice would be stylistically preferable.
- The idea *3,000 times more of the air* is awkward. The stylistic preference is for a more natural-sounding way of expressing this idea.

(D) Fin whales can empty followed by refilling their lungs in less than two seconds, half the time that humans take in spite of the whales' breathing in 3,000 times more air.
- The idea *can empty followed by refilling* is awkward. The stylistic preference is for a more natural-sounding way of expressing this idea.
- The idea *in spite of the whales' breathing in* is awkward. The stylistic preference is for a more natural-sounding way of expressing this idea.

(E) Fin whales can empty and then refill their lungs in less than two seconds, half the time humans take even though the whales breathe in 3,000 times more air.
- The conjunction *that* has been omitted in front of the subject and verb *humans take*. The stylistic preference on GMAT is to include the conjunction **that**.

5. This question tests **awkwardness**.

It is without surprise that large areas of both the United States and Australia are extremely fire-prone since aridity and drought conditions prevail in large swaths of both countries.

(A) *It is without surprise* that large areas of both the United States and Australia are extremely fire-prone since
  - The idea *It is without surprise* is awkward. The stylistic preference is for a more natural-sounding way of expressing this idea.

(B) *Without surprise it is* that large areas of both the United States and Australia are extremely fire-prone *in that*
  - The idea *Without surprise it is* is awkward. The stylistic preference is for a more natural-sounding way of expressing this idea.
  - The expression *in that* is considered stylistically awkward and overly formal by GMAT. The stylistic preference is for a more natural-sounding way of expressing this.

(C) *No surprise is it* that large areas of both the United States and Australia have an extreme *tending toward being* fire-prone since
  - The idea *No surprise is it* is awkward. The stylistic preference is for a more natural-sounding way of expressing this idea.
  - The part of the answer *tending toward being* is awkward. The stylistic preference is to avoid unnecessary gerunds (*-ing* verbal nouns) if possible.

(D) It is no surprise that large areas of both the United States and Australia *have an extreme fire-prone tendency* *in that*
  - The idea *have an extreme fire-prone tendency* is awkward. The stylistic preference is for a more natural-sounding way of expressing this idea.
  - The expression *in that* is considered stylistically awkward and overly formal by GMAT. The stylistic preference is for a more natural-sounding way of expressing this.

(E) It is no surprise that large areas of both the United States and Australia are extremely fire-prone since
  - This answer contains the stylistically preferable expressions **it is no surprise** and **are extremely fire-prone** in place of the more awkward expressions found in some of the other answers and uses the stylistically preferable conjunction **since** instead of the stylistically awkward expression *in that* found in some of the other answers. This answer is correct.

6. This question tests **awkwardness**.

Genghis Khan is believed to have fathered hundreds if not thousands of children, and, as a result, his Y chromosome has been estimated to be carried by 0.5 percent of the world's male population today.

(A) Genghis Khan *is believed to have fathered* hundreds if not thousands of children, and, as a result, his Y chromosome *has been estimated to be carried* by 0.5 percent of the world's male population today
- The passive voice *is believed to have fathered* is unnecessary here. The more direct active voice would be stylistically preferable.
- The passive voice *has been estimated to be carried* is unnecessary here. The more direct active voice would be stylistically preferable.

(B) Genghis Khan *is believed to have fathered* hundreds if not thousands of children, and, as a result, an estimated .5 percent of the world's male population today carries his Y chromosome.
- The passive voice *is believed to have fathered* is unnecessary here.. The more direct active voice would be stylistically preferable.

(C) Researchers believe *Genghis Khan fathered* hundreds if not thousands of children, and, as a result, his Y chromosome *has been estimated to be carried* by 0.5 percent of the world's male population today.
- The conjunction *that* has been omitted in front of the subject and verb *Genghis Khan fathered*. The stylistic preference on GMAT is to include the conjunction **that**.
- The passive voice *has been estimated to be carried* is unnecessary here. The more direct active voice would be stylistically preferable.

(D) Researchers **believe that** *Genghis Khan* **fathered** hundreds if not thousands of children and **that**, as a result, **an** estimated *.5 percent* of the world's male population today **carries** his Y chromosome.
- This answer contains the stylistically preferable active voice verbs **believe** and **fathered**, the adjective **estimated**, and the active voice verb **carries** in place of the more awkward passive expressions *is believed, to have fathered, has been estimated*, and *to be carried* found in some of the other responses. It also contains the stylistically preferable conjunction **that** in front of the subjects and verbs *Genghis Khan fathered* and *an estimated .5 percent...carries*. This answer is correct.

(E) Researchers believe *Genghis Khan fathered* hundreds if not thousands of children and, as a result, *his Y chromosome has been estimated* to be carried by 0.5 percent of the world's male population today.
- The conjunction *that* has been omitted in front of the subjects and verbs *Genghis Khan fathered* and *his Y chromosome has been estimated*. The stylistic preference on GMAT is to include the conjunction **that**.
- The passive voice *has been estimated* is unnecessary here. The more direct active voice would be stylistically preferable.

It Works! GMAT Sentence Correction

Lesson 10: Problems with DICTION

> **Diction** involves the dictionary definitions of words and whether or not words are used correctly according to these definitions. Problems with diction on the GMAT generally occur in the following situations:
> 1. when there are pairs of words with similar meanings that are commonly confused, such as *between* and *among*
> 2. when there are pairs of words with similar spellings that are easy to confuse, such as *averse* and *adverse*
> 3. when there are incorrect words that native speakers commonly use, such as *alot*
> 4. when there are individual words with meanings that native speakers commonly mistake, such as *allusion*

EXAMPLE 1: This example shows a pair of words with similar meanings that are commonly confused.

INCORRECT: The relationship *between* *the various candidates* was lukewarm early in the political season but turned to rancor *among* *the candidates* when the field had been *whittled down to two.*

CORRECT: The relationship **among** *the various candidates* was lukewarm early in the political season but turned to rancor **between** *the candidates* when the field had been *whittled down to two.*

In the incorrect example, *between* is used with *the various candidates* and *among* is used with *the candidates...whittled down to two*. *Between* should be used with a relationship involving only two people (or objects), and *among* should be used in a relationship involving more than two people (or objects). In the correct example, **among** is used with *the various candidates* -- clearly more than two -- and **between** is used with *the candidates...whittled down to two.*

- -

EXAMPLE 2: This example shows a pair of words with similar spellings that are commonly confused.

INCORRECT: The *voters* were adverse to the energy bill the legislature was considering because they were concerned about its possible averse *effects*.
CORRECT: The *voters* were averse to the energy bill the legislature was considering because they were concerned about its possible adverse *effects*.

In the incorrect example, the word *adverse* -- which means "harmful" -- is incorrectly used to describe the *voters*, and the word *averse* -- which means "opposed" -- is incorrectly used to describe the *effects* of the bill. In the correct example, the word **averse** is used correctly to describe the *voters* who are opposed, and **adverse** is used correctly to describe the *effects* which are harmful.

- -

EXAMPLE 3: This example shows an incorrect word that native speakers commonly use.

INCORRECT: The legislation has alot of proponents who are willing to do whatever it takes to get it passed.
CORRECT: The legislation has a lot of proponents who are willing to do whatever it takes to get it passed.

In the incorrect example, the word *alot* is not actually a correct word in English and should never be used. In the correct example, the correct expression **a lot** has replaced the incorrect word *alot*.

- -

EXAMPLE 4: This example shows a word with a meaning that is commonly mistaken.

INCORRECT: When a popular manager was *named* the new chief executive, the allusion was met with excitement.
CORRECT: An allusion to the *possibility* of having someone more popular named the new chief executive was met with excitement.

In the incorrect example, the word *allusion* is used inappropriately because an allusion is something that is deduced or understood and is not something that is directly stated, such as being *named* the new chief executive. In the correct example, the word **allusion** is used correctly because the specific information about the new chief executive only a *possibility* and is therefore only deduced or understood.

SKILLS PRACTICE: Find the problems with **diction** in the following sentences. (The number in parentheses indicates the number of problems you should find.) Then, study the explanations on the pages that follow.

1. The company stressed team-building and collusion over individual accomplishment and proscribed daily team meetings as the company's officious program to promote the efficacy of the teams. *(3)*

2. When the governor made a reference to potential tax increases, he inferred that anyone of a number of new taxes might be coming sooner than expected, and the audience implied from this that any one who herd about this would not respond in a, shall we say, positive fashion. *(5)*

3. Officials from areas along the border find that the situation there is in a serious state of demise and are holding talks aimed at diffusing the growing tensions over issues related to the border and the elicit activities taking place there. *(3)*

4. Any breeches of the confidentiality agreement by those who are less than discrete will be persecuted to the fullest extant possible, irregardless of any damage that may result. *(5)*

5. The enormity of the outpouring of love and affection left the crime victim with a plethora of feelings of gratitude and completely bereft of any feelings of animosity toward the perpetrator. *(3)*

6. It is unlikely that any permanent decision will be forthcoming until all interested parties have been appraised of the principle factors effecting the situation. *(3)*

7. The head of the agency quickly perused the report from the field agents and was able to glean that there was eminent danger ahead but still remained nonplussed about the situation, as was necessary for someone in his position. *(4)*

8. The antagonists were sucked into a vertex of escalating accusations, one that resulted in a bloody altercation and one that afterwards left everyone involved in the incident wondering what could of and should of been done to prevent it. *(4)*

EXPLANATIONS (I = incorrect, C = correct)

1. The company stressed team-building and *collusion* over individual accomplishment and *proscribed* daily team meetings as the company's *officious* program to promote the efficacy of the teams.

   - The word *collusion* -- which means "work together for fraudulent purposes" -- is illogical in this context. This word can be confused with **collaboration** -- which means "work together in a positive way."
     - I: *collusion*
     - C: **collaboration**

   - The word *proscribed* -- which means "prohibited" -- is illogical in this context. This word can be confused with **prescribed** -- which means "set down as a rule."
     - I: *proscribed*
     - C: **prescribed**

   - The word *officious* -- which means "objectionably aggressive or meddlesome" -- is illogical in this context. This word can be confused with **official** -- which means "bureaucratically authorized."
     - I: *officious*
     - C: **official**

---

2. When the governor made a reference to potential tax increases, he *inferred* that *anyone* of a number of new taxes might be coming sooner than expected, and the audience *implied* from this that *any one* who *herd* about this would not respond in a, shall we say, positive fashion.

   - The word *inferred* -- which means "concluded" and is something a listener or reader does -- is illogical in this context. This word can be confused with **implied** -- which means "insinuated" and is something a speaker or writer does.
     - I: *inferred*
     - C: **implied**

   - The word *anyone* -- which means "an unspecified person" -- is illogical in this context. This word can be confused with **any one** -- which means "one of many."
     - I: *anyone*
     - C: **any one**

   - The word *implied* -- which means "insinuated" and is something a speaker or writer does -- is illogical in this context. This word can be confused with **inferred** -- which means "concluded" and is something a listener or reader does.
     - I: *implied*
     - C: **inferred**

   - The expression *any one* -- which means "one of many" -- is illogical in this context. This expression can be confused with **anyone** -- which means "an unspecified person."

It Works! GMAT Sentence Correction

    I: *any one*
    C: **anyone**

- The word *herd* -- which means "a group of animals" -- is illogical in this context. This word can be confused with **heard** -- which means "perceived by sound."
    I: *herd*
    C: **heard**

- -

3. Officials from areas along the border find that the situation there is in a serious state of *demise* and are holding talks aimed at *diffusing* the growing tensions over issues related to the border and the *elicit* activities taking place there.

- The word *demise* -- which means "death" and not "decline" -- is illogical in this context. The word **decline** is more logical in this context.
    I: *demise*
    C: **decline**

- The word *diffusing* -- which means "scattering" -- is illogical in this context. This word can be confused with **defusing** -- which means "making less dangerous."
    I: *diffusing*
    C: **defusing**

- The word *elicit* -- which means "draw out" -- is illogical in this context. This word can be confused with **illicit** -- which means "illegal."
    I: *elicit*
    C: **illicit**

- -

4. Any *breeches* of the confidentiality agreement by those who are less than *discrete* will be *persecuted* to the fullest *extant* possible, *irregardless* of any damage that may result.

- The word *breeches* -- which means "lower parts of the body" -- is illogical in this context. This word can be confused with **breaches** -- which means "ruptures or violations."
    I: *breeches*
    C: **breaches**

- The word *discrete* -- which means "distinct" -- is illogical in this context. This word can be confused with **discreet** -- which means "showing good judgment."
    I: *discrete*
    C: **discreet**

- The word *persecuted* -- which means "harassed or oppressed" -- is illogical in this context. This word can be confused with **prosecuted** -- which means "initiated legal proceedings against."

I: *persecuted*
C: **prosecuted**

- The word *extant* -- which means "in existence" -- is illogical in this context. This word can be confused with **extent** -- which means "scope."
  I: *extant*
  C: **extent**

- The word *irregardless* is always incorrect. The correct word is **regardless**.
  I: *irregardless*
  C: **regardless**

- -

5. The *enormity* of the outpouring of love and affection left the crime victim with a *plethora* of feelings of gratitude and completely *bereft* of any feelings of animosity toward the perpetrator.

    - The word *enormity* -- which means "heinousness or atrocity" and not "great amount" -- is illogical in this context. The expression **great amount** is more logical in this context.
      I: *enormity*
      C: **great amount**

    - The word *plethora* -- which means "overabundance or excess" and not merely "large amount" -- is illogical in this context. The expression **large amount** is more logical in this context.
      I: *plethora*
      C: **large amount**

    - The expression *bereft of* -- which means "dispossessed of something you previously had" and not merely "lacking" -- is illogical in this context. The word **lacking** is more logical in this context.
      I: *bereft*
      C: **lacking**

- -

6. It is unlikely that any permanent decision will be forthcoming until all interested parties have been *appraised* of the *principle* factors *effecting* the situation.

- The word *appraised* -- which means "evaluated" -- is illogical in this context. This word can be confused with **apprised** -- which means "informed."
    - I: *appraised*
    - C: **apprised**

- The word *principle* -- which means "fundamental belief" -- is illogical in this context. This word can be confused with **principal** -- which means "most important."
    - I: *principle*
    - C: **principal**

- The word *effecting* -- which means "bringing about" -- is illogical in this context. This word can be confused with **affecting** -- which means "producing a change in."
    - I: *effecting*
    - C: **affecting**

- -

7. The head of the agency quickly *perused* the report from the field agents and was able to *glean* that there was *eminent* danger ahead but still remained *nonplussed* about the situation, as was necessary for someone in his position.

- The word *perused* -- which means "read with thoroughness" and not "skimmed" or "scanned" -- is illogical in this context. The word **scanned** is more logical in this context.
    - I: *perused*
    - C: **scanned**

- The word *glean* -- which means "gather painstakingly" and not "understand quickly" -- is illogical in this context. The expression **understand quickly** is more logical in this context.
    - I: *glean*
    - C: **understand quickly**

- The word *eminent* -- which means "prominent or noteworthy" -- is illogical in this context. This word can be confused with **imminent** -- which means "likely to occur at any moment."
    - I: *eminent*
    - C: **imminent**

- The word *nonplussed* -- which means "utterly perplexed or confused" and not "calm" or "unworried" -- is illogical in this context. The word **calm** is more logical in this context.
    - I: *nonplussed*
    - C: **calm**

- -

8. The antagonists were sucked into a *vertex* of escalating accusations, one that resulted in a bloody *altercation* and one that *afterwards* left everyone involved in the incident wondering what *could of* and *should of* been done to prevent it.

- The word *vertex* -- which means "highest point" -- is illogical in this context. This word can be confused with **vortex** -- which means "whirlwind."
    - I: *vertex*
    - C: **vortex**

- The word *altercation* -- which means "heated, angry dispute" but not **"physical fight"** -- is illogical in this context.
    - I: *altercation*
    - C: **physical fight**

- The word *afterwards* is always incorrect.
    - I: *afterwards*
    - C: **afterward**

- The expressions *could of* and *should of* are always incorrect. The correct expressions are **could have** and **should have**.
    - I: *could of...should of*
    - C: **could have...should have**

GMAT-STYLE SKILLS PRACTICE: Choose the letter of the answer to each question that best reflects the style and accuracy of standard written English. Then, study the explanations on the pages that follow.

1. Short-term disruptions in the banking system can cause <u>a lots of panic, and longer-term disruptions maybe responsible for wreaking havoc</u> throughout the entire world economy.

    (A) a lots of panic, and longer-term disruptions maybe responsible for wreaking havoc
    (B) a lot of panic, and longer-term disruptions may be responsible for wreaking havoc
    (C) a lot of panic, and longer-term disruptions maybe responsible for wrecking havoc
    (D) a lots of panic, and longer-term disruptions may be responsible for wrecking havoc
    (E) lots of panic, and longer-term disruptions maybe responsible for wreaking havoc

2. The fact that many supposedly educated people are unable identify Cape Agulhas as the southernmost point of Africa <u>is bemusing to those who are fully aware that Cape Agulhas extends 40 miles further south than</u> the Cape of Good Hope.

    (A) is bemusing to those who are fully aware that Cape Agulhas extends 40 miles further south than
    (B) bemuses those who are fully aware that Cape Agulhas extends 40 miles farther south then
    (C) is bemusing to those who are fully aware that Cape Agulhas extends 40 miles farther south then
    (D) amuses those who are fully aware that Cape Agulhas extends 40 miles further south then
    (E) is amusing to those who are fully aware that Cape Agulhas extends 40 miles farther south than

3. Inasmuch as the arbitrator stands to profit from the sale of the land, he cannot possibly be considered an uninterested party in the dispute and should recluse himself from involvement in it.

   (A) he cannot possibly be considered an uninterested party in the dispute and should recluse himself
   (B) he cannot possibly be considered an uninterested party in the dispute and should recuse himself
   (C) he cannot possibly be considered a disinterested party in the dispute and should recuse himself
   (D) he can not possibly be considered a disinterested party in the dispute and should recuse himself
   (E) he can not possibly be considered a disinterested party in the dispute and should recluse himself

4. After the historic inauguration, the president elect wanted to rest briefly to ensure that he was prepared for what everyone believed would be a joyous, boisterous, and noisy celebration that evening.

   (A) historic inauguration, the president elect wanted to rest briefly to ensure that he was prepared for what everyone believed would be a joyous, boisterous, and noisy
   (B) historic inauguration, the president elect wanted to rest briefly to insure that he was prepared for what everyone believed would be a joyous, boisterous, and noisome
   (C) historic inauguration, the president elect wanted to rest briefly to ensure that he was prepared for what everyone believed would be a joyous, boisterous, and noisome
   (D) historical inauguration, the president elect wanted to rest briefly to insure that he was prepared for what everyone believed would be a joyous, boisterous, and noisy
   (E) historical inauguration, the president elect wanted to rest briefly to ensure that he was prepared for what everyone believed would be a joyous, boisterous, and noisy

5. The regulator can publicly censure or fine a company or director that knowingly becomes involved in a serious infraction of government regulations, choosing to flaunt the law rather than abide by it.

    (A) censure or fine a company or director that knowingly becomes involved in a serious infraction of government regulations, choosing to flaunt
    (B) censure or fine a company or director that knowingly becomes involved in a serious infraction of government regulations, choosing to flout
    (C) censure or fine a company or director that knowingly becomes involved in a serious infarction of government regulations, choosing to flout
    (D) censor or fine a company or director that knowingly becomes involved in a serious infarction of government regulations, choosing to flout
    (E) censor or fine a company or director that knowingly becomes involved in a serious infraction of government regulations, choosing to flaunt

6. The United States of America is comprised of a federal district and fifty individual states, forty-eight of which are contiguous states lying between the Atlantic and Pacific Oceans, with Alaska in the northwest corner of the continent bordering Canada and Hawaii in the mid-Pacific.

    (A) is comprised of a federal district and fifty individual states, forty-eight of which are contiguous states lying between
    (B) is composed of a federal district and fifty individual states, forty-eight of which are continuous states lying between
    (C) composes a federal district and fifty individual states, forty-eight of which are continuous states lying among
    (D) comprises a federal district and fifty individual states, forty-eight of which are contiguous states lying between
    (E) is comprised of a federal district and fifty individual states, forty-eight of which are contiguous states lying among

EXPLANATIONS

1. This question tests **diction**.

   Short-term disruptions in the banking system can cause <u>a lots of panic, and longer-term disruptions maybe responsible for wreaking havoc</u> throughout the entire world economy.

(A) a *lots* of panic, and longer-term disruptions *maybe* responsible for wreaking havoc
   - The expression *a lots* is always incorrect. Use **a lot** instead.
   - The word *maybe* -- which is an adverb meaning "perhaps" -- is illogical in this context. Use the expression **may be** -- which is a verb meaning "possibly be" -- instead.

(B) a lot of panic, and longer-term disruptions may be responsible for wreaking havoc
   - This answer contains the correct expression **a lot** instead of the incorrect expression *a lots*, the logical expression **may be** instead of the illogical word *maybe*, and the logical word **wreaking** instead of the illogical word *wrecking*. This answer is correct.

(C) a lot of panic, and longer-term disruptions *maybe* responsible for *wrecking* havoc
   - The word *maybe* -- which is an adverb meaning "perhaps" -- is illogical in this context. Use the expression **may be** -- which is a verb meaning "possibly be" -- instead.
   - The word *wrecking* -- which means "damaging" -- is illogical in this context. Use **wreaking** -- which means "inflicting" -- instead.

(D) a *lots* of panic, and longer-term disruptions may be responsible for *wrecking* havoc
   - The expression *a lots* is always incorrect. Use **a lot** instead.
   - The word *wrecking* -- which means "damaging" -- is illogical in this context. Use **wreaking** -- which means "inflicting" -- instead.

(E) lots of panic, and longer-term disruptions *maybe* responsible for wreaking havoc
   - The word *maybe* -- which is an adverb meaning "perhaps" -- is illogical in this context. Use the expression **may be** -- which is a verb meaning "possibly be" -- instead.

2. This question tests **diction**.

The fact that many supposedly educated people are unable identify Cape Agulhas as the southernmost point of Africa is bemusing to those who are fully aware that Cape Agulhas extends 40 miles further south than the Cape of Good Hope.

(A) *is bemusing* to those who are fully aware that Cape Agulhas extends 40 miles *further* south than
   - The expression *is bemusing* -- which means "is bewildering" and not "is amusing"-- is illogical in this context. Use **is amusing** instead.
   - The word *further* -- which refers to concepts other than distance -- is incorrect in this context. Use the word **farther** -- which refers to distance -- instead.

(B) *bemuses* those who are fully aware that Cape Agulhas extends 40 miles farther south *then*
   - The word *bemuses* -- which means "bewilders" and not "amuses" -- is illogical in this context. Use **amuses** instead.
   - The word *then* -- which means "next" -- is illogical in this context. Use **than** -- which is used in comparisons -- instead.

(C) *is bemusing* to those who are fully aware that Cape Agulhas extends 40 miles farther south *then*
   - The expression *is bemusing* -- which means "is bewildering" and not "is amusing" -- is illogical in this context. Use **is amusing** instead.
   - The word *then* -- which means "next" -- is illogical in this context. Use **than** -- which is used in comparisons -- instead.

(D) amuses those who are fully aware that Cape Agulhas extends 40 miles *further* south *then*
   - The word *further* -- which refers to concepts other than distance -- is incorrect in this context. Use the word **farther** -- which refers to distance -- instead.
   - The word *then* -- which means "next" -- is illogical in this context. Use **than** -- which is used in comparisons -- instead.

(E) is amusing to those who are fully aware that Cape Agulhas extends 40 miles farther south than
   - This answer contains the logical expression **is amusing** instead of the illogical expression *is bemusing*, the correct word **farther** instead of the incorrect word *further*, and the logical word **than** instead of the illogical word *then*. This answer is correct.

3. This question tests **diction**.

Inasmuch as the arbitrator stands to profit from the sale of the land, he cannot possibly be considered an uninterested party in the dispute and should recluse himself from involvement in it.

(A) he cannot possibly be considered an *uninterested* party in the dispute and should *recluse* himself
   - The word *uninterested* -- which means "indifferent" -- is illogical in this context. Use **disinterested** -- which means "unbiased" -- instead.
   - The word *recluse* -- which means "a person who lives apart from society" -- is illogical in this context. Use **recuse** -- which means "withdraw from a position of judging" -- instead.

(B) he cannot possibly be considered an *uninterested* party in the dispute and should recuse himself
   - The word *uninterested* -- which means "indifferent" -- is illogical in this context. Use **disinterested** -- which means "unbiased" -- instead.

(C) he cannot possibly be considered a disinterested party in the dispute and should recuse himself
   - This answer contains the correct word **cannot** instead of the incorrect expression *can not*, the logical word **disinterested** instead of the illogical word *uninterested*, and the logical word **recuse** instead of the illogical word *recluse*. This answer is correct.

(D) he *can not* possibly be considered a disinterested party in the dispute and should recuse himself
   - The expression *can not* is always incorrect. Use **cannot** instead.

(E) he *can not* possibly be considered a disinterested party in the dispute and should *recluse* himself
   - The expression *can not* is always incorrect. Use **cannot** instead.
   - The word *recluse* -- which means "a person who lives apart from society" -- is illogical in this context. Use **recuse** -- which means "withdraw from a position of judging" -- instead.

4. This question tests **diction**.

   After the historic inauguration, the president elect wanted to rest briefly to ensure that he was prepared for what everyone believed would be a joyous, boisterous, and noisy celebration that evening.

(A) historic inauguration, the president elect wanted to rest briefly to **ensure** that he was prepared for what everyone believed would be a joyous, boisterous, and **noisy**
   - This answer contains the logical word **historic** instead of the illogical word *historical*, the logical word **ensure** instead of the illogical word *insure*, and the logical word **noisy** instead of the illogical word *noisome*. This answer is correct.

(B) historic inauguration, the president elect wanted to rest briefly to *insure* that he was prepared for what everyone believed would be a joyous, boisterous, and *noisome*
   - The word *insure* -- which means "take out a policy" -- is illogical in this context. Use **ensure** -- which means "guarantee" -- instead.
   - The word *noisome* -- which means "obnoxious or offensive to the senses" -- is illogical in this context. Use **noisy** -- which does not necessarily have a negative connotation -- instead.

(C) historic inauguration, the president elect wanted to rest briefly to ensure that he was prepared for what everyone believed would be a joyous, boisterous, and *noisome*
   - The word *noisome* -- which means "obnoxious or offensive to the senses" -- is illogical in this context. Use **noisy** -- which does not necessarily have a negative connotation -- instead.

(D) *historical* inauguration, the president elect wanted to rest briefly to *insure* that he was prepared for what everyone believed would be a joyous, boisterous, and noisy
   - The word *historical* -- which means "from the past" -- is illogical in this context. Use **historic** -- which means "of great importance" -- instead.
   - The word *insure* -- which means "take out a policy" -- is illogical in this context. Use **ensure** -- which means "guarantee" -- instead.

(E) *historical* inauguration, the president elect wanted to rest briefly to ensure that he was prepared for what everyone believed would be a joyous, boisterous, and noisy
   - The word *historical* -- which means "from the past" -- is illogical in this context. Use **historic** -- which means "of great importance" -- instead.

5. This question tests **diction**.

   The regulator can publicly censure or fine a company or director that knowingly becomes involved in a serious infraction of government regulations, choosing to flaunt the law rather than abide by it.

(A) censure or fine a company or director that knowingly becomes involved in a serious infraction of government regulations, choosing to *flaunt*
   - The word *flaunt* -- which means "display conspicuously" -- is illogical in this context. Use **flout** -- which means "treat with contempt" -- instead.

(B) censure or fine a company or director that knowingly becomes involved in a serious infraction of government regulations, choosing to flout
   - This answer contains the logical word **censure** instead of the illogical word *censor*, the logical word **infraction** instead of the illogical word *infarction*, and the logical word **flout** instead of the illogical word *flaunt*. This answer is correct.

(C) censure or fine a company or director that knowingly becomes involved in a serious *infarction* of government regulations, choosing to flout
   - The word *infarction* -- which means "blockage" -- is illogical in this context. Use **infraction** -- which means "violation" -- instead.

(D) *censor* or fine a company or director that knowingly becomes involved in a serious *infarction* of government regulations, choosing to flout
   - The word *censor* -- which means "delete objectionable material" -- is illogical in this context. Use **censure** -- which means "reprimand" -- instead.
   - The word *infarction* -- which means "blockage" -- is illogical in this context. Use **infraction** -- which means "violation" -- instead.

(E) *censor* or fine a company or director that knowingly becomes involved in a serious infraction of government regulations, choosing to *flaunt*
   - The word *censor* -- which means "delete objectionable material" -- is illogical in this context. Use **censure** -- which means "reprimand" -- instead.
   - The word *flaunt* -- which means "display conspicuously" -- is illogical in this context. Use **flout** -- which means "treat with contempt" -- instead.

It Works! GMAT Sentence Correction

6. This question tests **diction**.

The United States of America is comprised of a federal district and fifty individual states, forty-eight of which are contiguous states lying between the Atlantic and Pacific Oceans, with Alaska in the northwest corner of the continent bordering Canada and Hawaii in the mid-Pacific.

(A) *is comprised of* a federal district and fifty individual states, forty-eight of which are contiguous states lying between
- The expression *is comprised of* -- which means "makes up" and not "is made up of"-- is illogical in this context. Use **comprises** -- which means "is made up of" -- instead.

(B) is composed of a federal district and fifty individual states, forty-eight of which are *continuous* states lying between
- The word *continuous* -- which means "uninterrupted in time" -- is illogical in this context. Use **contiguous** -- which means "bordering upon" -- instead.

(C) *composes* a federal district and fifty individual states, forty-eight of which are *continuous* states lying *among*
- The word *composes* -- which means "makes up" and not "is made up of"-- is illogical in this context. Use **comprises** -- which means "is made up of" -- instead.
- The word *continuous* -- which means "uninterrupted in time" -- is illogical in this context. Use **contiguous** -- which means "bordering upon" -- instead.
- The word *among* -- which is used when three or more people or objects are related -- is incorrect in this context. Use **between** -- which is used when two people or objects are related-- instead.

(D) comprises a federal district and fifty individual states, forty-eight of which are contiguous states lying between
- This answer contains the logical word **comprises** instead of the illogical expression *is comprised of* or the illogical word *composes,* the logical word **contiguous** instead of the illogical word *continuous,* and correct word **between** instead of the incorrect word *among*. This answer is correct.

(E) *is comprised of* a federal district and fifty individual states, forty-eight of which are contiguous states lying *among*
- The expression *is comprised of* -- which means "makes up" and not "is made up of" -- is illogical in this context. Use **comprises** -- which means "is made up of" -- instead.
- The word *among* -- which is used when three or more people or objects are related -- is incorrect in this context. Use **between** -- which is used two people or objects are related -- instead.

Lesson 10: Problems with DICTION

Lesson 11: Problems with IDIOMS

> **Idioms** are groups of words that have meanings that are not related literally to the meanings of the individual words in the expressions. The following problems with idioms are common on the GMAT:
> 1. the incorrect use of prepositions in certain expressions
> 2. the casual rather than formal use of prepositions in certain expressions
> 3. the inaccurate expression of common idioms

EXAMPLE 1: This example shows an idiomatic expression that includes an incorrect preposition.

INCORRECT: The news analyst *commented in* the president's recent actions.
CORRECT: The news analyst **commented on** the president's recent actions.

In the incorrect example, the incorrect preposition *in* is used in the expression *commented in*. The correct preposition to use with *commented* is *on* and not *in*. In the correct example, the correct preposition *on* is used in the expression **commented on**.

- -

EXAMPLE 2: This example shows an idiomatic expression that includes the casual use of a preposition.

INCORRECT: The product should be on the market *inside of* a month.
CORRECT: The product should be on the market **within** a month.

In the incorrect example, the preposition *inside of* is used casually but is not formally acceptable. In the correct example, the formally acceptable **within** is used.

- -

EXAMPLE 3: This example shows a common idiom that is expressed inaccurately.

INCORRECT: When pink slips were issued, the supervisor said he couldn't help because his hands were tied up.
CORRECT: When pink slips were issued, the supervisor said he couldn't help because his hands were tied.

In the incorrect example, the expression *his hands were tied up* is an incorrect idiom. The correct expression is *his hands were tied* and not *tied up*. In the correct example, the idiomatic expression **his hand were tied** is used correctly.

SKILLS PRACTICE: Find the problems with **idioms** in the following sentences. (The number in parentheses indicates the number of problems you should find.) Then, study the explanations on the pages that follow.

1. The debates among the county supervisors have turned ugly, with polite interchanges far and few between; according with the county charter, if worse comes to worse and the supervisors are unable to fix up the situation, the mayor can call for elections. *(4)*

2. When prosecutors wanted to try and charge Albert DeSalvo as the Boston Strangler, this was problematic, despite of his confession, because witnesses were unable to identify him beyond a shadowy doubt and because he was diagnosed from schizophrenia. *(4)*

3. Though the candidate won the election by only a hair's breath, it was taken for granite that he would have free reign to pass all and any legislation from his far-reaching platform. *(4)*

4. As an echolocating bat closes on a flying insect, it increases its call emission to rates beyond 160 calls per second, a type of high call rate phase that has proven to be enigmatic because it is unknown how bats are able to bring this off so quickly. *(3)*

5. The proposed university sports complex has been on the back of a burner and off of the current agenda for so long that now it is virtually dead water with its fate hanging out of balance. *(4)*

6. Cognitive psychologist Howard Gardner has been on the forefront of creativity studies throughout his career – from his early work in which he use to focus in the role of the arts in human development to his landmark theory of multiple intelligences and cutting-edged work on the essential links between creativity and leadership effectiveness. *(4)*

7. The reign of Mughal emperor Shah Jahan (1628-58) is considered to be notable in a large part for its architectural achievements, for all intensive purposes the most famous of which is the Taj Mahal, the magnificent tomb built from the behest of Shah Jahan for his beloved wife, Mumtaz Mahal. *(4)*

8. With the company in the brink of financial ruin and investors on tenderhooks about its future, the company managed at the eleventh hour to make major strides in resolving the issues but knew that it had a long road to hoe to become a preeminent company once again. *(4)*

EXPLANATIONS (I = incorrect, C = correct)

1. The debates among the county supervisors have turned ugly, with polite interchanges *far and few between*; *according with* the county charter, if *worse comes to worse* and the supervisors are unable to *fix up* the situation, the mayor can call for elections.

    - The expression *far and few between* is an incorrect idiom.
        - I: far and few between
        - C: **few and far between**

    - The incorrect preposition *with* is used in the expression *according with*.
        - I: according with
        - C: **according to**

    - The expression *if worse comes to worse* is an incorrect idiom.
        - I: if worse comes to worst
        - C: **if worse comes to worse**

    - The idiomatic expression *fix up* is too casual for formal writing.
        - I: fix up
        - C: **fix**

- -

2. When prosecutors wanted to *try and charge* Albert DeSalvo as the Boston Strangler, this was problematic, *despite of* his confession, because witnesses were unable to identify him *beyond a shadowy doubt* and because he was *diagnosed from* schizophrenia.

    - The idiomatic expression *try and charge* is too casual for formal writing.
        - I: try and charge
        - C: **try to charge**

    - The expression *despite of* is an incorrect expression. *Of* should never be used with *despite*.
        - I: despite of
        - C: **despite**

    - The expression *beyond a shadowy doubt* is an incorrect idiom.
        - I: beyond a shadowy doubt
        - C: **beyond the shadow of a doubt**

    - The incorrect preposition *from* is used in the expression *diagnosed from*.
        - I: diagnosed from
        - C: **diagnosed with**

- -

3. Though the candidate won the election *by only a hair's breath*, it was *taken for granite* that he would have *free reign* to pass *all and any* legislation from his far-reaching platform.

- The expression *by only a hair's breath* is an incorrect idiom.
    - I: by only a hair's breath
    - C: **by only a hair's breadth**

- The expression *taken for granite* is an incorrect idiom.
    - I: taken for granite
    - C: **taken for granted**

- The expression *free reign* is an incorrect idiom.
    - I: free reign
    - C: **free rein**

- The expression *all and any* is an incorrect idiom.
    - I: all and any
    - C: **any and all**

- -

4. As an echolocating bat *closes on* a flying insect, it increases its call emission to rates beyond 160 calls per second, a type of high call rate phase that has *proven to be* enigmatic because it is unknown how bats are able to *bring this off* so quickly.

- The expression *closes on* is an incorrect idiom.
    - I: closes on
    - C: **closes in on**

- The expression *proven to be* is an incorrect idiom. The word *proven* should never be followed by *to be*.
    - I: proven to be
    - C: **proven**

- The idiomatic expression *bring this off* is too casual for formal writing.
    - I: bring this off
    - C: **accomplish this**

- -

5. The proposed university sports complex has been *on the back of a burner* and *off of* the current agenda for so long that now it is virtually *dead water* with *its fate hanging out of balance*.

- The expression *on the back of a burner* is an incorrect idiom.
    - I: *on the back of a burner*
    - C: **on a back burner**

- The idiomatic expression *off of* is too casual for formal writing.
    - I: *off of*
    - C: **off**

- The expression *dead water* is an incorrect idiom.
    - I: *dead water*
    - C: **dead in the water**

- The expression *its fate hanging out of balance* is an incorrect idiom.
    - I: *its fate hanging out of balance*
    - C: **its fate hanging in the balance**

- -

6. Cognitive psychologist Howard Gardner has been *on the forefront* of creativity studies throughout his career — from his early work in which he *use to* *focus in* the role of the arts in human development to his landmark theory of multiple intelligences and *cutting-edged* work on the essential links between creativity and leadership effectiveness.

- The incorrect preposition *on* is used in the expression *on the forefront*.
    - I: *on the forefront*
    - C: **at the forefront**

- The expression *use to* is an incorrect idiom. The actual verb in this expression should be the past tense *used*.
    - I: *use to*
    - C: **used to**

- The incorrect preposition *in* is used in the expression *focus in*.
    - I: *focus in*
    - C: **focus on**

- The expression *cutting-edged* is an incorrect idiom.
    - I: *cutting-edged*
    - C: **cutting-edge**

7. The reign of Mughal emperor Shah Jahan (1628-58) is *considered to be* notable *in a large part* for its architectural achievements, *for all intensive purposes* the most famous of which is the Taj Mahal, the magnificent tomb built *from the behest of* Shah Jahan for his beloved wife, Mumtaz Mahal.

- The expression *considered to be* is an incorrect idiom. The word *considered* should never be followed by either *as* or *to be*.
  - I: *considered to be*
  - C: **considered**

- The expression *in a large part* is an incorrect idiom.
  - I: *in a large part*
  - C: **in large part**

- The expression *for all intensive purposes* is an incorrect idiom.
  - I: *for all intensive purposes*
  - C: **for all intents and purposes**

- The incorrect preposition *from* is used in the expression *from the behest of*.
  - I: *from the behest of*
  - C: **at the behest of**

- -

8. With the company *in the brink of* financial ruin and investors *on tenderhooks* about its future, the company managed at the eleventh hour to *make major strides in* resolving the issues but knew that it had *a long road to hoe* to become a preeminent company once again.

- The incorrect preposition *in* is used in the expression *in the brink of*.
  - I: *in the brink of*
  - C: **on the brink of**

- The expression *on tenderhooks* is an incorrect idiom.
  - I: *on tenderhooks*
  - C: **on tenterhooks**

- The expression *make major strides in* is an incorrect idiom.
  - I: *make major strides in*
  - C: **take major strides toward**

- The expression *a long road to hoe* is an incorrect idiom.
  - I: *a long road to hoe*
  - C: **a long row to hoe**

GMAT-STYLE SKILLS PRACTICE: Choose the letter of the answer to each question that best reflects the style and accuracy of standard written English. Then, study the explanations on the pages that follow.

1. Norse creation myths were permeated <u>from the natural elements of fire, ice, and water that were by and large regular features found in the environment</u> where people lived.

    (A) from the natural elements of fire, ice, and water that were by and large regular features found in the environment
    (B) with the natural elements of fire, ice, and water that were by and large regular features found in the environment
    (C) with the natural elements of fire, ice, and water that were by and large regular features found at the environment
    (D) with the natural elements of fire, ice, and water that were by in large regular features found at the environment
    (E) from the natural elements of fire, ice, and water that were by in large regular features found in the environment

2. In early twentieth century America, many women pinched their cheeks and bit their lips to achieve a rosy look, while the more daring resorted to using tinted lip salves and rouges, a practice that <u>caught the fantasy of some and was considered by others to be rather vulgar</u>.

    (A) caught the fantasy of some and was considered by others to be rather vulgar
    (B) caught the fantasy of some and was considered as rather vulgar by others
    (C) caught the fantasy of some and was regarded by others to be rather vulgar
    (D) caught the fancy of some and was considered rather vulgar by others
    (E) caught the fancy of some and was regarded as if rather vulgar by others

3. When the repeat offender was unable to tow the line during his umpteenth chance at parole, the judge basically threw a book at him and remanded him to prison for a long stretch, feeling that the criminal had received his just deserts.

   (A) tow the line during his umpteenth chance at parole, the judge basically threw a book at him and remanded him to prison for a long stretch, feeling that the criminal had received his just deserts
   (B) tow the line during his umpteenth chance at parole, the judge basically threw the book at him and remanded him to prison for a long stretch, feeling that the criminal had received his just deserts
   (C) toe the line during his umpteenth chance at parole, the judge basically threw a book at him and remanded him to prison for a long stretch, feeling that the criminal had received his just desserts
   (D) tow the line during his umpteenth chance at parole, the judge basically threw the book at him and remanded him to prison for a long stretch, feeling that the criminal had received his just desserts
   (E) toe the line during his umpteenth chance at parole, the judge basically threw the book at him and remanded him to prison for a long stretch, feeling that the criminal had received his just deserts

4. The Indus Valley civilization was thriving until the mid-second millennium BCE, when its abrupt demise coincided with and was quite possibly related to the arrival of the Indo-European Aryans, whose culture apparently replaced rather than existed alongside the Indus Valley civilization.

   (A) until the mid-second millennium BCE, when its abrupt demise coincided with and was quite possibly related to the arrival of the Indo-European Aryans, whose culture apparently replaced rather than existed alongside
   (B) until the mid-second millennium BCE, when its abrupt demise coincided and was quite possibly related to the arrival of the Indo-European Aryans, whose culture apparently replaced rather than existed alongside of
   (C) until the mid-second millennium BCE, when its abrupt demise coincided with and was quite possibly related to the arrival of the Indo-European Aryans, whose culture apparently replaced rather than existed alongside of
   (D) up until the mid-second millennium BCE, when its abrupt demise coincided and was quite possibly related to the arrival of the Indo-European Aryans, whose culture apparently replaced rather than existed alongside
   (E) up until the mid-second millennium BCE, when its abrupt demise coincided with and was quite possibly related to the arrival of the Indo-European Aryans, whose culture apparently replaced rather than existed alongside

5. As a youth serving a stiff nine-year term in Indiana, John Dillinger <u>came to contact for the first time with a host of seasoned lawbreakers who believed that crime was not too big a deal</u> and were happy to instruct him in the finer points of robbing banks and succeeding at various other criminal pursuits.

    (A) came to contact for the first time with a host of seasoned lawbreakers who believed that crime was not too big a deal
    (B) came to contact for a first time with a host of seasoned lawbreakers who believed that crime was not too big of a deal
    (C) came into contact for the first time with a host of seasoned lawbreakers who believed that crime was not too big a deal
    (D) came into contact for a first time with a host of seasoned lawbreakers who believed that crime was not too big a deal
    (E) came into contact for the first time with a host of seasoned lawbreakers who believed that crime was not too big of a deal

6. The renowned French poet Arthur Rimbaud (1854-1891) wrote his much of his poetry of note before he turned twenty; at the age of twenty-five he suddenly became <u>bored of this, disavowed his art, opened a business in Ethiopia, and spent the rest of his life there engaged to commerce and disengaged from</u> the world of art.

    (A) bored of this, disavowed his art, opened a business in Ethiopia, and spent the rest of his life there engaged to commerce and disengaged from
    (B) bored of this, disavowed his art, opened up a business in Ethiopia, and spent the rest of his life there engaged in commerce and disengaged from
    (C) bored with this, disavowed his art, opened up a business in Ethiopia, and spent the rest of his life there engaged in commerce and disengaged out of
    (D) bored with this, disavowed his art, opened a business in Ethiopia, and spent the rest of his life there engaged to commerce and disengaged out of
    (E) bored with this, disavowed his art, opened a business in Ethiopia, and spent the rest of his life there engaged in commerce and disengaged from

EXPLANATIONS

1. This question tests **idioms**.

   Norse creation myths were *permeated* from the natural elements of fire, ice, and water that were by and large regular features found in the environment where people lived.

   (A) *from* the natural elements of fire, ice, and water that were by and large regular features found in the environment
   - The incorrect preposition *from* is used with the verb *permeated*. The correct preposition to use with **permeated** is **with**.

   (B) with the natural elements of fire, ice, and water that were by and large regular features found in the environment
   - This answer contains the correct preposition **with** with the verb **permeated**, the correct idiom **by and large**, and the correct preposition **in** with **the environment**. This answer is correct.

   (C) with the natural elements of fire, ice, and water that were by and large regular features found *at the environment*
   - The incorrect preposition *at* is used in the expression *at the environment*. The correct preposition to use with **the environment** is **in**.

   (D) with the natural elements of fire, ice, and water that were *by in large* regular features found *at the environment*
   - The expression *by in large* is an incorrect idiom. The correct idiomatic expression is **by and large**.
   - The incorrect preposition *at* is used in the expression *at the environment*. The correct preposition to use with **the environment** is **in**.

   (E) *from* the natural elements of fire, ice, and water that were *by in large* regular features found in the environment
   - The incorrect preposition *from* is used with the verb *permeated*. The correct preposition to use with *permeated* is **with**.
   - The expression *by in large* is an incorrect idiom. The correct idiomatic expression is **by and large**.

2. This question tests **idioms**.

In early twentieth century America, many women pinched their cheeks and bit their lips to achieve a rosy look, while the more daring resorted to using tinted lip salves and rouges, a practice that caught the fantasy of some and was considered by others to be rather vulgar.

(A) caught the fantasy of some and was considered by others to be rather vulgar
- The expression caught the fantasy is an incorrect idiom. The correct idiomatic expression is **caught the fancy**.
- The expression considered...to be is an incorrect idiom. The word *considered* should never be followed by either *as* or *to be*.

(B) caught the fantasy of some and was considered as rather vulgar by others
- The expression caught the fantasy is an incorrect idiom. The correct idiomatic expression is **caught the fancy**.
- The expression considered as is an incorrect idiom. The word *considered* should never be followed by either *as* or *to be*.

(C) caught the fantasy of some and was regarded by others to be rather vulgar
- The expression caught the fantasy is an incorrect idiom. The correct idiomatic expression is **caught the fancy**.
- The expression regarded...to be is an incorrect idiom. The correct idiomatic expression is **regarded...as**.

(D) caught the fancy of some and was considered rather vulgar by others
- This answer correctly contains the correct idioms **caught the fancy** and **considered** without *as* or *to be*. This answer is correct.

(E) caught the fancy of some and was regarded as if rather vulgar by others
- The expression regarded as if is an incorrect idiom. The correct idiomatic expression is **regarded as**.

3. This question tests **idioms**.

   When the repeat offender was unable to <u>tow the line during his umpteenth chance at parole, the judge basically threw a book at him and remanded him to prison for a long stretch, feeling that the criminal had received his just deserts</u>.

(A) *tow the line* during his umpteenth chance at parole, the judge basically *threw a book at* him and remanded him to prison for a long stretch, feeling that the criminal had received his just deserts
   - The expression *tow the line* is an incorrect idiom. The correct idiomatic expression is **toe the line**.
   - The expression *threw a book at* is an incorrect idiom. The correct idiomatic expression is **threw the book at**.

(B) *tow the line* during his umpteenth chance at parole, the judge basically threw the book at him and remanded him to prison for a long stretch, feeling that the criminal had received his just deserts
   - The expression *tow the line* is an incorrect idiom. The correct idiomatic expression is **toe the line**.

(C) toe the line during his umpteenth chance at parole, the judge basically *threw a book at* him and remanded him to prison for a long stretch, feeling that the criminal had received his *just desserts*
   - The expression *threw a book at* is an incorrect idiom. The correct idiomatic expression is **threw the book at**.
   - The expression *just desserts* is an incorrect idiom. The correct idiomatic expression is **just deserts**.

(D) *tow the line* during his umpteenth chance at parole, the judge basically threw the book at him and remanded him to prison for a long stretch, feeling that the criminal had received his *just desserts*
   - The expression *tow the line* is an incorrect idiom. The correct idiomatic expression is **toe the line**.
   - The expression *just desserts* is an incorrect idiom. The correct idiomatic expression is **just deserts**.

(E) toe the line during his umpteenth chance at parole, the judge basically threw the book at him and remanded him to prison for a long stretch, feeling that the criminal had received his just deserts
   - This answer contains the correct idiomatic expressions **toe the line, threw the book at,** and **just deserts**. This answer is correct.

4. This question tests **idioms**.

The Indus Valley civilization was thriving until the mid-second millennium BCE, when its abrupt demise coincided with and was quite possibly related to the arrival of the Indo-European Aryans, whose culture apparently replaced rather than existed alongside the Indus Valley civilization.

(A) until the mid-second millennium BCE, when its abrupt demise coincided with and was quite possibly related to the arrival of the Indo-European Aryans, whose culture apparently replaced rather than existed alongside
- This answer contains the more formal prepositions **until**, the correct expression **coincided with**, and the more formal preposition **alongside**. This answer is correct.

(B) until the mid-second millennium BCE, when its abrupt demise *coincided* and was quite possibly related to the arrival of the Indo-European Aryans, whose culture apparently replaced rather than existed *alongside of*
- The verb *coincided* is missing a necessary preposition. The correct expression is **coincided with**.
- The idiomatic expression *alongside of* is too casual for formal writing. It is stylistically preferable to use the preposition **alongside**.

(C) until the mid-second millennium BCE, when its abrupt demise coincided with and was quite possibly related to the arrival of the Indo-European Aryans, whose culture apparently replaced rather than existed *alongside of*
- The idiomatic expression *alongside of* is too casual for formal writing. It is stylistically preferable to use the preposition **alongside**.

(D) *up until* the mid-second millennium BCE, when its abrupt demise *coincided* and was quite possibly related to the arrival of the Indo-European Aryans, whose culture apparently replaced rather than existed alongside
- The idiomatic expression *up until* is too casual for formal writing. It is stylistically preferable to use the preposition **until**.
- The verb *coincided* is missing a necessary preposition. The correct expression is **coincided with**.

(E) *up until* the mid-second millennium BCE, when its abrupt demise coincided with and was quite possibly related to the arrival of the Indo-European Aryans, whose culture apparently replaced rather than existed alongside
- The idiomatic expression *up until* is too casual for formal writing. It is stylistically preferable to use the preposition **until**.

5. This question tests **idioms**.

   As a youth serving a stiff nine-year term in Indiana, John Dillinger came to contact for the first time with a host of seasoned lawbreakers who believed that crime was not too big a deal and were happy to instruct him in the finer points of robbing banks and succeeding at various other criminal pursuits.

(A) came to contact for the first time with a host of seasoned lawbreakers who believed that crime was not too big a deal
   - The incorrect preposition *to* is used in the expression *came to contact*. The correct preposition to use with **came...contact** is **into**.

(B) came to contact for a first time with a host of seasoned lawbreakers who believed that crime was not too big of a deal
   - The incorrect preposition *to* is used in the expression *came to contact*. The correct preposition to use with **came...contact** is **into**.
   - The expression *for a first time* is an incorrect idiom. The correct idiomatic expression is **for the first time**.
   - The idiomatic expression *not too big of a deal* is too casual for formal writing. It is stylistically preferable to use the expression **not too big a deal**.

(C) came into contact for the first time with a host of seasoned lawbreakers who believed that crime was not too big a deal
   - This answer contains the correct expressions **came into contact** and **for the first time** and the less casual expression **not too big a deal**. This answer is correct.

(D) came into contact for a first time with a host of seasoned lawbreakers who believed that crime was not too big a deal
   - The expression *for a first time* is an incorrect idiom. The correct idiomatic expression is **for the first time**.

(E) came into contact for the first time with a host of seasoned lawbreakers who believed that crime was not too big of a deal
   - The idiomatic expression *not too big of a deal* is too casual for formal writing. It is stylistically preferable to use the expression **not too big a deal**.

6. **This question tests idioms.**

The renowned French poet Arthur Rimbaud (1854-1891) wrote his much of his poetry of note before he turned twenty; at the age of twenty-five he suddenly became <u>bored of this, disavowed his art, opened a business in Ethiopia, and spent the rest of his life there engaged to commerce and disengaged from</u> the world of art.

(A) bored of this, disavowed his art, opened a business in Ethiopia, and spent the rest of his life there engaged to commerce and disengaged from
- The incorrect preposition *of* is used in the expression *bored of*. The correct preposition to use with **bored** is **with**.
- The incorrect preposition *to* is used in the expression *engaged to*. The correct preposition to use with **engaged** in this situation is **in**.

(B) bored of this, disavowed his art, opened up a business in Ethiopia, and spent the rest of his life there engaged in commerce and disengaged from
- The incorrect preposition *of* is used in the expression *bored of*. The correct preposition to use with **bored** is **with**.
- The idiomatic expression *opened up* is too casual for formal writing. It is stylistically preferable to use the verb **opened**.

(C) bored with this, disavowed his art, opened up a business in Ethiopia, and spent the rest of his life there engaged in commerce and disengaged out of
- The idiomatic expression *opened up* is too casual for formal writing. It is stylistically preferable to use the verb **opened**.
- The incorrect prepositions *out* and *of* are used in the expression *disengaged out of*. The correct preposition to use with **disengaged** is **from**.

(D) bored with this, disavowed his art, opened a business in Ethiopia, and spent the rest of his life there engaged to commerce and disengaged out of
- The incorrect preposition *to* is used in the expression *engaged to*. The correct preposition to use with **engaged** in this situation is **in**.
- The incorrect prepositions *out* and *of* are used in the expression *disengaged out of*. The correct preposition to use with **disengaged** is **from**.

(E) **bored with this, disavowed his art, opened a business in Ethiopia, and spent the rest of his life there engaged in commerce and disengaged from**
- This answer contains the correct expressions **bored with, engaged in,** and **disengaged from** and avoids the problem with the casual expression *opened up* by using **opened**. This answer is **correct**.

Lesson 12: Problems with CLARITY

> Problems with **clarity** are stylistic problems involving language that, while it may not actually be grammatically incorrect, is not expressed in the clearest and most accurate way possible. The following kinds of problems with clarity are common on the GMAT:
> 1. ideas that are imprecise
> 2. ideas that are ambiguous
> 3. ideas that are illogical
> 4. infinitives of purpose that are misused
> 5. pronouns that lack clear referents

EXAMPLE 1: This example shows a sentence with ideas that are imprecise. These are ideas in which the reader is fairly certain what is meant but what is meant is not clearly stated.

INCORRECT: Chocolate is massively popular in Belgium, and even the smallest town has at least a couple of shops.
CORRECT: Chocolate is massively popular in Belgium, and even the smallest town has at least a couple of shops that sell chocolate.

In the incorrect example, the idea of shops is imprecise. From the context, it is understood that the intended meaning is that the shops that are mentioned sell chocolate, but this is not clearly stated. The correct example contains the more precise **shops that sell chocolate**.

- -

EXAMPLE 2: This example shows a sentence with ideas that are ambiguous. These are ideas in which there are two possible meanings and the reader is not sure of the intended meaning.

INCORRECT: A former *employer* recommended this *candidate* with no qualifications.
CORRECT: A former employer recommended this candidate in spite of the fact that the *candidate* had no qualifications.

In the incorrect example, the meaning of *with no qualifications* is ambiguous. This sentence could meaning either that the former *employer* had no qualifications or that this *candidate* had no qualifications. In the correct example, it is clear that it is the *candidate* who **has no qualifications**.

EXAMPLE 3: This example shows ideas that are illogical. These are ideas that do not actually make sense.

INCORRECT: Brazil occupies nearly half the area of South America and touches on all the countries of South America except Chile and Ecuador.

CORRECT: Brazil occupies nearly half the area of South America and touches on all the **other** countries of South America except Chile and Ecuador.

In the incorrect example, the expression *all the countries in South America except Chile and Ecuador* is not logical. It does not make sense that Brazil touches itself. In the correct example, the idea has been modified with the word **other** to exclude Brazil.

- -

EXAMPLE 4: This example shows the misuse of an infinitive of purpose. An infinitive of purpose is problematic if it is attributed to something inanimate or inhuman that is not capable of feeling purpose.

INCORRECT: Flu viruses enter your body through the mucous membranes of your nose, eyes, or mouth to make you ill.

CORRECT: Flu viruses enter your body through the mucous membranes of your nose, eyes, or mouth **and result in making you ill**.

In the incorrect example, there is a misused infinitive of purpose *to make* that causes the sentence to be illogical. According to the incorrect sentence, flu viruses enter the body with the purpose of making *you ill*. However, a flu virus cannot experience a sense of purpose. In the correct example, flu viruses enter the body **and result in making you ill**; this is a more logical meaning.

- -

EXAMPLE 5: This example shows a pronoun with an unclear referent. A pronoun should have one clear referent and is problematic if it has either no referent or two possible referents.

INCORRECT: The *members* of the legislature announced to the *citizens* that *they* would have thirty days of vacation per year.

CORRECT: The members of the legislature announced that **each citizen** would have thirty days of vacation per year.

In the incorrect example, the pronoun *they* has two possible referents, *members* and *citizens*, so the meaning of this sentence is ambiguous. This sentence could mean either that the members of the legislature would have thirty days of vacation or that the citizens would have thirty days of vacation. In the correct example, it is clear that it is **each citizen** who would have thirty days of vacation.

SKILLS PRACTICE: Find the problems with **clarity** in the following sentences. (The number in parentheses indicates the number of problems you should find.) Then, study the explanations on the pages that follow.

1. Following an altercation in a local tavern, the police officer arrested the suspected instigator with a gun. *(1)*

2. Now believed to be between fifteen and twenty billion years old, the universe was, as recently as two centuries ago, widely known to be only six thousand years old. *(1)*

3. An old wives' tale that seems to work is that the temperature can be determined by counting the number of cricket chirps and adding 40. *(1)*

4. Computerized traffic lights can tell how many vehicles have passed through a particular light, and they can adapt according to the volume of traffic. *(1)*

5. Until the mid sixteenth century, comets were believed to be not astronomical phenomena but burning vapors that had arisen from distant swamps to propel themselves across the sky by fire and light. *(1)*

6. High winds combine with low pressure in the eye of a hurricane to suck up the seawater; the effect, as the eye makes landfall, is a wall of water known as storm surge. *(1)*

7. The Old English alphabet was quite similar to today's alphabet, though a number of letters had somewhat different shapes and only lower-case letters. *(1)*

8. Not wishing to spend months as a lame-duck president, Woodrow Wilson planned to turn the government over to his successor immediately after the election unless his reelection bid failed. *(1)*

EXPLANATIONS (I = incorrect, C = correct)

1. Following an altercation in a local tavern, the *police officer* arrested the suspected *instigator* with a gun.

   - The meaning of *with a gun* is ambiguous. This sentence could mean either that the *police officer* used a gun to arrest the instigator or that the police officer arrested an *instigator* who had a gun.
     - I: *The suspected instigator with a gun*
     - C: **the suspected instigator who was holding a gun**

---

2. Now believed to be between fifteen and twenty billion years old, the universe was, as recently as two centuries ago, widely known to be only six thousand years old.

   - The meaning of *widely known to be only six thousand years old* is illogical. It does not make sense that one could "know" something that is not true.
     - I: *known*
     - C: **believed**

---

3. An old wives' tale that seems to work is that the temperature can be determined by counting the number of cricket chirps and adding 40.

   - The meaning of *counting the number of cricket chirps* is imprecise. It is not possible to count the number of cricket chirps unless you know how long to count them.
     - I: *counting the number of cricket chirps*
     - C: **counting the number of cricket chirps for a minute**

---

4. Computerized *traffic lights* can tell how many *vehicles* have passed through a particular light, and *they* can adapt according to the volume of traffic.

   - The pronoun *they* has two possible referents, *traffic lights* and *vehicles*, so the meaning of this sentence is ambiguous. This sentence could mean either that the traffic lights can adapt or that the vehicles can adapt.
     - I: *they*
     - C: **these lights**

5. Until the mid sixteenth century, comets were believed to be not astronomical phenomena but burning vapors that had arisen from distant swamps *to propel* themselves across the sky by fire and light.

   - This sentence has a misused infinitive of purpose *to propel* that makes the sentence illogical. According to this sentence, the burning vapors have the purpose of propelling themselves across the sky. However, vapors cannot experience a sense of purpose.
     - I: *to propel themselves*
     - C: **propelled**

- -

6. High winds combine with low pressure in the eye of a hurricane to suck up the seawater; the effect, *as the eye makes landfall*, is a wall of water known as storm surge.

   - The idea of *as the eye makes landfall* is imprecise. From the context describing when the storm surge occurs, it is understood that this occurs, not when the eye makes landfall, but when the hurricane itself makes landfall.
     - I: *the eye*
     - C: **the hurricane**

- -

7. The Old English alphabet was quite similar to today's alphabet, though a number of letters had somewhat different shapes and *only lower-case letters*.

   - The meaning of *only lower case letters* is ambiguous. This sentence could mean either that the Old English alphabet had only lower-case letters or that the letters with different shapes had only lower case letters.
     - I: *only lower-case letters*
     - C: **the entire alphabet had only lower-case letters**

- -

8. Not wishing to spend months as a lame-duck president, Woodrow Wilson planned to turn the government over to his successor immediately after the election *unless his reelection bid failed*.

   - The meaning of *unless his reelection bid failed* is illogical. It does not make sense that the president would turn the government over to his successor *unless his reelection bid failed*, an idea meaning *if his reelection bid succeeded*.
     - I: *unless*
     - C: **if**

It Works! GMAT Sentence Correction

GMAT-STYLE SKILLS PRACTICE: Choose the letter of the answer to each question that best reflects the style and accuracy of standard written English. Then, study the explanations on the pages that follow.

1. Doctors now know that tuberculosis is caused by a bacterium and can be treated with antibiotics, but in the 19th century the only known <u>cure for doctors to prescribe</u> was plenty of clean, warm, fresh air.

   (A) treatment for doctors to prescribe
   (B) treatment for doctors to try
   (C) cure for patients to try
   (D) treatment for patients to prescribe
   (E) cure for doctors to prescribe

2. XYZ Touring Company is conducting <u>tours to the Père LaChaise Cemetery where numerous famous people are buried daily</u>.

   (A) tours to the Père LaChaise Cemetery where numerous famous people are buried daily
   (B) daily tours to the Père LaChaise Cemetery, where numerous famous people are buried
   (C) tours to see where numerous famous people are buried daily in the Père LaChaise Cemetery
   (D) tours to show where numerous famous people are buried daily in the Père LaChaise Cemetery
   (E) daily tours to the Père LaChaise Cemetery to see where numerous famous people are buried

3. It is energy-efficient to turn off a fluorescent light because it will be used again within an hour or more due to the high voltage needed to turn it on.

    (A) because it will be used again
    (B) although it will be used again
    (C) if it will be used again
    (D) unless it will not be used again
    (E) only if it will not be used again

4. In 359 AD the Franks entered into an alliance with the Romans, but in 481 AD Clovis became king of the Salian Franks and within five years had begun a campaign of aggression against them to prove their superiority.

    (A) against them to prove their superiority
    (B) against the Romans to prove their superiority
    (C) against them to prove the superiority of the Franks
    (D) against the Franks to prove the superiority of the Romans
    (E) against the Romans to prove the superiority of the Franks

5. Elizabeth 1 of Russia used to change her outfits at least two or three times per evening; when she died in 1762, her royal closet contained more than 15,000 <u>dresses to contribute to the narrative of her extreme profligacy.</u>

    (A) dresses to contribute to the narrative of her extreme profligacy
    (B) dresses, a fact that was intended to contribute to the narrative of her extreme profligacy
    (C) dresses to prove to her subjects that she was extremely profligate
    (D) dresses, a fact that contributed to the narrative of her extreme profligacy
    (E) dresses to demonstrate her extreme profligacy to her subjects

6. By law, creditors cannot ask purchasers to pledge as collateral any <u>clothes, furniture, or personal property unless these items are</u> the actual credit purchases.

    (A) clothes, furniture, or personal belongings unless these items are
    (B) clothes, furniture, or personal items if it is
    (C) clothes, furniture, or other personal items because it is
    (D) clothes, furniture, or other personal belongings unless these items are
    (E) clothes, furniture, or personal belongings if these items are

EXPLANATIONS

1. This question tests **clarity**.

   Doctors now know that tuberculosis is caused by a bacterium and can be treated with antibiotics, but in the 19th century the only known <u>cure for doctors to prescribe</u> was plenty of clean, warm, fresh air.

   (A) treatment for doctors to prescribe
   - This answer is more precise than the other answers in its use of **treatment** and **prescribe**. This answer is correct.

   (B) treatment *for doctors to try*
   - The expression *for doctors to try* is imprecise. It was the patients who tried the treatment, and not the doctors. It is more precise to say that the doctors prescribed the treatment.

   (C) *cure* for patients to try
   - The word *cure* is imprecise. *Plenty of clean, warm, fresh air* was a treatment but was not a cure.

   (D) treatment for *patients* to prescribe
   - The word *patients* is illogical. *Patients* are not the ones who prescribe a treatment.

   (E) *cure* for doctors to prescribe
   - The word *cure* is imprecise. *Plenty of clean, warm, fresh air* was a treatment but was not a cure.

2. This question tests **clarity**.

XYZ Touring Company is conducting <u>tours to the Père LaChaise Cemetery where numerous famous people are buried daily</u>.

(A) *tours* to the Père LaChaise Cemetery where numerous famous people are buried *daily*
- The meaning of *daily* is ambiguous. This answer could mean either that the *tours* are daily or that or that famous people are buried daily.

(B) daily *tours* to the Père LaChaise Cemetery, where numerous famous people are buried
- This answer uses the expression **daily tours** instead of the ambiguous use of *daily* and the misused infinitive of purpose *to see* found in some of the other answers. This answer is correct.

(C) *tours* *to see* where numerous famous people are buried *daily* in the Père LaChaise Cemetery
- This answer has a misused infinitive of purpose *to see* that makes the sentence illogical. According to this answer, the *tours* have the purpose of seeing where famous people are buried. However, *tours* cannot experience a sense of purpose.
- The meaning of *daily* is ambiguous. This answer could mean either that the tours are daily or that or that famous people are buried daily.

(D) *tours* to show where numerous famous people are buried *daily* in the Père LaChaise Cemetery
- The meaning of *daily* is ambiguous. This answer could mean either that the tours are daily or that or that famous people are buried daily.

(E) daily *tours* to the Père LaChaise Cemetery *to see* where numerous famous people are buried
- This answer has a misused infinitive of purpose *to see* that makes the sentence illogical. According to this answer, the *tours* have the purpose of seeing where famous people are buried. However, *tours* cannot experience a sense of purpose.

3. **This question tests clarity.**

   It is energy-efficient to turn off a fluorescent light <u>because it will be used again</u> within an hour or more due to the high voltage needed to turn it on.

   (A) because it will be used again
   - The meaning of *because* is illogical in this context.

   (B) although it will be used again
   - The meaning of *although* is illogical in this context.

   (C) if it will be used again
   - The meaning of *if* is illogical in this context.

   (D) unless it will not be used again
   - The meaning of *unless* is illogical in this context.

   (E) only if it will not be used again
   - The meaning of the sentence is logical because of the use of the expression **only if**. This answer is correct.

4. **This question tests clarity.**

In 359 AD *the Franks* entered into an alliance with *the Romans*, but in 481 AD Clovis became king of the Salian Franks and within five years had begun a campaign of aggression <u>against them to prove their superiority</u>.

(A) against *them* to prove *their* superiority
- The pronoun *them* has two possible referents, *the Franks* and *the Romans*, so the meaning of the sentence is ambiguous.
- The possessive *their* has two possible referents, *the Franks* and *the Romans*, so the meaning of the sentence is ambiguous.

(B) against the Romans to prove *their* superiority
- The possessive *their* has two possible referents, *the Franks* and *the Romans*, so the meaning of the sentence is ambiguous.

(C) against *them* to prove the superiority of the Franks
- The pronoun *them* has two possible referents, *the Franks* and *the Romans*, so the meaning of the sentence is ambiguous.

(D) against the Franks to prove the superiority of the Romans
- The phrase *against the Franks to prove the superiority of the Romans* makes the meaning of this sentence is illogical. Clovis, the king of the Salian Franks began a campaign of aggression against the Romans, and not against the Franks, to prove the superiority of the Franks, and not against the Romans.

(E) against the Romans to prove the superiority of the Franks
- This answer lacks the pronouns and possessives with unclear referents of some of the other answers and logically has Clovis, king of the Salian Franks, campaigning **against the Romans to prove the superiority of the Franks**. This answer is correct.

5. This question tests **clarity**.

Elizabeth 1 of Russia used to change her outfits at least two or three times per evening; when she died in 1762, *her royal closet contained more than 15,000* dresses to contribute to the narrative of her extreme profligacy.

(A) *dresses* to contribute *to the narrative of her extreme profligacy*
- This answer has a misused infinitive of purpose *to contribute* that makes the sentence illogical. According to this answer, the idea that *her royal closet contained more than 15,000 dresses* had the purpose of contributing to a narrative. However, this idea cannot experience a sense of purpose.

(B) *dresses*, a fact that was intended *to contribute to the narrative of her extreme profligacy*
- The meaning of *intended* is illogical. It does not make sense that the idea that *her royal closet contained more than 15,000 dresses* experienced a sense of intention.

(C) *dresses* to prove *to her subjects that she was extremely profligate*
- This answer has a misused infinitive of purpose *to prove* that makes the sentence illogical. According to this answer, the idea that *her royal closet contained more than 15,000 dresses* had the purpose of proving something to her subjects. However, this idea cannot experience a sense of purpose.

(D) dresses, **a fact that contributed** to the narrative of her extreme profligacy
- This answer includes the expression **a fact that contributed** to avoid the problems with intentions and purpose of the other answers. This answer is correct.

(E) *dresses* to demonstrate *her extreme profligacy to her subjects*
- This answer has a misused infinitive of purpose *to demonstrate* that makes the sentence illogical. According to this answer, the idea that *her royal closet contained more than 15,000 dresses* has the purpose of contributing to a narrative. However, this idea cannot experience a sense of purpose.

It Works! GMAT Sentence Correction

6. **This question tests clarity.**

    By law, creditors cannot ask purchasers to pledge as collateral any <u>clothes, furniture, or personal property unless these items are</u> the actual credit purchases.

(A) *clothes, furniture, or personal belongings* unless these items are
   - The meaning of *clothes, furniture, or personal belongings* is imprecise because *clothes* and *furniture* are kinds of *personal belongings*.

(B) *clothes, furniture, or personal items* *if* *it* is
   - The meaning of *clothes, furniture, or personal items* is imprecise because *clothes* and *furniture* are kinds of *personal items*.
   - The meaning of *if* is illogical in this context.
   - The pronoun *it* has no clear referent.

(C) clothes, furniture, or other personal items *because* *it* is
   - The meaning of *because* is illogical in this context.
   - The pronoun *it* has no clear referent.

(D) clothes, furniture, or **other** personal belongings **unless these items are**
   - This answer includes **other** in the expression *clothes, furniture, or other personal belongings* to make the expression more precise. It also includes the logical conjunction **unless** and uses the subject and verb **items are** to avoid a pronoun with an unclear referent. This answer is correct.

(E) *clothes, furniture, or personal belongings* *if* these items are
   - The meaning of *clothes, furniture, or personal belongings* is imprecise because *clothes* and *furniture* are kinds of *personal belongings*.
   - The meaning of *if* is illogical in this context.

THE GMAT-STYLE TESTS

GMAT-Style Tests
TEST 1

Choose the letter of the answer to each question that best reflects the style and accuracy of standard written English. Then, study the explanations on the pages that follow.

1. In the nineteenth century, mathematician William Shanks calculated the mathematical value of pi (π) to 707 places, which took up fifteen years of his life.

    (A) which took up fifteen years of his life
    (B) a task which involved spending fifteen years to complete
    (C) which was a fifteen-year-long feat
    (D) a feat that took fifteen years to complete
    (E) and that was something that had cost him fifteen years of his life

2. The Sherman Antitrust Act of 1890 and the Clayton Act of 1914 was passed specifically in order to limit the control and influence a single business could gain in any given market.

    (A) was passed specifically in order to limit the control and influence a single business could gain
    (B) were passed specifically to limit the control and influence that a single business could gain
    (C) was passed specifically to limit the control and influence of a single business
    (D) were passed in order to limit specifically the control and influence of a single business
    (E) were passed to specifically limit the control and influence a single business could gain

3. The key to the process of making rational decisions is generating a list of alternatives and then knowing how best to select or eliminate it from the list.

   (A) is generating a list of alternatives and then knowing how best to select or eliminate it
   (B) are generating a list of alternatives and then to know how best to select or eliminate it
   (C) is generating a list of alternatives and then knowing how best to select or eliminate them
   (D) is creating a list of alternatives and then knowing how to best select or eliminate them
   (E) are creating a list of alternatives and then knowing how best to select or to eliminate them

4. The narrow body of water separating northeastern Africa from the Arabian Peninsula, the designation of the Red Sea comes from the masses of reddish seaweed found in its waters.

   (A) the designation of the Red Sea comes from
   (B) the naming of the Red Sea was based on
   (C) the Red Sea was so dubbed because of
   (D) the Red Sea dubbed itself in this way based on
   (E) the Red Sea so designated itself because of

5. The camel originated in North America and, from there, has migrated to Asia and South America before becoming extinct and dying out in its native homeland.

    (A) has migrated to Asia and South America before becoming extinct and dying out in its native homeland
    (B) migrated to Asia and South America before dying out in its homeland
    (C) has migrated to Asia and South America before becoming extinct in their native homeland
    (D) migrated to Asia and South America before becoming extinct and dying out in its homeland
    (E) migrated to Asia and South America before dying out in their native homeland

6. While the English language only distinguishes singular and plural, other languages, such as Sanskrit, make a distinction among singular, dual, and plural.

    (A) While the English language only distinguishes singular and plural, other languages, such as Sanskrit, make a distinction among singular, dual, and plural.
    (B) While the English language distinguishes only singular and plural, other languages, including Sanskrit, make a distinction between singular, dual, and plural.
    (C) The English language only distinguishes singular and plural, however other languages, such as Sanskrit, make a distinction among singular, dual, and plural.
    (D) The English language distinguishes only singular and plural, but other languages, such as Sanskrit, make a distinction among singular, dual, and plural.
    (E) The English language makes a distinction only between singular and plural, but other languages, including Sanskrit, maybe distinguished by their use of

7. Half of the cost of the construction of the Erie Canal was paid for through a tax of 12.5% on salt purchased in New York State <u>on top of tolls already being charged by the state</u> for shipments of salt.

   (A) on top of tolls already being charged by the state
   (B) irregardless of the fact that the state was already charging tolls
   (C) in addition to the tolls the state was already charging
   (D) on top of the already assessed tolls the state was charging
   (E) in addition to the tolls that the state was already charging

8. Most of the evidence of a ballad tradition in the British Isles before 1500 can be found in Francis J. Child's monumental work, *The English and Scottish Popular Ballads*, <u>which provides not only a lengthy foreword but also all the texts that Child was able to amass</u>.

   (A) which provides not only a lengthy foreword but also all the texts that Child was able to amass
   (B) which provides not only a foreword that was long but also provides all the texts that Child could accrue
   (C) which not only provides a lengthy introductory foreword but also all the texts Child could amass
   (D) which provides not only long introductory notes but also all the texts Child was able to amass
   (E) which provides not only long introductory notes but also all the texts that Child was able to accrue

9. Oddly enough, it takes only about 3 normal-sized carrots per day to come down with hypercarotenemia, which is an excess consumption of carotene that turns one's skin orange.

   (A) to come down with hypercarotenemia, which is
   (B) for a medium-sized person to come down with hypercarotenemia, this is
   (C) for medium-sized people to come down with hypercarotenemia, which is
   (D) for medium-sized people to come down with hypercarotenemia, this is
   (E) for a medium-sized person to come down with hypercarotenemia, which is

10. Although a company's work environment is partly a heritage of its past leaders, shaping that environment is a critically important part of every incumbent manager's job.

    (A) Although a company's work environment is partly a heritage of
    (B) Unless the work environment of a company is, at least partly, a heritage of
    (C) While the environment of a company's workers exists, at least in part, to reflect
    (D) Though the workers and the environment in which they work in a company could partly reflect the heritage of
    (E) Only if the environment in which a company works is at least in part a reflection of the heritage of

11. Vowel sounds differ from consonant sounds primarily in that they are produced not by blocking air in its passage from the lungs and by passing air through different shapes of the mouth and different positions of the tongue and lips.

    (A) Vowel sounds differ from consonant sounds primarily in that they are produced not by blocking air in its passage from the lungs and by passing
    (B) Vowel sounds are different than consonant sounds in that primarily vowel sounds are produced not by blocking the surge of air from the lips but that they pass
    (C) The primary way that vowel sounds differ from consonant sounds is that vowel sounds are produced not by blocking air in its passage from the lungs but by passing
    (D) The way that vowel sounds are different, primarily, than consonant sounds is that vowel sounds are produced not by blocking air in its passage from the lungs but by passing
    (E) The way vowel sounds primarily differ from consonant sounds is that they are not produced by blocking air in its passage from the lungs but produced by passing

12. Medieval alchemists' failed endeavors had at their basic core the incorrect belief that all matter in the universe was comprised in varying amounts of the four basic elements of earth, fire, air, and water and that creating gold required only the determination of the exact proportions of these basic elements.

    (A) had at their basic core the incorrect belief that all matter in the universe was comprised in
    (B) were based in the incorrect belief that all matters in the universe were composed of
    (C) were based on the incorrect belief that all matter in the universe was comprised of
    (D) had as their basis the mistaken belief that all matters in the universe were comprised of
    (E) were based on the incorrect belief that all matter in the universe was comprised in

EXPLANATIONS

1. This question tests **pronouns**, **awkwardness**, and **wordiness**.

   In the nineteenth century, mathematician *William Shanks calculated the mathematical value of pi (π) to 707 places, which took up fifteen years of his life.*

   (A) *which* took up fifteen years of his life
   - The relative pronoun *which* is used incorrectly. This relative pronoun should be used to refer to a specific noun and not to a complete idea such as *William Shanks calculated the mathematical value of pi (π) to 707 places.*

   (B) *a task which involved spending* fifteen years to complete
   - The idea *a task which involved spending* is awkward. The stylistic preference on GMAT is for a more natural-sounding way of expressing this idea.

   (C) *which* was a fifteen-year-long feat
   - The relative pronoun *which* is used incorrectly. This relative pronoun should be used to refer to a specific noun and not to a complete idea such as *William Shanks calculated the mathematical value of pi (π) to 707 places.*

   (D) **a feat that** took fifteen years to complete
   - This answer uses **a feat that** to avoid the issue of the incorrect use of *which* and avoids the awkwardness and wordiness found in some of the other answers.

   (E) and that was *something that had cost him fifteen years of his life*
   - The part of the answer *something that had cost him fifteen years of his life* is overly wordy and complex. The stylistic preference on GMAT is for more simple and concise language.

2. This question tests **agreement**, **wordiness**, **awkwardness**, and **modifiers**.

The *Sherman Antitrust Act* of 1890 *and* the *Clayton Act* of 1914 <u>was passed specifically in order to limit the control and influence a single business could gain</u> in any given market.

(A) *was passed* specifically *in order to limit* the control and influence *a single business could gain*
   - The singular verb *was passed* does not agree with the plural subject *Sherman Antitrust Act...and...Clayton Act*.
   - The idea *in order to limit* is overly wordy. The stylistic preference on GMAT is for more concise language.
   - The conjunction *that* has been omitted in front of the subject and verb *a single business could gain*. The stylistic preference on GMAT is to include the conjunction **that**.

(B) were passed specifically to limit the control and influence that *a single business could gain*
   - This answer contains the correct plural past tense verb **were passed** and the correctly positioned adverb **specifically**. It also includes **that** in front of the subject and verb *a single business could gain*.

(C) *was passed* specifically to limit the control and influence of a single business
   - The singular verb *was passed* does not agree with the plural subject *Sherman Antitrust Act...and...Clayton Act*.

(D) were passed *in order to limit* *specifically* the *control and influence* of a single business
   - The idea *in order to limit* is overly wordy. The stylistic preference on GMAT is for more concise language.
   - The modifier *specifically* is positioned incorrectly because an adverb cannot be positioned between a verb or verbal *to limit* and its direct object *control and influence*.

(E) were passed to *specifically* limit the control and influence *a single business could gain*
   - The modifier *specifically* is positioned incorrectly because an adverb cannot be used between the two parts of an infinitive, *to* and *limit*. This is called a split infinitive.
   - The conjunction *that* has been omitted in front of the subject and verb *a single business could gain*. The stylistic preference on GMAT is to include the conjunction **that**.

3. This question tests **agreement**, **parallelism**, and **modifiers**.

The *key* to the process of making rational decisions <u>is generating a list of alternatives and then knowing how best to select or eliminate it</u> from the list.

(A) is generating a list of *alternatives* and then knowing how best to select or eliminate *it*
   - The singular pronoun *it* does not agree with the plural noun *alternatives*, to which it refers.

(B) *are generating* a list of *alternatives and* then *to know* how best to select or eliminate *it*
   - The plural verb *are generating* does not agree with the singular subject *key*.
   - The expression *to know* is not parallel to the expression *generating*. The structure *and* indicates that these expressions should be parallel.
   - The singular pronoun *it* does not agree with the plural noun *alternatives*, to which it refers.

(C) is generating a list of alternatives and then knowing how best to select or eliminate them
   - This answer contains the correct singular verb **is generating** to agree with the subject *key* and the parallel expressions **generating** and **knowing** connected with **and**, and the parallel expressions **select** and **eliminate** connected with **or**.

(D) is *creating* a list of alternatives *and* then knowing how to *best* select or eliminate them
   - The modifier *best* is positioned incorrectly because an adverb cannot be used between the two parts of an infinitive, *to* and *select*. This is called a split infinitive.

(E) *are creating* a list of alternatives and then knowing how best to select or to eliminate them
   - The plural verb *are creating* does not agree with the singular subject *key*.

4. This question tests **modifiers** and **diction**.

The narrow body of water separating northeastern Africa from the Arabian Peninsula, <u>the designation of the Red Sea comes from</u> the masses of reddish seaweed found in its waters.

(A) the designation of the Red Sea comes from
- The use of *the designation* following the comma (,) creates a sentence with a dangling modifier, *The narrow body of water separating northeastern Africa from the Arabian Peninsula*. An introductory modifier should modify the subject of the main clause directly following the comma (,). The expression *The narrow body of water separating northeastern Africa from the Arabian Peninsula* should modify **the Red Sea** and not *the designation*.

(B) the naming of the Red Sea was based on
- The use of *the naming* following the comma (,) creates a sentence with a dangling modifier, *The narrow body of water separating northeastern Africa from the Arabian Peninsula*. An introductory modifier should modify the subject of the main clause directly following the comma (,). The expression *The narrow body of water separating northeastern Africa from the Arabian Peninsula* should modify **the Red Sea** and not *the naming*.

(C) the Red Sea was so dubbed because of
- This answer contains **the Red Sea** following the comma so that the introductory modifier is not dangling. It also uses the verb **was...dubbed** according to its dictionary definition.

(D) the Red Sea dubbed itself in this way based on
- The word *dubbed* has an inappropriate meaning for this context. It is not possible for *the Red Sea* to dub something. Humans dub something, and inanimate objects do not.

(E) the Red Sea so designated itself because of
- The word *designated* has an inappropriate meaning for this context. It is not possible for *the Red Sea* to designate something. Humans designate something, and inanimate objects do not.

5. This question tests **verbs**, **wordiness**, and **agreement**.

    The *camel* originated in North America and, from there, has migrated to Asia and South America before becoming extinct and dying out in its native homeland.

(A) *has migrated* to Asia and South America before *becoming extinct* and *dying out* in its *native* homeland
   - The present perfect tense *has migrated* is used incorrectly. The present perfect tense should be used when an action occurs in the period from the past to the present. Here the verb refers to period before the camel became extinct in North America.
   - The expression *dying out* is redundant because its meaning is included within the expression *becoming extinct*.
   - The word *native* is redundant because its meaning is included within the word *homeland*.

(B) **migrated** to Asia and South America before dying out in its homeland
   - This answer contains the correct simple past tense **migrated** and the correct singular possessive **its** to refer to *camel*. It also avoids the problems with wordiness found in some of the other answers.

(C) *has migrated* to Asia and South America before becoming extinct in *their* *native* homeland
   - The present perfect tense *has migrated* is used incorrectly. The present perfect tense should be used when an action occurs in the period from the past to the present. Here the verb refers to period before the camel became extinct in North America.
   - The plural possessive *their* does not agree with the singular noun *camel*, to which it refers.
   - The word *native* is redundant because its meaning is included within the word *homeland*.

(D) migrated to Asia and South America before *becoming extinct* and *dying out* in its homeland
   - The expression *dying out* is redundant because its meaning is included within the expression *becoming extinct*.

(E) migrated to Asia and South America before dying out in *their* native homeland
   - The plural possessive *their* does not agree with the singular noun *camel*, to which it refers.

6. This question tests **modifiers**, **diction**, and **sentences**.

   While the English language only distinguishes singular and plural, other languages, such as Sanskrit, make a distinction among singular, dual, and plural.

(A) While the English language |only| distinguishes *singular and plural*, other languages, such as Sanskrit, make a distinction among singular, dual, and plural.
   • The modifier |only| is positioned incorrectly because it is not directly in front of the idea *singular and plural*, which it modifies.

(B) While the English language distinguishes only singular and plural, other languages, including Sanskrit, make a distinction |between| singular, dual, and plural.
   • The word *between* is used incorrectly with to relate, *singular, dual, and plural*. The word *between* should be used to relate only two ideas. Use **among** -- which is used when three or more people or objects are related -- instead.

(C) The *English language* |only| distinguishes singular and plural, however |other languages|, such as Sanskrit, |make| a distinction among singular, dual, and plural.
   • The modifier |only| is positioned incorrectly because it is not directly in front of the idea *singular and plural*, which it modifies.
   • This answer creates a run-on sentence because the two subjects and verbs *English language...distinguishes* and |other languages...make| are connected with only a comma *(,)*. A comma cannot be used to connect two subjects and verbs without a conjunction, and *however* is an adverb and is not a conjunction.

(D) The English language distinguishes only *singular and plural*, but other languages, such as Sanskrit, make a distinction **among** *singular, dual, and plural*.
   • This answer has the modifier **only** in the correct position in front of *singular and plural* and correctly uses **among** with the three ideas *singular, dual, and plural*. It also avoids the problem with a run-on sentence which is found in one of the other answers.

(E) The English language makes a distinction |only| between *singular and plural*, but other languages, including Sanskrit, |maybe| distinguished by their use of
   • The modifier |only| is positioned incorrectly because it is not directly in front of the idea *singular and plural*, which it modifies.
   • The expression |maybe| -- which is an adverb meaning "perhaps" -- should not be confused with the verb *may be* -- which means "could possibly be." Use the verb **may be** instead.

7. This question tests **awkwardness**, **diction**, and **wordiness**.

   Half of the cost of the construction of the Erie Canal was paid for through a tax of 12.5% on salt purchased in New York State on top of tolls already being charged by the state for shipments of salt.

(A) on top of tolls already being charged by the state
   - The passive voice *already being charged by* is unnecessary here. The more direct active voice would be stylistically preferable on GMAT.

(B) irregardless of the fact that the state was already charging tolls
   - The word *iregardless* is always incorrect. Use **regardless** instead.

(C) in addition to the tolls the state was already charging
   - The conjunction *that* has been omitted in front of the subject and verb *the state was already charging*. The stylistic preference on GMAT is to include the conjunction **that**.

(D) on top of the already assessed tolls the state was charging
   - The word *assessed* is redundant because its meaning is included within the word *charging*.
   - The conjunction *that* has been omitted in front of the subject and verb *the state was charging*. The stylistic preference on GMAT is to include the conjunction **that**.

(E) in addition to the tolls that the state was already charging
   - This answer avoids the problems with the unnecessary passive voice, the omitted *that*, diction, and redundancy that are found in some of the other answers.

8. This question tests **wordiness**, **parallelism**, **diction**, and **awkwardness**.

   Most of the evidence of a ballad tradition in the British Isles before 1500 can be found in Francis J. Child's monumental work, *The English and Scottish Popular Ballads*, which provides not only a lengthy foreword but also all the texts that Child was able to amass.

(A) which provides not only a lengthy foreword but also all the texts *that Child was* able to amass
   - This answer contains the conjunction *that* in front of the subject and verb *Child was* and the correctly used word *amass*. This answer also avoids the problems with wordiness and parallelism that are found in some of the other answers.

(B) which provides *not only* a foreword that was long *but also* provides all the texts that Child could accrue
   - The idea *a foreword that was long* is overly wordy and complex. The stylistic preference on GMAT is for more concise and simpler language.
   - The expression *provides all the texts* is not parallel to the expression *a foreword that was long*. The structure *not only...but also* indicates that these expressions should be parallel.
   - The word *accrue* -- which means "accumulate as a result of natural growth" and not "accumulate intentionally"-- is illogical in this context. Use **amass** -- which means "accumulate intentionally" -- instead.

(C) which *not only provides a lengthy* introductory *foreword but also* all the texts Child could amass
   - The word *introductory* is redundant because its meaning is included within the word *foreword*.
   - The expression *all the texts Child could amass* is not parallel to the expression *provides a lengthy introductory foreword*. The structure *not only...but also* indicates that these expressions should be parallel.
   - The conjunction *that* has been omitted in front of the subject and verb *Child could amass*. The stylistic preference on GMAT is to include the conjunction **that**.

(D) which provides not only long introductory notes but also all the texts *Child was* able to amass
   - The conjunction *that* has been omitted in front of the subject and verb *Child was*. The stylistic preference on GMAT is to include the conjunction **that**.

(E) which provides not only long introductory notes but also all the texts that Child was able to accrue
   - The word *accrue* -- which means "accumulate as a result of natural growth" and not "accumulate intentionally" -- is illogical in this context. Use **amass** -- which means "accumulate intentionally" -- instead.

9. This question tests **clarity**, **sentences**, and **agreement**.

Oddly enough, *it takes* only about 3 normal-sized carrots per day to come down with hypercarotenemia, which is an excess consumption of carotene that turns *one's* skin orange.

(A) *to come down with hypercarotenemia*, which is
- The meaning of the part of the answer *to come down with hypercarotenemia* is imprecise because it is not clear who or what would develop hypercarotenemia after eating 3 carrots. From the context, it is understood that the intended meaning is that a person would, but this is not clearly stated.

(B) for a medium-sized person to come down with hypercarotenemia, *this is*
- This answer creates a run-on sentence because the two subjects and verbs *it takes* and *this is* are connected with only a comma (,). A comma cannot be used to connect two subjects and verbs without a conjunction.

(C) for medium-sized *people* to come down with hypercarotenemia, which is
- The plural noun *people* does not agree with the singular possessive *one's*, to which it refers.

(D) for medium-sized *people* to come down with hypercarotenemia, *this is*
- The plural noun *people* does not agree with the singular possessive *one's*, to which it refers.
- This answer creates a run-on sentence because the two subjects and verbs *it takes* and *this is* are connected with only a comma (,). A comma cannot be used to connect two subjects and verbs without a conjunction.

(E) for a medium-sized person to come down with hypercarotenemia, which is
- This answer avoids the issues with clarity, run-on sentences, and agreement found in some of the other answers.

10. This question tests **clarity**, **wordiness**, and **agreement**.

   Although a company's work environment *is* partly a heritage of its past leaders, shaping that environment is a critically important part of every incumbent manager's job.

   (A) **Although** a company's work environment is partly a heritage of
   - This answer contains the logical conjunction **Although** and avoids the problems with wordiness and agreement found in some of the other answers.

   (B) *Unless* the work environment of a company is, at least partly, a heritage of
   - The meaning of this answer is illogical. This answer does not make sense when it includes *Unless*.

   (C) While *the environment of a company's workers exists*, at least in part, *to reflect*
   - This answer has a misused infinitive of purpose *to reflect* that makes the sentence illogical. According to this answer, the idea that *the environment of a company's workers exists* has the purpose of shaping that environment. However, this idea cannot experience a sense of purpose.

   (D) Though *the workers and the environment in which they work in a company* could partly reflect the heritage of
   - The idea *the workers and the environment in which they work in a company* is overly wordy. The stylistic preference on GMAT is for more concise language.
   - The plural subject *the workers and the environment* does not agree with the singular verb *is*.

   (E) *Only if* the environment in which a company works is at least in part a reflection of the heritage of
   - The meaning of this answer is illogical. This answer does not make sense when it includes *Only if*.
   - The idea *the environment in which a company works* is overly wordy. The stylistic preference on GMAT is for more concise language.

11. This question tests **awkwardness**, **clarity**, **comparisons**, and **parallelism**.

   <u>Vowel sounds differ from consonant sounds primarily *in that they* are produced not by blocking air in its passage from the lungs *and* by passing</u> air through different shapes of the mouth and different positions of the tongue and lips.

(A) *Vowel sounds* differ from *consonant sounds* primarily *in that* *they* are produced not by blocking air in its passage from the lungs *and* by passing
   - The expression *in that* is considered stylistically awkward and overly formal on GMAT. The stylistic preference on GMAT is for a more natural-sounding way of expressing this idea.
   - The pronoun *they* has two possible referents, *Vowel sounds* and *consonant sounds*, so the meaning of the sentence is ambiguous.

(B) Vowel sounds are *different than* consonant sounds *in that* primarily vowel sounds are produced *not by blocking* the surge of air from the lips *but that they pass*
   - The comparative expression *different than* is considered stylistically unacceptable on GMAT. The stylistic preference on GMAT is for **different from**.
   - The expression *in that* is considered stylistically awkward and overly formal on GMAT. The stylistic preference on GMAT is for a more natural-sounding way of expressing this idea.
   - The expression *that they pass* is not parallel to the expression *by blocking*. The structure *not...but* indicates that these expressions should be parallel.

(C) The primary way that vowel sounds differ from consonant sounds is that vowel sounds are produced *not* by blocking air in its passage from the lungs *but* by passing
   - This answer contains the parallel expressions **by blocking** and **by passing** following *not* and *but*. It also avoids the problems with awkwardness, clarity, and comparisons that are found in some of the other responses.

(D) The way that vowel sounds *are different, primarily, than* consonant sounds is that vowel sounds are produced not by blocking air in its passage from the lungs but by passing
   - The comparative expression *different...than* is considered stylistically unacceptable on GMAT. The stylistic preference on GMAT is for **different from**.
   - The part of the answer *are different, primarily, than* is awkward. The stylistic preference on GMAT is for a more natural-sounding way of expressing this idea.

(E) The way *vowel sounds* primarily *differ* from *consonant sounds* is that *they* are not produced by blocking air in its passage from the lungs but produced by passing
   - The conjunction *that* has been omitted in front of the subject and verb *vowel sounds...differ*. The stylistic preference on GMAT is to include the conjunction **that**.
   - The pronoun *they* has two possible referents, *vowel sounds* and *consonant sounds*, so the meaning of the sentence is ambiguous.

12. This question tests **wordiness**, **idioms**, and **nouns**.

   Medieval alchemists' failed endeavors had at their basic core the incorrect belief that all matter in the universe was comprised in varying amounts of the four basic elements of earth, fire, air, and water and that creating gold required only the determination of the exact proportions of these basic elements.

(A)   had at their basic core the incorrect belief that all matter in the universe was comprised in
   - The part of the answer *had at their basic core* is overly wordy. The stylistic preference on GMAT is for more concise language.
   - An incorrect preposition is used in the expression *comprised in*. Use **comprised of** instead.

(B)   were based in the incorrect belief that all matters in the universe were composed of
   - An incorrect preposition is used in the expression *based in*. Use **based on** instead.
   - The countable plural *matters* is incorrect. The noun *matter* can be countable *(a matter/ many matters)* or uncountable *(some matter)*, and the countable and uncountable versions of this noun have different meanings. Use the uncountable **matter** instead.

(C)   were based on the incorrect belief that all matter in the universe was comprised of
   - This answer contains the correct idioms **based on** and **comprised of** and the correct uncountable noun **matter** and avoids the problems with wordiness found in some of the other answers.

(D)   had as their basis the mistaken belief that all matters in the universe were comprised of
   - The part of the answer *had as their basis* is overly wordy. The stylistic preference on GMAT is for more concise language.
   - The countable plural *matters* is incorrect. The noun *matter* can be countable *(a matter/ many matters)* or uncountable *(some matter)*, and the countable and uncountable versions of this noun have different meanings. Use the uncountable **matter** instead.

(E)   were based on the incorrect belief that all matter in the universe was comprised in
   - An incorrect preposition is used in the expression *comprised in*. Use **comprised of** instead.

GMAT-Style Tests
TEST 2

Choose the letter of the answer to each question that best reflects the style and accuracy of standard written English. Then, study the explanations on the pages that follow.

1. <u>Someone who thinks on their feet does not require a lot of extra time</u> to come up with workable solutions to problems.

    (A) Someone who thinks on their feet does not require a lot of extra time
    (B) Someone who thinks on their feet does not need many extra times
    (C) People who think on their feet does not require alot of extra time
    (D) Those who think on their feet do not require much extra time
    (E) People who think on their feet do not require a lots of extra time

2. In 1788, some political leaders in New York City worked <u>to actively urge the city to succeed from New York State and to perhaps</u> join another state, New Jersey or Connecticut, for example.

    (A) to actively urge the city to succeed from New York State and to perhaps
    (B) actively to encourage the city to secede from New York State and perhaps to
    (C) to actively encourage the city to secede from New York State and maybe
    (D) actively to urge the city to succeed from New York State and to perhaps
    (E) to actively encourage the city to secede from New York State and maybe to

3. Though an alligator can close its jaws with enough force to break a human bone or tear a human appendage from its body, the muscles that open its jaws are so weak, resulting in a person being able to hold an alligator's jaws closed fairly easily.

    (A) that open its jaws are so weak, resulting in a person being able to hold an alligator's jaws closed fairly easily
    (B) that open their jaws are quite weak, with the result that a person can hold an alligator's jaws closed fairly easy
    (C) opening their jaws are so weak that a person can hold an alligator's jaws closed fairly easy
    (D) that open its jaws are so weak, causing a person to be able to hold an alligator's jaws closed fairly easily
    (E) that open its jaws are so weak that a person is able to hold an alligator's jaws closed fairly easily

4. A hurricane sucks heat from the ocean and funnels it up into the atmosphere, which causes the temperature of the ocean to drop.

    (A) ocean and funnels it up into the atmosphere, which causes the temperature of the ocean to drop
    (B) ocean and funnels it into the atmosphere, something that causes the temperature of the ocean to drop
    (C) ocean, funneling it up into the atmosphere to cause the temperature of the area to drop
    (D) ocean and funnels it into the atmosphere, which causes the temperature of the ocean to drop down
    (E) ocean, funneling it into the atmosphere and causing the temperature of the ocean to drop down

5. The empire created by Alexander the Great was divided among his officers upon his abrupt death at the age of thirty-three and endured for centuries until the Romans had conquered them.

    (A) until the Romans had conquered them
    (B) until they were conquered by the Romans
    (C) until its conquest by the Romans
    (D) up until the Romans conquered it
    (E) up until it had been conquered by the Romans

6. Stretching across a distance equal to the full breadth of the United States, there is a system of canyons on Mars that dwarf any such geological formations on Earth.

    (A) there is a system of canyons on Mars that dwarf
    (B) Mars has a system of canyons dwarfing
    (C) a system of canyons on Mars dwarfs
    (D) a system of canyons on Mars that dwarf
    (E) Mars has a system of canyons that dwarfs

7. Without a question, Tyrannosaurus was one of the largest terrestrial carnivores ever, but what is the subject of active debate was whether it was an active hunter or merely a scavenger.

    (A) Without a question, Tyrannosaurus was one of the largest terrestrial carnivores ever, but what is the subject of active debate was whether it was
    (B) Without question, Tyrannosaurus was among the largest terrestrial carnivores ever; however, what is under active discussion is whether it would have been
    (C) Without doubt, Tyrannosaurus is one of the largest terrestrial carnivores ever, but what is actively debated in discussions is whether it was
    (D) Without a doubt, Tyrannosaurus was one of the largest terrestrial carnivores ever; what is the subject of active debate, however, is whether it was
    (E) Without question, Tyrannosaurus was among the largest terrestrial carnivores ever, however what is under active discussion was whether it was

8. Like Bahasa Malay, the national language of Malaysia, Bahasa Indonesia has no tones, no verb tenses, and no articles and has plurals that are created simply by saying a noun twice.

    (A) Bahasa Indonesia has no tones, no verb tenses, and no articles and has plurals that are
    (B) Bahasa Indonesia lacks tones, verb tenses, and articles, on top of which it has unusual plurals
    (C) there are no tones, no verb tenses, and no articles in Bahasa Indonesia, and plurals are
    (D) the characteristics of Bahasa Indonesia are similar, with no tones, no verb tenses, and no articles and with plurals that are
    (E) Bahasa Indonesia is a closely related language that lacks tones, verb tenses, and articles but does have plurals

9. The Académie Royale de Danse (Royal Dance Academy) opened in Paris in 1661 with an all-male ensemble but by 1681 began training women.

   (A) began training women
   (B) began the training of women
   (C) began as well training women
   (D) began also training women
   (E) began training women as well

10. Astronauts brought back about 800 pounds of lunar rock from the Moon to Earth, most of which has not been analyzed.

   (A) Astronauts brought back about 800 pounds of lunar rock from the Moon to Earth, most of which has not been analyzed.
   (B) Astronauts brought back approximately 800 pounds of lunar rocks from the Moon to Earth, most of which have not been analyzed.
   (C) Astronauts returned to Earth with somewhere around 800 pounds of lunar rock, most of which has not underwent scientific analysis.
   (D) Astronauts brought back about 800 pounds of rocks from the Moon to Earth, most of which has not been analyzed.
   (E) Astronauts returned to Earth with around 800 pounds of lunar rock, most of which has not been analyzed.

11. In the early nineteenth century, Britain signed treaties with the leaders of each Emirate to protect its shipping routes from pirates.

    (A) its shipping routes from pirates
    (B) its shipping routes from pirates attacking ships on these routes
    (C) its shipping routes from the activities of pirates on the sea
    (D) Britain's shipping routes from pirates
    (E) shipping routes used by Britain from the activities of pirates on the sea

12. In 1507, after Scotsman John Damian broke his leg leaping from the walls of a castle with wings made from chicken feathers, he concluded that his jump would have been more successful if he had used the feathers of a bird that could actually fly.

    (A) he concluded that his jump would have been more successful if he had used
    (B) he arrived at the conclusion his jump would have had greater success if he would have used
    (C) he concluded his jump would have been a greater success had he used
    (D) he arrived at the unavoidable conclusion that his jump would have succeeded better if he would have used
    (E) he concluded, unavoidably, that his jump would turned out more successfully if he had used

EXPLANATIONS

1. This question tests **agreement**, **nouns**, and **diction**.

   <u>Someone who thinks on their feet does not require a lot of extra time</u> to come up with workable solutions to problems.

(A) Someone who thinks on *their* feet does not require a lot of extra time
   - The plural possessive *their* does not agree with the singular noun *Someone*, to which it refers.

(B) Someone who thinks on *their* feet does not need *many* extra *times*
   - The plural possessive *their* does not agree with the singular noun *Someone*, to which it refers.
   - The countable plural *many*...*times* is used incorrectly. The noun *time* can be countable *(one time/many times)* or uncountable *(some time)*, and the countable and uncountable versions of this noun have different meanings. Use the uncountable **much...time** instead.

(C) People who think on their feet *does* not *require* alot of extra time
   - The singular verb *does*...*require* does not agree with the plural subject *People*.
   - The expression *alot of* is always incorrect. Use **a lot of** instead.

(D) Those who think on their feet do not require much extra time
   - This answer contains the plural possessive **their**, which correctly refers to the plural subject *Those*. It also contains the uncountable quantifier **much** and the correctly used uncountable noun **time**.

(E) People who think on their feet do not require *a lots of* extra time
   - The expression *a lots of* is always incorrect. Use **a lot of** instead.

2. This question tests **modifiers** and **diction**.

In 1788, some political leaders in New York City worked <u>to actively urge the city to succeed from New York State and to perhaps *join* another state</u>, New Jersey or Connecticut, for example.

(A) *to* |actively| urge the city to |succeed from| New York State and *to* |perhaps|
   - The modifier |actively| is positioned incorrectly because an adverb cannot be used between the two parts of an infinitive, *to* and *urge*. This is called a split infinitive.
   - The expression |succeed from| -- which means "achieve success because of" and not "withdraw from" -- is illogical in this context. Use **secede from** -- which means "withdraw from" -- instead.
   - The modifier |perhaps| is positioned incorrectly because an adverb cannot be used between the two parts of an infinitive, *to* and *join*. This is called a split infinitive.

(B) actively to encourage the city to secede from New York State and perhaps to
   - This answer contains the correctly positioned modifiers **actively** and **perhaps** and the correctly used expression **secede from**.

(C) *to* |actively| *encourage* the city to secede from New York State and maybe
   - The modifier |actively| is positioned incorrectly because an adverb cannot be used between the two parts of an infinitive, *to* and *encourage*. This is called a split infinitive.

(D) actively to urge the city to |succeed from| New York State and *to* |perhaps|
   - The expression |succeed from| -- which means "achieve success because of" and not "withdraw from" -- is illogical in this context. Use **secede from** -- which means "withdraw from" -- instead.
   - The modifier |perhaps| is positioned incorrectly because an adverb cannot be used between the two parts of an infinitive, *to* and *join*. This is called a split infinitive.

(E) *to* |actively| *encourage* the city to secede from New York State and maybe to
   - The modifier |actively| is positioned incorrectly because an adverb cannot be used between the two parts of an infinitive, *to* and *encourage*. This is called a split infinitive.

3. This question tests **wordiness**, **agreement**, and **modifiers**.

   Though an *alligator* can close its jaws with enough force to break a human bone or tear a human appendage from its body, the muscles that open its jaws are so weak, resulting in a person being able to hold an alligator's jaws closed fairly easily.

(A) that open its jaws are so weak, *resulting in a person being able to hold* an alligator's jaws closed fairly easily
   - The idea *resulting in a person being able to hold* is overly wordy and complex. The stylistic preference on GMAT is for more concise and simpler language.

(B) that open *their* jaws are quite weak, *with the result that* a person can *hold* an alligator's jaws closed *fairly easy*
   - The plural possessive *their* does not agree with the singular noun *alligator*, to which it refers.
   - The idea *with the result that* is overly complex. The stylistic preference on GMAT is for simpler language.
   - In the expression *fairly easy*, the adjective *easy* is used incorrectly. *Fairly* is a correctly used adverb that modifies *easy*, but the adjective *easy* should be an adverb (**easily**) that modifies the verb *hold*.

(C) opening *their* jaws are so weak that a person can hold an alligator's jaws closed *fairly easy*
   - The plural possessive *their* does not agree with the singular noun *alligator*, to which it refers.
   - In the expression *fairly easy*, the adjective *easy* is used incorrectly. *Fairly* is a correctly used adverb that modifies *easy*, but the adjective *easy* should be an adverb (**easily**) that modifies the verb *hold*.

(D) that open its jaws are so weak, *causing a person to be able to hold* an alligator's jaws closed fairly easily
   - I The idea *causing a person to be able to hold* is overly wordy and complex. The stylistic preference on GMAT is for more concise and simpler language.

(E) that open its jaws are so weak that a person is able to *hold* an alligator's jaws closed fairly easily
   - This answer contains the correct singular possessive **its** to agree with *alligator* and the correct adverb **easily** to modify the verb *hold*. It also avoids the problems with wordiness that are found in some of the other answers.

4. This question tests **wordiness**, **pronouns**, and **clarity**.

    A hurricane sucks heat from the ocean and funnels it up into the atmosphere, which causes the temperature of the ocean to drop.

(A) *ocean and funnels it up into the atmosphere, which causes the temperature of the ocean to drop*
    - The word *up* is redundant because its meaning is included within the expression *funnels it...into the atmosphere*.
    - The relative pronoun *which* is used incorrectly. This relative pronoun should be used to refer to a specific noun and not to a complete idea such as *A hurricane sucks heat from the ocean and funnels it*.

(B) ocean and funnels it into the atmosphere, something that causes the temperature of the ocean to drop
    - This answer avoids the problems with wordiness, the pronoun *which*, and clarity found in some of the other answers.

(C) ocean, funneling it up into the atmosphere *to cause* the temperature of the area to drop
    - This answer has a misused infinitive of purpose *to cause* that makes the sentence illogical. According to this answer, the idea that *A hurricane sucks heat from the ocean* has the purpose of contributing to the drop in temperature. However, a hurricane cannot experience a sense of purpose.

(D) *ocean and funnels it* into the atmosphere, *which* causes the temperature of the ocean to *drop down*
    - The relative pronoun *which* is used incorrectly. This relative pronoun should be used used to refer to a specific noun and not to a complete idea such as *A hurricane sucks heat from the ocean and funnels it*.
    - The word *down* is redundant because its meaning is included within the word *drop*.

(E) ocean, funneling it into the atmosphere and causing the temperature of the ocean to *drop down*
    - The word *down* is redundant because its meaning is included within the word *drop*.

5. This question tests **verbs**, **clarity**, **awkwardness**, and **wordiness**.

   The *empire* created by Alexander the Great was divided among his officers upon his abrupt death at the age of thirty-three and endured for centuries until the Romans had conquered them.

   (A) until the Romans *had conquered* *them*
   - The past perfect tense *had conquered* is used incorrectly. The past perfect tense should be used when one past action is completed prior to another. From the context, it can be determined that the action of conquering Alexander the Great's forces did not occur prior to the time that the *empire...was divided*.
   - The pronoun *them* does not have a clear referent. The sentence most likely means that the Romans conquered Alexander's empire, but the plural pronoun *them* could not refer to the singular noun *empire*.

   (B) until *they* *were conquered by* the Romans
   - The pronoun *they* does not have a clear referent. The sentence most likely means that the Romans conquered Alexander's empire, but the plural pronoun *they* could not refer to the singular noun *empire*.
   - The passive voice *were conquered by* is unnecessary here. The more direct active voice would be stylistically preferable.

   (C) until its conquest by the Romans
   - This answer avoids the problems with verbs, clarity, awkwardness, and wordiness that are found in some of the other answers.

   (D) *up* *until* the Romans conquered it
   - The word *up* is redundant because its meaning is included within the word *until*.

   (E) *up* *until* it *had been conquered* by the Romans
   - The word *up* is redundant because its meaning is included within the word *until*.
   - The past perfect tense *had been conquered* is used incorrectly. The past perfect tense should be used when one past action is completed prior to another. From the context, it can be determined that the action of conquering Alexander the Great's forces did not occur prior to the time that the *empire...was divided*.

6. This question tests **modifiers** and **agreement**.

    Stretching across a distance equal to the full breadth of the United States, there is a system of canyons on Mars that dwarf any such geological formations on Earth.

(A) *there* is a *system* of canyons on Mars *that* dwarf
   - The use of *there* following the comma (,) creates a sentence with a dangling modifier, *Stretching across a distance*.... An introductory adjective should modify the subject of the main clause directly following the comma (,). The expression *Stretching across a distance*... should modify **a system** and not *there*.
   - The plural verb *dwarf* does not agree with the subject *that*, which refers to the singular noun *system*.

(B) *Mars* has a *system* of canyons dwarfing
   - The use of *there* following the comma (,) creates a sentence with a dangling modifier, *Stretching across a distance*.... An introductory adjective should modify the subject of the main clause directly following the comma (,). The expression *Stretching across a distance*... should modify **a system** and not *Mars*.

[(C)] a *system* of canyons on Mars dwarfs
   - This answer has the subject **system** following the comma so that the introductory modifier is not dangling, and it contains the correct singular verb **dwarfs**.

(D) a *system* of canyons on Mars *that* dwarf
   - The plural verb *dwarf* does not agree with the subject *that*, which refers to the singular noun *system*.

(E) *Mars* has a *system* of canyons that dwarfs
   - The use of *Mars* following the comma (,) creates a sentence with a dangling modifier, *Stretching across a distance*.... An introductory adjective should modify the subject of the main clause directly following the comma (,). The expression *Stretching across a distance*... should modify **a system** and not *Mars*.

7. This question tests **idioms**, **verbs**, **wordiness**, and **sentences**.

   Without a question, Tyrannosaurus *was* one of the largest terrestrial carnivores ever, but what is the subject of active debate was whether it was an active hunter or merely a scavenger.

(A) *Without a question*, Tyrannosaurus *was* one of the largest terrestrial carnivores ever, but *what is the subject of active debate* *was* whether it was
   - The expression *Without a question* is an incorrect idiom. Use **Without question** instead.
   - The simple past tense *was* is used incorrectly. Although the simple past tense *was* is used correctly earlier in the sentence, the second use of *was* should be in the present tense (**is**) because the time period of the second *was* is the present, *what is the subject of active debate*. The present and past tenses can be used in one sentence if the meaning is logical.

(B) Without question, Tyrannosaurus was among the largest terrestrial carnivores ever; however, what is under active discussion is *whether* it *would have been*
   - The conditional perfect tense *would have been* following *whether* is used incorrectly. A conditional tense with *would* is never used in a clause directly following *whether*.

(C) *Without doubt*, Tyrannosaurus *is* one of the largest terrestrial carnivores ever, but what *is* actively *debated* in *discussions* *is* whether it was
   - The expression *Without doubt* is an incorrect idiom. Use **Without a doubt** instead.
   - The simple present tense *is* is used incorrectly. Although the present tense *is* is used correctly later in the sentence, the first use of *is* should be in the simple past tense (**was**) because the time period of the first *is* is the past, during the time of *Tyrannosaurus*. The present and past tenses can be used in one sentence if the meaning is logical.
   - The word *discussions* is redundant because its meaning is included within the word *debated*.

(D) Without a doubt, Tyrannosaurus was one of the largest terrestrial carnivores ever; what is the subject of active debate, however, is whether it was
   - This answer contains the correct idiom **Without a doubt** and the correct simple past tense verb **was**, the correct simple present tense verb **is**, and the correct simple past tense **was**. It also avoids the problems with wordiness and run-on sentences found in some of the other answers.

(E) Without question, Tyrannosaurus *was* among the largest terrestrial carnivores ever, however *what is* under active discussion *was* whether it was
   - This answer creates a run-on sentence because the two subjects and verbs *Tyrannosaurus was* and *what is* are connected with only a comma (,). A comma cannot be used to connect two subjects and verbs without a conjunction, and *however* is an adverb and is not a conjunction.
   - The simple past tense *was* is used incorrectly. Although the simple past tense *was* is used correctly earlier in the sentence, the second use of *was* should be in the present tense (**is**) because the time period of the second *was* is the present, *what is under active discussion*. The present and past tenses can be used in one sentence if the meaning is logical.

8. This question tests **wordiness** and **comparisons**.

   Like Bahasa Malay, the national language of Malaysia, <u>Bahasa Indonesia has no tones, no verb tenses, and no articles and has plurals that are</u> created simply by saying a noun twice.

(A) Bahasa Indonesia has no tones, no verb tenses, and no articles and has plurals that are
   - This answer contains the expression **Bahasa Indonesia**, which is parallel to *Bahasa Malay*. It also avoids the problems with wordiness that are found in some of the other answers.

(B) Bahasa Indonesia lacks tones, verb tenses, and articles, *on top of which* it has unusual plurals
   - The idea *on top of which* is overly complex. The stylistic preference on GMAT is for simpler language.

(C) *there are* no tones, no verb tenses, and no articles in Bahasa Indonesia, and plurals are
   - The expression *there are* following the comma (,) is not parallel to the expression *Bahasa Malay*. The comparative *Like* indicates that these expressions should be parallel.

(D) *the characteristics of Bahasa Indonesia* are *similar*, with no tones, no verb tenses, and no articles and with plurals that are
   - The expression *the characteristics of Bahasa Indonesia* is not parallel to the expression *Bahasa Malay*. The comparative *Like* indicates that these expressions should be parallel.
   - The idea *similar* is redundant because its meaning is included within the idea *Like*.

(E) Bahasa Indonesia is *a closely related language* that lacks tones, verb tenses, and articles but does have plurals
   - The idea *a closely related language* is redundant because its meaning is included within the idea *Like Bahasa Malay*.

9. This question tests **clarity**, **awkwardness**, and **modifiers**.

   The Académie Royale de Danse (Royal Dance Academy) opened in Paris in 1661 with an all-male ensemble but by 1681 began training women.

   (A) began training women
   - The meaning of *began training women* is imprecise. From the context, it is understood that the intended meaning is most likely that the academy began training women in addition to men, but this is not clearly stated.

   (B) began the training of women
   - The meaning of *began the training of women* is imprecise. From the context, it is understood that the intended meaning is most likely that the academy began training women in addition to men, but this is not clearly stated.
   - The part of the answer *the training* is awkward. The stylistic preference on GMAT is to avoid unnecessary gerunds (*-ing* verbal nouns) if possible.

   (C) began as well training women
   - The modifier *as well* is positioned incorrectly because an adverb phrase cannot be positioned between a verb *began* and its direct object *training*.

   (D) began also training women
   - The modifier *also* is positioned incorrectly because an adverb cannot be positioned between a verb *began* and its direct object *training*.

   (E) began training women **as well**
   - This answer uses the adverb phrase **as well** in the correct position to clarify that the academy was training women in addition to men and not in place of men.

10. This question tests **wordiness**, **verbs**, and **agreement**.

Astronauts brought back about 800 pounds of lunar rock from the Moon to Earth, most of which has not been analyzed.

(A) Astronauts brought back about 800 pounds of *lunar* rock *from the Moon* to Earth, most of which has not been analyzed.
   • The expression *from the Moon* is redundant because its meaning is included within the word *lunar*.

(B) Astronauts brought back approximately 800 pounds of *lunar* rocks *from the Moon* to Earth, most of which have not been analyzed.
   • The expression *from the Moon* is redundant because its meaning is included within the word *lunar*.

(C) Astronauts returned to Earth with somewhere around 800 pounds of lunar *rock, most of which* has not *underwent* scientific analysis.
   • The form of the verb *underwent* is incorrect. *Underwent* is the simple past tense and is not the past participle. Use the past participle **undergone** following *has* instead.

(D) Astronauts brought back about 800 pounds of *rocks* from the Moon to Earth, *most of which* **has** not been analyzed.
   • The singular verb *has* does not agree with the subject *most of which*, which refers to the plural noun *rocks*.

(E) Astronauts returned to Earth with around 800 pounds of lunar *rock, most of which* **has** not been analyzed.
   • In this answer, the singular verb **has** agrees with the subject *most of which*, which refers to the singular noun *rock*. This answer also avoids the problem with redundancy found in some of the other answers.

11. This question tests **clarity** and **wordiness**.

In the early nineteenth century, *Britain* signed treaties with the leaders of *each Emirate* to protect its shipping routes from pirates.

(A) *its* shipping routes from pirates
  - The possessive *its* has two possible referents, *Britain* and *each Emirate*, so the meaning of the sentence is ambiguous.

(B) *its* shipping routes from pirates *attacking ships on these routes*
  - The possessive *its* has two possible referents, *Britain* and *each Emirate*, so the meaning of the sentence is ambiguous.
  - The idea *attacking ships on these routes* is overly wordy. The stylistic preference on GMAT is for more concise language.

(C) *its* shipping routes from *the activities of pirates on the sea*
  - The possessive *its* has two possible referents, *Britain* and *each Emirate*, so the meaning of the sentence is ambiguous.
  - The idea *the activities of pirates on the sea* is overly wordy. The stylistic preference on GMAT is for more concise language.

(D) Britain's shipping routes from pirates
  - This answer avoids the problems with clarity and wordiness found in some of the other answers.

(E) *shipping routes used by Britain* from *the activities of pirates on the sea*
  - The ideas *shipping routes used by Britain* and *the activities of pirates on the sea* are overly wordy. The stylistic preference on GMAT is for more concise language.

12. This question tests **awkwardness**, **verbs**, and **wordiness**.

In 1507, after Scotsman John Damian broke his leg leaping from the walls of a castle with wings made from chicken feathers, he concluded that his jump would have been more successful if he had used the feathers of a bird that could actually fly.

(A) he concluded that *his jump would have been* more successful *if* he had used
- This answer contains the conjunction **that** in front of the subject and verb *his jump would have been* and the correct verb tense **had used**, which does not contain *would*, following *if*. This answer also avoids the problem with wordiness found in one of the other answers.

(B) he arrived at the conclusion *his jump would have had* greater success *if* he *would have used*
- The conjunction *that* has been omitted in front of the subject and verb *his jump would have had*. The stylistic preference on GMAT is to include the conjunction **that**.
- The conditional perfect tense *would have used* following *if* is used incorrectly. A conditional tense with *would* is never used in a clause directly following *if*.

(C) he concluded *his jump would have been* a greater success had he used
- The conjunction *that* has been omitted in front of the subject and verb *his jump would have been*. The stylistic preference on GMAT is to include the conjunction **that**.

(D) he *arrived at the unavoidable conclusion* that his jump would have succeeded better *if* he *would have used*
- The idea *arrived at the unavoidable conclusion* is overly wordy and complex. The stylistic preference on GMAT is for more concise and simpler language.
- The conditional perfect tense *would have used* following *if* is used incorrectly. A conditional tense with *would* is never used in a clause directly following *if*.

(E) he *concluded, unavoidably, that* his jump would turned out more successfully if he had used
- The idea *concluded, unavoidably, that* is awkward. The stylistic preference on GMAT is for a more natural-sounding way of expressing this idea.

GMAT-Style Tests
TEST 3

Choose the letter of the answer to each question that best reflects the style and accuracy of standard written English. Then, study the explanations on the pages that follow.

1. British colonists at the time of the French and Indian Wars (1756-1763) wanted to expand westward, but <u>the French dominance of the west</u> by virtue of three key advantages: outposts in the territory, dominance of strategic rivers, and good relations with their Native American allies.

    (A) the French dominance of the west
    (B) France's dominance of the west
    (C) the French have dominated the west
    (D) France's dominating the west
    (E) the French dominated the west

2. As a propeller rotates, air flows around the propeller blades and <u>moving more rapidly over the curved leading edge, which</u> reduces the air pressure in front of the blade and pulls the aircraft forward.

    (A) moving more rapidly over the curved leading edge, which
    (B) moves more rapidly over the curved leading edge, something that
    (C) move faster over the curved leading edge, which
    (D) move more fast over the leading edge which is curved, something that
    (E) moves faster over the leading edge which is curved, which

3. When Charles Darwin published *The Descent of Man,* his pioneering work on human evolution, in 1871, not a single pre-human fossil known to support the ideas he presented in the book had been discovered.

   (A) not a single pre-human fossil known to support the ideas he presented in the book had been discovered
   (B) what was known was that the discovery of not a single pre-human fossil to support his ideas had taken place
   (C) there was not a single pre-human fossil to support the ideas he presented in the book
   (D) not a single pre-human fossil had been discovered to support the ideas that he presented in the book
   (E) not a single pre-human fossil that would support the ideas in his book was known to have been discovered

4. Both large and small schools of business are "internationalizing" their programs to do the best job in preparing the next generation for the changing global economy.

   (A) Both large and small schools of business are "internationalizing" their programs to do the best job in preparing the next generation for the changing global economy.
   (B) Large as well as small schools of business are currently "internationalizing" their programs to best prepare the coming generation for the changing global economy.
   (C) Large as well as small schools of business are "internationalizing" currently their programs to do the best job of preparing the coming generation for the changing of the global economy.
   (D) Both large schools of business and small schools of business are currently "internationalizing" their programs in order to best prepare the next generation with the changing global economy.
   (E) Schools of business both large and small are currently "internationalizing" their programs to do the best job in preparing the current generation with the changing of the global economy.

5. The exact causes of schizophrenia are unknown, though the leading theories attribute it to a combination of genetic predispositions and a series of environmental conditions and external stresses that trigger the onset.

    (A) that trigger the onset
    (B) that triggers the onset
    (C) that cause the onset to trigger
    (D) that cause the triggering of
    (E) that causes the onset to trigger

6. Emigration had a profound influence on the world in the 18th, 19th, and 20th centuries, when millions of people left Europe, though U.S. government policies limiting emigration in the 1920s put a damper on mass immigration from Europe.

    (A) Europe, though U.S. government policies limiting emigration in the 1920s put a damper on mass immigration from Europe
    (B) Europe, however, U.S. government restrictions on emigration in the early Twenties brought the age of mass emigration from Europe to an end
    (C) Europe; though limitations on immigration by the U.S. government in the 1920s brought the age of mass immigration from Europe to an end
    (D) Europe, although U.S. government policies limiting emigration in the 1920s resulted in a greatly decreased amount of emigration from Europe
    (E) Europe; however, restrictions on immigration put in place by the U.S. government in the early Twenties tamped down on mass emigration from Europe

7. Thomas Stewart was an early researcher on intellectual capital, a field including and dedicated to understanding and managing intangible assets.

    (A) an early researcher on intellectual capital, a field including and dedicated to understanding and managing
    (B) an early pioneer in intellectual capital, a field including and dedicated to the understanding and managing of
    (C) a pioneer in the field of intellectual capital, a field dedicated to understanding and managing
    (D) an early pioneer in the field of intellectual capitol, a field that includes the understanding and managing of
    (E) an early researcher on intellectual capitol, a field that is dedicated to the understanding and managing of

8. After suffering left-sided strokes, serious speech disorders are often suffered by many individuals who, surprisingly, are often able to sing complete text relatively fluently.

    (A) serious speech disorders are often suffered by many individuals who, surprisingly, are often able to sing complete texts relatively fluently
    (B) serious speech disorders often impact many individuals who, it may seem amazing, often have the ability to sing complete texts relatively fluently
    (C) many individuals may be impacted by a serious speech disorder but are often able to sing complete texts relatively fluently
    (D) many individuals suffer from serious speech disorders but are, astonishingly, often able to sing complete texts relatively fluently
    (E) many individuals who suffer from serious speech disorders are often able, quite amazingly, to relatively fluently sing complete texts

9. Event organizers were stunned by the <u>unexpectedly abysmal conference enrolling, with less people in attendance than there had been</u> in each of the preceding eight years.

   (A) unexpectedly abysmal conference enrolling, with less people in attendance than there had been
   (B) conference enrollment, as unexpectedly abysmal as it was, with less people than there were
   (C) unexpectedly abysmal conference enrollment, with fewer attendees than there had been
   (D) conference enrolling, which was quite unexpectedly abysmal, with not as many people as there was
   (E) unexpectedly abysmal conference enrollment, which had fewer people in attendance than there had been

10. Two collections of historic black-and-white photographs depicting Staten Island neighborhoods of a century ago have been released for study by the Staten Island Historical Society, and interested parties <u>have been pouring over the treasure trove, hoping that a better sense of the history of the area could be developed</u>.

    (A) have been pouring over the treasure trove, hoping that a better sense of the history of the area could be developed
    (B) have been attentively pouring over the valuable discovery in the hope that a better understanding of the history of the area could perhaps be obtained
    (C) have taken to poring over the treasure to develop something of a better understanding of the area's history
    (D) have been poring over the treasure trove in the hope of developing a better sense of the history of the area
    (E) have been astutely poring over the valuable treasure in the hope of developing a better sensitivity toward the area's history

11. For today's Kalahari bushman, an ostrich egg is a valuable vessel in which he keeps scarce water and from which he makes jewelry for his wife and children.

    (A) an ostrich egg is a valuable vessel in which he keeps scarce water and from which he makes jewelry
    (B) the shell of an ostrich egg is valuable both because it can be used to hold scarce water and because of its use in making jewelry.
    (C) the shell of an ostrich egg is a valuable vessel in which he holds scarce water and from which he can make jewelry
    (D) an ostrich egg is a valuable vessel which he uses to keep scarce water and to make jewelry
    (E) the shell of an ostrich egg is valuable because of its use as a container for scarce water and as a material for making jewelry

12. In 1799, England's war office secretly commissioned astronomer William Herschel to build a spy telescope to mount on the walls of Walmer Castle on the southeast coast of Kent to provide the earliest warning of a possible invasion by the French fleet.

    (A) to build a spy telescope to mount on the walls of Walmer Castle on the southeast coast of Kent to provide
    (B) to build a spy telescope for mounting on the walls of Walmer Castle in the southeast coast of Kent in order to provide
    (C) for building a spy telescope for mounting on the walls of Walmer Castle on the southeast coast of Kent to provide
    (D) for the building of a spy telescope mounted on the walls of Walmer Castle in the southeast coast of Kent with the intention of providing
    (E) for the building of a spy telescope to be mounted on the walls of Walmer Castle on the southeast coast of Kent in order to provide

EXPLANATIONS

1. This question tests **sentences** and **verbs**.

   British colonists at the time of the French and Indian Wars (1756-1763) wanted to expand westward, *but* the French dominance of the west by virtue of three key advantages: outposts in the territory, dominance of strategic rivers, and good relations with their Native American allies.

   (A) the French dominance of the west
   - The part of this sentence *the French dominance of the west* following the comma *(,)* and *but* is a fragment because a subject and a verb are required following a comma *(,)* and *but*. This answer has a subject *dominance* but no verb.

   (B) France's dominance of the west
   - The part of this sentence *France's dominance of the west* following the comma *(,)* and *but* is a fragment because a subject and a verb are required following a comma *(,)* and *but*. This answer has a subject *dominance* but no verb.

   (C) the French have dominated the west
   - The present perfect tense *have dominated* is used incorrectly. The present perfect tense should be used when an action occurs in the period from the past to the present, and this action occurs only in the past *(1756-1763)*.

   (D) France's dominating the west
   - The part of this sentence *France's dominating the west* following the comma *(,)* and *but* is a fragment because a subject and a verb are required following a comma *(,)* and *but*. This answer has a subject *dominating* but no verb.

   (E) the French dominated the west
   - This sentence has a subject **the French** and a verb **dominated** following the comma *(,)* and *but*. The verb **dominated** is correctly in the simple past tense because of the past time frame *(1756-1763)*.

2. This question tests **parallelism**, **pronouns**, **wordiness**, and **comparisons**.

   As a propeller rotates, *air flows* around the propeller blades *and* moving more rapidly over the curved leading edge, which reduces the air pressure in front of the blade and pulls the aircraft forward.

(A) *moving* more rapidly over the curved leading edge, *which*
   - The expression *moving* is not parallel to the expression *flows*. The structure *and* indicates that these expressions should be parallel.
   - The relative pronoun *which* is used incorrectly. This relative pronoun should be used to refer to a specific noun and not to a complete idea such as *air flows...and moving* (should be **moves**) *more rapidly....*

(B) moves more rapidly over the curved leading edge, something that
   - This answer contains the correct parallel expression **moves**, the correct comparative adverb **more rapidly**, and the correctly used pronoun **something** and avoids the problems with wordiness found in some of the other answers.

(C) *move* faster over the curved leading edge, *which*
   - The expression *move* is not parallel to the expression *flows*. The structure *and* indicates that these expressions should be parallel.
   - The relative pronoun *which* is used incorrectly. This relative pronoun should be used to refer to a specific noun and not to a complete idea such as *air flows...and move* (should be **moves**) *faster....*

(D) *move more fast* over *the leading edge which is curved*, something that
   - The expression *move* is not parallel to the expression *flows*. The structure *and* indicates that these expressions should be parallel.
   - The comparative *more fast* is incorrectly formed. The comparative form of a one-syllable word such as *fast* should be formed with *-er* (**faster**) rather than *more*.
   - The part of the answer *the leading edge which is curved* is overly wordy and complex. The stylistic preference on GMAT is for more concise and simpler language.

(E) *moves faster* over *the leading edge which is curved*, *which*
   - The part of the answer *the leading edge which is curved* is overly wordy and complex. The stylistic preference on GMAT is for more concise and simpler language.
   - The relative pronoun *which* is used incorrectly. This relative pronoun should be used to refer to a specific noun and not to a complete idea such as *air flows...and moves faster....*

3. This question tests **awkwardness** and **wordiness**.

When Charles Darwin published *The Descent of Man,* his pioneering work on human evolution, in 1871, not a single pre-human fossil known to support the ideas he presented in the book had been discovered.

(A) not a single pre-human fossil known to support the ideas *he presented* in the book had been discovered
- The conjunction *that* has been omitted in front of the subject and verb *he presented*. The stylistic preference on GMAT is to include the conjunction **that**.

(B) *what was known was that* the discovery of not a single pre-human fossil to support his ideas had taken place
- The idea *what was known was that* is overly complex. The stylistic preference on GMAT is for simpler language.

(C) there was not a single pre-human fossil to support the ideas *he presented* in the book
- The conjunction *that* has been omitted in front of the subject and verb *he presented*. The stylistic preference on GMAT is to include the conjunction **that**.

(D) not a single pre-human fossil had been discovered to support the ideas that *he presented* in the book
- This answer contains the conjunction **that** in front of the subject and verb *he presented* and avoids the problems with the passive voice and wordiness that are found in some of the other answers.

(E) not a single pre-human fossil that would support the ideas in his book *was known to have been discovered*
- The passive voice *was known to have been discovered* is unnecessary here. The more direct active voice would be stylistically preferable on GMAT.

4. This question tests **modifiers**, **awkwardness**, **wordiness**, and **idioms**.

   Both large and small schools of business are "internationalizing" their programs to do the best job in preparing the next generation for the changing global economy.

(A) Both large and small schools of business are "internationalizing" their programs to do the best job in preparing the next generation for the changing global economy.
   - This answer avoids the problems of incorrectly placed modifiers, awkwardness, wordiness, and idioms found in some of the other answers.

(B) Large as well as small schools of business are currently "internationalizing" their programs *to best prepare* the coming generation for the changing global economy.
   - The modifier *best* is positioned incorrectly because an adverb cannot be used between the two parts of an infinitive (*to* and *prepare*). This is called a split infinitive.

(C) Large as well as small schools of business *are "internationalizing" currently* their *programs* to do the best job of preparing the coming generation for *the changing of the global economy*.
   - The modifier *currently* is positioned incorrectly because an adverb cannot be positioned between a verb *are "internationalizing"* and its direct object *programs*.
   - The part of the answer *the changing of the global economy* is awkward. The stylistic preference on GMAT is to avoid unnecessary *-ing* verbal nouns.

(D) *Both large schools of business and small schools of business* are currently "internationalizing" their programs in order *to best prepare* the next generation *with* the changing global economy.
   - The part of the answer *Both large schools of business and small schools of business* is overly wordy. The stylistic preference on GMAT is for more concise language.
   - The modifier *best* is positioned incorrectly because an adverb cannot be used between the two parts of an infinitive (*to* and *prepare*). This is called a split infinitive.
   - An incorrect preposition is used in the expression *prepare...with*. Use **prepare...for** instead.

(E) Schools of business both large and small are currently "internationalizing" their programs to do the best job in *preparing* the current generation *with the changing of the global economy*.
   - An incorrect preposition is used in the expression *preparing...with*. Use **preparing...for** instead.
   - The part of the answer *the changing of the global economy* is awkward. The stylistic preference on GMAT is to avoid unnecessary *-ing* verbal nouns.

5. This question tests **agreement** and **wordiness**.

The exact causes of schizophrenia are unknown, though the leading theories attribute it to a combination of genetic predispositions and a *series* of environmental conditions and external stresses that trigger the onset.

(A) that *trigger* the onset
- The plural verb *trigger* does not agree with the subject *that*, which refers to the singular noun *series*.

(B) that **triggers** the onset
- This answer contains the correct singular verb **triggers** and avoids the problem with redundancy found in some of the other answers.

(C) that *cause* the onset to *trigger*
- The plural verb *cause* does not agree with the subject *that*, which refers to the singular noun *series*.
- The word *trigger* is redundant because its meaning is included within the word *cause*.

(D) that *cause* the *triggering* of
- The plural verb *cause* does not agree with the subject *that*, which refers to the singular noun *series*.
- The word *triggering* is redundant because its meaning is included within the word *cause*. (The word *triggering* is also an unnecessary gerund (-*ing* verbal noun).

(E) that *causes* the onset to *trigger*
- The word *trigger* is redundant because its meaning is included within the word *causes*.

6. This question tests **diction** and **sentences**.

   Emigration had a profound influence on the world in the 18th, 19th, and 20th centuries, when millions of people left Europe, though U.S. government policies limiting emigration in the 1920s put a damper on mass immigration from Europe.

(A) Europe, though U.S. government policies limiting emigration in the 1920s put a damper on mass immigration from Europe
   - The word emigration -- which means "to leave one region to settle in another" and not "to enter another region to settle there"-- is illogical in this context. Use **immigration** -- which means "to enter another region to settle there" -- instead.
   - The word immigration -- which means "to enter another region to settle there" and not "to leave one region to settle in another "-- is illogical in this context. Use **emigration** -- which means "to leave one region to settle in another" -- instead.

(B) Europe, *however,* U.S. government restrictions on emigration in the early Twenties brought the age of mass emigration from Europe to an end
   - This answer creates a run-on sentence because the two subjects and verbs *Emigration had* and restrictions...brought are connected with only a comma (,). A comma cannot be used to connect two subjects and verbs without a conjunction, and *however* is an adverb and is not a conjunction.
   - The word emigration -- which means "to leave one region to settle in another" and not "to enter another region to settle there"-- is illogical in this context. Use **immigration** -- which means "to enter another region to settle there" -- instead.

(C) *Europe; though limitations* on immigration by the U.S. government in the 1920s brought the age of mass immigration from Europe to an end
   - This sentence has an incorrectly used semi-colon (;). There must be a main subject and verb on either side of a semi-colon (;). This sentence has a subordinate clause though limitations...brought following the semi-colon, so the semi-colon is not needed.
   - The word immigration -- which means "to enter another region to settle there" and not "to leave one region to settle in another "-- is illogical in this context. Use **emigration** -- which means "to leave one region to settle in another" -- instead.

(D) Europe, although U.S. government policies limiting emigration in the 1920s resulted in a greatly decreased amount of emigration from Europe
   - The word emigration -- which means "to leave one region to settle in another" and not "to enter another region to settle there"-- is illogical in this context. Use **immigration** -- which means "to enter another region to settle there" -- instead.

(E) Europe; however, restrictions on immigration put in place by the U.S. government in the early Twenties tamped down on mass emigration from Europe
   - This answer contains the correct sentence structure with a semi-colon (;) in front of the adverb **however** and the main clause **restrictions...tamped** as well as the correctly used words **immigration** and **emigration**.

7. This question tests **clarity**, **wordiness**, **awkwardness**, and **diction**.
Thomas Stewart was <u>an early researcher on intellectual capital, a field including and dedicated to understanding and managing</u> intangible assets.

(A) an early researcher on intellectual capital, a field *including and dedicated to* understanding and managing
- The meaning of *included and dedicated to* is illogical. One field cannot both include something and be dedicated to trying to achieve it.

(B) an *early* pioneer in intellectual capital, a field *including and dedicated to* *the understanding and managing* of
- The word *early* is redundant because its meaning is included within the word *pioneer*.
- The meaning of *included and dedicated to* is illogical. One field cannot both include something and be dedicated to trying to achieve it.
- The part of the answer *the understanding and managing* is awkward. The stylistic preference on GMAT is to avoid unnecessary gerunds (*-ing* verbal nouns) if possible.

(C) a pioneer in the field of intellectual capital, a field dedicated to understanding and managing
- This answer contains the correctly used word **capital** and avoids the problems with clarity, wordiness, and awkwardness found in some of the other answers.

(D) an *early* pioneer in the field of intellectual *capitol*, a field that includes *the understanding and managing* of
- The word *early* is redundant because its meaning is included within the word *pioneer*.
- The word *capitol* -- which means "a building for a law-making body" and not "wealth"-- is illogical in this context. Use **capital** -- which means "wealth" -- instead.
- The part of the answer *the understanding and managing* is awkward. The stylistic preference on GMAT is to avoid unnecessary gerunds (*-ing* verbal nouns) if possible.

(E) an early researcher on intellectual *capitol*, a field that is dedicated to the understanding and managing of
- The word *capitol* -- which means "a building for a law-making body" and not "wealth"-- is illogical in this context. Use **capital** -- which means "wealth" -- instead.

8. This question tests **modifiers**, **awkwardness**, **wordiness**, and **agreement**.

   After suffering left-sided strokes, serious speech disorders are often suffered by many individuals who, surprisingly, are often able to sing complete text relatively fluently.

(A) serious speech disorders are often suffered by many *individuals* who, surprisingly, are often able to sing complete texts relatively fluently
   - The use of serious speech disorders following the comma (,) creates a sentence with a dangling modifier, *After suffering left-sided strokes*. An introductory adjective should modify the subject of the main clause directly following the comma (,). The expression *After suffering left-sided strokes* should modify **individuals** and not *serious speech disorders*.
   - The passive voice are...suffered by is unnecessary here. The more direct active voice would be stylistically preferable on GMAT.

(B) serious speech disorders often impact many *individuals* who, it may seem amazing, often have the ability to sing complete texts relatively fluently
   - The use of serious speech disorders following the comma (,) creates a sentence with a dangling modifier, *After suffering left-sided strokes*. An introductory adjective should modify the subject of the main clause directly following the comma (,). The expression *After suffering left-sided strokes* should modify **individuals** and not *serious speech disorders*.
   - The idea it may seem amazing is overly wordy and complex. The stylistic preference on GMAT is for more concise and simpler language.

(C) many *individuals* may be impacted by a serious speech disorder but are often able to sing complete texts relatively fluently
   - The passive voice may be impacted by is unnecessary here. The more direct active voice would be stylistically preferable on GMAT.
   - The singular noun phrase a serious speech disorder does not make sense when used with the plural noun *individuals*.

(D) many individuals suffer from serious speech disorders but are, astonishingly, often able to sing complete texts relatively fluently
   - This answer avoids the problems with modifiers, awkwardness, wordiness, and agreement found in some of the other answers.

(E) many individuals who suffer from serious speech disorders are often able, quite amazingly, to relatively fluently sing complete texts
   - The modifiers *relatively* and *fluently* are positioned incorrectly because adverbs cannot be used between the two parts of an infinitive, *to* and *sing*. This is called a split infinitive.

— *It Works!* GMAT Sentence Correction —

9. This question tests **awkwardness**, **nouns**, **wordiness**, **agreement**, and **clarity**.

   Event organizers were stunned by the unexpectedly abysmal conference enrolling, with less people in attendance than there had been in each of the preceding eight years.

(A) unexpectedly abysmal *conference enrolling*, with *less people* in attendance than there had been
   - The part of the answer *conference enrolling* is awkward. The stylistic preference on GMAT is to avoid unnecessary gerunds (*-ing* verbal nouns).
   - The uncountable quantifier *less* should not be used with the countable noun *people*.

(B) conference enrollment, *as unexpectedly abysmal as it was*, with *less people* than there were
   - The part of the answer *as unexpectedly abysmal as it was* is overly wordy and complex. The stylistic preference on GMAT is for more concise and simpler language.
   - The uncountable quantifier *less* should not be used with the countable noun *people*.

(C) unexpectedly abysmal conference enrollment, with fewer *attendees* than there had been
   - This answer uses the correct countable quantifier **fewer** with the countable noun *attendees* and avoids the problems of the unnecessary *enrolling*, the relative pronoun *which*, wordiness, and agreement found in some of the other answers.

(D) *conference enrolling*, *which was quite unexpectedly abysmal*, with not as many *people* as there *was*
   - The part of the answer *conference enrolling* is awkward. The stylistic preference on GMAT is to avoid unnecessary gerunds (*-ing* verbal nouns).
   - The part of the answer *which was quite unexpectedly abysmal* is overly wordy and complex. The stylistic preference on GMAT is for more concise and simpler language.
   - The singular verb *was* does not agree with the plural subject *people*.

(E) unexpectedly abysmal conference enrollment, *which* had *fewer people* in attendance than there had been
   - The referent of the relative pronoun *which* is unclear. *Which* should refer to *enrollment* because *which* follows this noun; however, the context suggests that *which* refers to *conference*.

10. This question tests **idioms** and **wordiness**.

   Two collections of historic black-and-white photographs depicting Staten Island neighborhoods of a century ago have been released for study by the Staten Island Historical Society, and interested parties have been pouring over the treasure trove, hoping that a better sense of the history of the area could be developed.

(A) have been pouring over the treasure trove, hoping that a better sense of the history of the area could be developed
   - The expression pouring over is an incorrect idiom. Use **poring over** instead.

(B) have been attentively pouring over the valuable discovery in the hope that a better understanding of the history of the area could perhaps be obtained
   - The word attentively is redundant because its meaning is included within the expression pouring over (should be **poring over**).
   - The expression pouring over is an incorrect idiom. Use **poring over** instead.
   - The word perhaps is redundant because its meaning is included within the word could.

(C) have taken to poring over the treasure to develop something of a better understanding of the area's history
   - The idiomatic expression taken to is too casual for formal writing. A more formal style is preferable on GMAT.
   - The idiomatic expression something of is too casual for formal writing. A more formal style is preferable on GMAT.

(D) have been poring over the treasure trove in the hope of developing a better sense of the history of the area
   - This answer contains the correct expression **poring over** and avoids the problems with casual expressions and wordiness found in some of the other answers.

(E) have been astutely poring over the valuable treasure in the hope of developing a better sensitivity toward the area's history
   - The word astutely is redundant because its meaning is included within the expression poring over.
   - The word valuable is redundant because its meaning is included within the word treasure.

11. This question tests **clarity** and **parallelism**.

For today's Kalahari bushman, <u>an ostrich egg is a valuable vessel in which he keeps scarce water and from which he makes jewelry</u> for his wife and children.

(A) an *ostrich egg* is a valuable *vessel* in `which` he keeps *scarce water* and from `which` he makes *jewelry*
   - The two uses of `which` in this answer have different referents, and this is not logical. The first use of *which* refers to *vessel* because *he keeps scarce water* in it, while the second use of *which* refers to *an ostrich egg* because *he makes jewelry* from it.

(B) the *shell of an ostrich egg* is valuable both *because it can be used* to hold scarce water *and* `because of its use` in making jewelry
   - The expression `because of its use` is not parallel to the expression *because it can be used*. The structure *and* indicates that these expressions should be parallel.

(C) the *shell of an ostrich egg* is a valuable *vessel* in `which` he holds *scarce water* and from `which` he can make *jewelry*
   - The two uses of `which` in this answer have different referents, and this is not logical. The first use of *which* refers to *vessel* because *he holds scarce water* in it, while the second use of *which* refers to *shell of an ostrich egg* because *he can make jewelry* from it.

(D) an *ostrich egg* is a valuable *vessel* `which` he uses *to keep scarce water* and *to make jewelry*
   - The use of `which` in this answer has two possible referents, and this is not logical. *Which* could refer to *vessel...to keep scarce water* or to *ostrich egg...to make jewelry*.

(E) the shell of an ostrich egg is valuable because of its use **as a container** for scarce water *and* **as a material** for making jewelry
   - This answer contains the parallel expressions **as a container** and **as a material** joined with *and* and avoids the problems with clarity found in some of the other answers.

12. This question tests **awkwardness**, **idioms**, and **wordiness**.

In 1799, England's war office secretly commissioned astronomer William Herschel <u>to build a spy telescope to mount on the walls of Walmer Castle on the southeast coast of Kent to provide</u> the earliest warning of a possible invasion by the French fleet.

(A) to build a spy telescope to mount on the walls of Walmer Castle on the southeast coast of Kent to provide
- This answer contains the correct preposition **on** and avoids the problems with awkwardness and wordiness found in some of the other answers.

(B) to build a spy telescope *for mounting* on the walls of Walmer Castle *in the southeast coast* of Kent *in order to provide*
- The part of the answer *for mounting* is awkward. The stylistic preference on GMAT is to avoid unnecessary gerunds (*-ing* verbal nouns) if possible.
- An incorrect preposition is used in the expression *in the southeast coast*. Use **on the southeast coast** instead.
- The idea *in order to provide* is overly wordy. The stylistic preference on GMAT is for more concise language.

(C) *for building* a spy telescope *for mounting* on the walls of Walmer Castle on the southeast coast of Kent to provide
- The part of the answer *for building* is awkward. The stylistic preference on GMAT is to avoid unnecessary gerunds (*-ing* verbal nouns) if possible.
- The part of the answer *for mounting* is awkward. The stylistic preference on GMAT is to avoid unnecessary gerunds (*-ing* verbal nouns) if possible.

(D) *for the building of* a spy telescope mounted on the walls of Walmer Castle *in the southeast coast* of Kent *with the intention of providing*
- The part of the answer *for the building of* is awkward. The stylistic preference on GMAT is to avoid unnecessary gerunds (*-ing* verbal nouns) if possible.
- An incorrect preposition is used in the expression *in the southeast coast*. Use **on the southeast coast** instead.
- The idea *with the intention of providing* is overly wordy and complex. The stylistic preference on GMAT is for more concise and simpler language.

(E) *for the building of* a spy telescope to be mounted on the walls of Walmer Castle on the southeast coast of Kent *in order to provide*
- The part of the answer *for the building of* is awkward. The stylistic preference on GMAT is to avoid unnecessary gerunds (*-ing* verbal nouns) if possible.
- The idea *in order to provide* is overly wordy. The stylistic preference on GMAT is for more concise language.

GMAT-Style Tests
TEST 4

Choose the letter of the answer to each question that best reflects the style and accuracy of standard written English. Then, study the explanations on the pages that follow.

1. The Kingdom of Thailand was established in the mid-14th century and <u>has succeeded in the maintenance of its independence</u> from foreign sovereignty since that time.

    (A) has succeeded in the maintenance of its independence
    (B) maintained its successful independence
    (C) has managed to successfully maintain its independence
    (D) succeeded in maintaining its independence
    (E) has successfully maintained its independence

2. Egyptians created hieroglyphs either by carving pictographs into stone <u>or painting them onto walls</u> or papyrus using reed instruments.

    (A) or painting them onto walls
    (B) or by painting it onto walls
    (C) and painting them onto walls
    (D) or by painting them onto walls
    (E) nor by painting it onto walls

3. Psychologist Abraham Maslow's hierarchy of human needs proposed that human needs can be classified into five basic types and that they can be arranged in a hierarchy according to their importance.

   (A) Psychologist Abraham Maslow's hierarchy of human needs proposed
   (B) In his hierarchy of human needs, psychologist Abraham Maslow proposed
   (C) The hierarchy of needs developed by psychologist Abraham Maslow proposed
   (D) Psychologist Abraham Maslow developed a hierarchy of needs that proposed
   (E) Psychologist Abraham Maslow, in the hierarchy describing human needs that he created, proposed

4. Ocean crust is more dense than continental crust; therefore, they subduct beneath the latter, forming underwater trenches and volcanoes.

   (A) more dense than continental crust; therefore, they subduct
   (B) denser as continental crust; they therefore subduct
   (C) denser than continental crust; therefore, it subducts
   (D) more dense than continental crust; it therefore subducts
   (E) denser than continental crust, thereby subducting itself

5. When a company must rely heavily on external sources of capital, it has an overriding goal to restore <u>itself to a position of financial self-sufficiency, a goal that can have a profound effect on</u> strategic decision-making.

    (A) itself to a position of financial self-sufficiency, a goal that can have a profound effect on
    (B) it to a financial position based on self-sufficiency, which can profoundly effect
    (C) itself to a financial position that is based on self-sufficiency, and this can have a profound effect in
    (D) it to a position of self-sufficiency in finances, which can profoundly affect
    (E) itself to a position of self-sufficiency in financial matters, and this can have a profound affect on

6. Charles Lindbergh was an airmail pilot on the St. Louis-to-Chicago route <u>when a group of St. Louis businessmen agreed to finance his attempt to try to make</u> the historic New York-to-Paris transatlantic crossing.

    (A) when a group of St. Louis businessmen agreed to finance his attempt to try to make
    (B) when a consortium of St. Louis businessmen had agreed to finance the attempt by Lindbergh to try to make
    (C) at the time that some businessmen in St. Louis arrived at an accord on the financing of his attempt at making
    (D) when a consortium of St. Louis businessmen agreed to finance his attempt to make
    (E) when a group of St. Louis businessmen joined up in an accord to finance his attempt at making

7. When Columbus returned to Spain from his second voyage to the New World with 500 Native Americans to be sold as slaves, Queen Isabella of Spain ordered him returned to the homeland in Haiti.

    (A) him returned to the homeland in Haiti
    (B) them to be returned to Haiti, their homeland
    (C) them returned to their Haitian homeland
    (D) their return by Columbus to their homeland on Haiti
    (E) their Haitian homeland return

8. Sentences have a linear order that is obvious and a constituent structure that is less so but is nonetheless understood by native speakers.

    (A) Sentences have a linear order that is obvious and a constituent structure that is less so but is nonetheless understood by native speakers.
    (B) Sentences have an obvious linear order and a constituent structure that is less so but nonetheless understood by native speakers.
    (C) Sentences have an obvious linear order and a constituent structure that is less so but is nonetheless understood by native speakers.
    (D) Sentences have a linear order that is obvious and a constituent structure that is less so but native speakers nonetheless understand.
    (E) Sentences have a linear order that is obvious and a constituent structure that is less so but nonetheless native speakers understand it.

9. There are far more craters on the surface of the Moon than <u>on the Earth because, unlike the Earth, there is no atmosphere on the Moon, so even very small meteoroids are</u> able to strike its surface.

   (A) on the Earth because, unlike the Earth, there is no atmosphere on the Moon, so even very small meteoroids are
   (B) on the Earth since, unlike the Earth, the Moon does not have an atmosphere, thus even very small meteoroids are
   (C) on the surface of the Earth because the Moon, unlike the Earth, has no atmosphere, so even the smallest meteoroids are
   (D) the Earth's surface because, unlike the Earth, there is no atmosphere on the Moon, so the smallest of meteoroids are
   (E) the surface of the Earth since, unlike the Earth, the Moon has no atmosphere, thus even very small meteoroids are

10. The phrase "good night, sleep tight" came into usage during Shakespeare's time based on the custom of securing <u>a mattress to bed frames with ropes and then tightening the ropes to make the mattress firmer</u>.

   (A) a mattress to bed frames with ropes and then tightening the ropes to make the mattress firmer
   (B) a mattress to a bed frame with ropes and then tighten the rope to make more firm the mattress
   (C) mattresses to a bed frame with ropes and then tighten the ropes to make the mattress firmer
   (D) a mattress to a bed frame with ropes and then tightening the ropes to make more firm the mattress
   (E) a mattress to a bed frame with ropes and then tightening the ropes to make the mattress firmer

11. In a survey of the 1,000 words that are used most frequently in English, it was found that what the percentage was that had Old English origins was roughly 61.7 percent.

   (A) In a survey of the 1,000 words that are used most frequently in English, it was found that what the percentage was that had Old English origins was roughly 61.7 percent.
   (B) In a survey covering the 1,000 most frequently used words in English, researchers found the percentage of the words with Old English origins was something close to 61.7 percent.
   (C) A survey of the 1,000 most frequently used English words found that the percentage with Old English origins was roughly 61.7 percent.
   (D) A researcher conducting a survey of the 1,000 words that are most frequently used in English found that roughly 61.7 percent had Old English origins.
   (E) Based on a survey of the 1,000 most frequently used English words, researchers have determined the percentage of words with Old English origins to be approximately 61.7 percent.

12. In *The Wealth of Nations*, Adam Smith (1723-1790) laid out the various philosophical foundations and bases of modern capitalism and the modern market society.

   (A) Adam Smith (1723-1790) laid out the various philosophical **foundations** and **bases** of modern capitalism and the modern market society
   (B) Adam Smith (1723-1790) laid out the varied philosophical bases of the modern capitalist society
   (C) an outline of the philosophical foundations at the core of the modern market society were laid out by Adam Smith (1723-1790)
   (D) various philosophical foundations and bases of the modern capitalist society had been laid out by Adam Smith (1723-1790)
   (E) Adam Smith (1723-1790) lay out an outline of the philosophical foundations of capitalism and the modern market society

EXPLANATIONS

1. This question tests **wordiness**, **verbs**, and **modifiers**.

   The Kingdom of Thailand was established in the mid-14th century and has succeeded in the maintenance of its independence from foreign sovereignty *since* that time.

(A) has *succeeded in the maintenance* of its independence
   - The part of the answer *succeeded in the maintenance* is overly wordy. The stylistic preference on GMAT is for more concise language.

(B) *maintained* its successful independence
   - The simple past tense *maintained* is used incorrectly. Because the word *since* indicates a period of time from the past to the present, the main verb should be in the present perfect tense (**has maintained**) and not the simple past tense.

(C) has managed *to successfully maintain* its independence
   - The modifier *successfully* is positioned incorrectly because an adverb cannot be used between the two parts of an infinitive (*to* and *maintain*). This is called a split infinitive.

(D) *succeeded* in maintaining its independence
   - The simple past tense *succeeded* is used incorrectly. Because the word *since* indicates a period of time from the past to the present, the main verb should be in the present perfect tense (**has succeeded**) and not the simple past tense.

(E) has successfully maintained its independence
   - This answer contains the correct present perfect tense **has...maintained** and the correctly positioned modifier **successfully**. It also avoids the problem with wordiness found in one of the other answers.

2. This question tests **parallelism** and **agreement**.

Egyptians created hieroglyphs *either by carving pictographs* into stone or painting them onto walls or papyrus using reed instruments.

(A) or *painting* them onto walls
   - The expression *painting* is not parallel to the expression *by carving*. The structure *either...or* indicates that these expressions should be parallel.

(B) or by painting *it* onto walls
   - The singular pronoun *it* does not agree with the plural noun *pictographs*, to which it refers.

(C) *and painting* them onto walls
   - The word *and* is used incorrectly. *Either...or* is a paired conjunction. Use **or** -- and not *and* -- with *either*.
   - The expression *painting* is not parallel to the expression *by carving*. The structure *either...and* (should be **or**) indicates that these expressions should be parallel.

[(D)] or by painting them onto walls
   - This answer contains **or** to create the parallel expression *either...or* and includes the expression **by painting** following **or** to be parallel to *by carving* following *either*.

(E) *nor* by painting *it* onto walls
   - The word *nor* is used incorrectly. *Either...or* is a paired conjunction. Use **or** -- and not *nor* -- with *either*.
   - The singular pronoun *it* does not agree with the plural noun *pictographs*, to which it refers.

3. This question tests **diction** and **wordiness**.

<u>Psychologist Abraham Maslow's hierarchy of human needs proposed</u> that human needs can be classified into five basic types and that they can be arranged in a hierarchy according to their importance.

(A) Psychologist Abraham Maslow's *hierarchy* of human needs proposed
   - The word *proposed* has an inappropriate meaning for this context. It is not possible for *a hierarchy* to propose something. Humans propose, and inanimate objects do not.

(B) In his hierarchy of human needs, psychologist Abraham Maslow **proposed**
   - This answer uses the word **proposed** correctly, with *Abraham Maslow* as its subject, in an answer that is stylistically concise.

(C) The *hierarchy* of needs developed by psychologist Abraham Maslow proposed
   - The word *proposed* has an inappropriate meaning for this context. It is not possible for *a hierarchy* to propose something. Humans propose, and inanimate objects do not.

(D) Psychologist Abraham Maslow developed a *hierarchy* of needs that proposed
   - The word *proposed* has an inappropriate meaning for this context. It is not possible for *a hierarchy* to propose something. Humans propose, and inanimate objects do not.

(E) Psychologist Abraham Maslow, in the hierarchy describing human needs that he created, proposed
   - The part of the answer *the hierarchy describing human needs that he created* is overly wordy. The stylistic preference on GMAT is for more concise language.

4. This question tests **comparisons**, **agreement**, and **clarity**.

   Ocean *crust* is more dense than continental crust; therefore, they subduct beneath the latter, forming underwater trenches and volcanoes.

   (A) more dense than continental crust; therefore, they subduct
   - The comparative *more dense* is formed incorrectly. The comparative form of a one-syllable word such as *dense* should be formed with *-er* (**denser**) rather than *more*.
   - The plural pronoun *they* does not agree with the singular noun *crust*, to which it refers.

   (B) denser as continental crust; they therefore subduct
   - The comparative *denser as* is formed incorrectly. The comparative *denser* should be completed with *than* (**denser than**) rather than *as*.
   - The plural pronoun *they* does not agree with the singular noun *crust*, to which it refers.

   (C) denser than continental crust; therefore, it subducts
   - This answer has the correctly formed comparative **denser than** and avoids the problems with agreement and clarity that are found in some of the other answers.

   (D) more dense than continental crust; it therefore subducts
   - The comparative *more dense* is formed incorrectly. The comparative form of a one-syllable word such as *dense* should be formed with *-er* (**denser**) rather than *more*.

   (E) denser than continental crust, thereby subducting itself
   - The meaning of *subducting itself* is ambiguous. This answer could mean either that the *Ocean crust* or the *continental crust* subducts itself.

5. This question tests **pronouns**, **diction**, **clarity**, and **idioms**.

When *a company must rely heavily on external sources of capital, it has an overriding goal to restore* itself to a position of financial self-sufficiency, a goal that can have a profound effect on *strategic decision-making.*

(A) itself to a position of financial self-sufficiency, a goal that can have a profound effect on
- This answer contains the correct reflexive object pronoun **itself**, which refers to *company*, and avoids the problems with the pronoun *which*, diction, clarity, and idioms that are found in some of the other answers.

(B) *it to a financial position based on self-sufficiency, which can profoundly effect*
- The object pronoun *it* is used incorrectly. A reflexive pronoun should be used as an object when it refers to the subject. Since the subject of the verb *has* is *it*, which refers to *company*, and the object pronoun *it* refers to the subject *company*, a reflexive pronoun (**itself**) should be used.
- The relative pronoun *which* is used incorrectly. This relative pronoun should be used to refer to a specific noun and not to a complete idea such as *it has an overriding goal to restore it* (should be **itself**) *to a financial position based on self-sufficiency*.

(C) *itself to a financial position that is based on self-sufficiency, and this can have a profound effect in*
- The referent of the pronoun *this* is unclear. This pronoun could possibly refer to the idea that *a company must rely heavily on external sources of capital*, or to the idea *an overriding goal*, or to the idea that it wants *to restore itself to a financial position that is based on self-sufficiency*.
- An incorrect preposition is used in the expression *have a profound effect in*. Use **have a profound effect on** instead.

(D) *it to a position of self-sufficiency in finances, which can profoundly affect*
- The object pronoun *it* is used incorrectly. A reflexive pronoun should be used as an object when it refers to the subject. Since the subject of the verb *has* is *it*, which refers to *company*, and the object pronoun *it* refers to the subject *company*, a reflexive pronoun (**itself**) should be used.
- The relative pronoun *which* is used incorrectly. This relative pronoun should be used to refer to a specific noun and not to a complete idea such as *it has an overriding goal to restore it* (should be **itself**) *to a position of self-sufficiency in finances*.
- The word *affect* -- which is a verb meaning "influence" and not a noun meaning "result"-- is illogical in this context. Use **effect** -- which is a noun meaning "result" -- instead.

(E) *itself to a position of self-sufficiency in financial matters, and this can have a profound affect on*
- The referent of the pronoun *this* is unclear. This pronoun could possibly refer to the idea that *a company must rely heavily on external sources of capital*, or to *an overriding goal*, or to the idea that it wants *to restore itself to a position of self-sufficiency in financial matters*.
- The word *affect* -- which is a verb meaning "influence" and not a noun meaning "result"-- is illogical in this context. Use **effect** -- which is a noun meaning "result" -- instead.

6. This question tests **wordiness**, **verbs**, **awkwardness**, and **idioms**.

Charles Lindbergh *was an airmail pilot* on the St. Louis-to-Chicago route <u>when a group of St. Louis businessmen agreed to finance his attempt to try to make</u> the historic New York-to-Paris transatlantic crossing.

(A) when a group of St. Louis businessmen agreed to finance his *attempt* *to try* to make
- The idea *to try* is redundant because its meaning is included within the word *attempt*.

(B) when a consortium of St. Louis businessmen *had agreed* to finance the *attempt* by Lindbergh *to try* to make
- The past perfect tense *had agreed* is used incorrectly. The past perfect tense should be used when one past action is completed prior to another. It is not the case that the agreement occurred before Charles Lindbergh *was an airmail pilot*.
- The idea *to try* is redundant because its meaning is included within the word *attempt*.

(C) at the time that some businessmen in St. Louis *arrived at an accord* on *the financing* of his attempt at making
- The idea *arrived at an accord* is overly wordy. The stylistic preference on GMAT is for more concise language.
- The part of the answer *the financing* is awkward. The stylistic preference on GMAT is to avoid unnecessary gerunds (*-ing* verbal nouns).

[(D)] when a consortium of St. Louis businessmen **agreed** to finance his attempt to make
- This answer uses the correct simple past tense **agreed** and avoids the problems with wordiness, awkwardness, and idioms found in some of the other answers.

(E) when a group of St. Louis businessmen *joined up* in an accord to finance *his attempt at making*
- The idiomatic expression *joined up* is too casual for formal writing. It is stylistically preferable to use only the verb **joined**.
- The part of the answer *his attempt at making* is awkward. The stylistic preference on GMAT is for a more natural-sounding way of expressing this idea.

It Works! GMAT Sentence Correction

7. This question tests **agreement** and **awkwardness**.

    When Columbus returned to Spain from his second voyage to the New World with 500 *Native Americans* to be sold as slaves, Queen Isabella of Spain ordered him returned to the homeland in Haiti.

(A) him returned to the homeland in Haiti
   - The singular pronoun *him* does not agree with the plural noun phrase *Native Americans*, to which it refers.

(B) them to be returned to Haiti, their homeland
   - The idea *Haiti, their homeland* is awkward. The stylistic preference on GMAT is for a more natural-sounding way of expressing this idea.

(C) them returned to their Haitian homeland
   - This answer contains the correct plural pronoun **them** and avoids the problems with awkwardness found in some of the other answers.

(D) their return by Columbus to their homeland on Haiti
   - The idea *their return by Columbus* is awkward. The stylistic preference on GMAT is for a more natural-sounding way of expressing this idea.

(E) their Haitian homeland return
   - The idea *their Haitian homeland return* is awkward. The stylistic preference on GMAT is for a more natural-sounding way of expressing this idea.

8. This question tests **parallelism**.

   Sentences have a linear order that is obvious and a constituent structure that is less so but is nonetheless understood by native speakers.

   (A) Sentences have a linear order that is obvious *and* a constituent structure that is less so *but* is nonetheless understood by native speakers.
   - This sentence contains the parallel structures **a linear order that is obvious** and **a constituent structure that is less so** connected with the conjunction *and*. It also contains the parallel structures **is less so** and **is nonetheless understood** connected with the conjunction *but*.

   (B) Sentences have an obvious linear order and a constituent structure that *is less so* but nonetheless understood by native speakers.
   - The expression nonetheless understood is not parallel to the expression *is less so*. The structure *but* indicates that these expressions should be parallel.

   (C) Sentences have *an obvious linear order and* a constituent structure that is less so but is nonetheless understood by native speakers.
   - The expression a constituent structure that is less so is not parallel to the expression *an obvious linear order*. The structure *and* indicates that these expressions should be parallel.

   (D) Sentences have a linear order that is obvious and a constituent structure *that is less so but* native speakers nonetheless understand.
   - The expression native speakers nonetheless understand is not parallel to the expression *that is less so*. The structure *but* indicates that these expressions should be parallel.

   (E) Sentences have a linear order that is obvious and *a constituent structure that is less so but* nonetheless native speakers understand it.
   - The expression nonetheless native speakers understand it is not parallel to the expression *a constituent structure that is less so*. The structure *but* indicates that these expressions should be parallel.

9. This question tests **comparisons** and **sentences**.

   There *are* far *more craters on the surface of the Moon than* on *the Earth* because, unlike the Earth, *there is no* atmosphere on the Moon, so even very small *meteoroids are* able to strike its surface.

(A) on the Earth because, unlike the Earth, there is no atmosphere on the Moon, so even very small meteoroids are
   - The expression on the Earth is not parallel to the expression *on the surface of the Moon*. The comparative *more...than* indicates that these expressions should be parallel.
   - The expression there is no atmosphere following the comma (,) is not parallel to the expression *the Earth*. The comparative *unlike* indicates that these expressions should be parallel.

(B) on the Earth since, unlike the Earth, the Moon does not have an atmosphere, *thus* even very small meteoroids are
   - The expression on the Earth is not parallel to the expression *on the surface of the Moon*. The comparative *more...than* indicates that these expressions should be parallel.
   - This answer creates a run-on sentence because the two subjects and verbs *are..craters* and meteoroids are are connected with only a comma (,). A comma cannot be used to connect two subjects and verbs without a conjunction, and *thus* is an adverb and is not a conjunction.

(C) on the surface of the Earth because *the Moon*, unlike the Earth, has no atmosphere, so even the smallest meteoroids are
   - This answer contains the expression **on the surface of the Earth**, which is parallel to *on the surface of the Moon* and the expression **the Earth**, which is parallel to *the Moon*. It also avoids the problem with sentences found in some of the other answers.

(D) the Earth's surface because, unlike the Earth, there is no atmosphere on the Moon, so the smallest of meteoroids are
   - The expression the Earth's surface is not parallel to the expression *the surface of the Moon*. The comparative *more...than* indicates that these expressions should be parallel.
   - The expression there is no atmosphere is not parallel to the expression *the Earth*. The comparative *unlike* indicates that these expression should be parallel.

(E) the surface of the Earth since, unlike the Earth, the Moon has no atmosphere, *thus* even very small meteoroids are
   - This answer creates a run-on sentence because the two subjects and verbs *are...craters* and meteoroids are are connected with only a comma (,). A comma cannot be used to connect two subjects and verbs without a conjunction, and *thus* is an adverb and is not a conjunction.

10. **This question tests, agreement, parallelism, and comparisons.**

   The phrase "good night, sleep tight" came into usage during Shakespeare's time based on the custom of *securing a mattress to bed frames with ropes and then tightening the ropes to make the mattress firmer*.

   (A)   a *mattress* to bed *frames* with ropes and then tightening the ropes to make the mattress firmer
   - The plural noun *frames* does not make sense when used with the singular noun *mattress*.

   (B)   a mattress to a bed frame with *ropes and* then *tighten* the *rope* to *make more firm* the *mattress*
   - The expression *tighten* is not parallel to the expression *securing*. The structure *and* indicates that these expressions should be parallel.
   - The singular noun *rope* does not make sense when used with the plural noun *ropes*.
   - The comparative *more firm* is formed incorrectly. The comparative form of a one-syllable word such as *firm* should be formed with *-er* (**firmer**) rather than *more*.

   (C)   *mattresses* to a bed frame with ropes *and* then *tighten* the ropes to make the *mattress* firmer
   - The expression *tighten* is not parallel to the expression *securing*. The structure *and* indicates that these expressions should be parallel.
   - The singular noun *mattress* does not make sense when used with the plural noun *mattresses*.

   (D)   a mattress to a bed frame with ropes and then tightening the ropes to *make more firm* the *mattress*
   - The comparative *more firm* is formed incorrectly. The comparative form of a one-syllable word such as *dense* should be formed with *-er* (**firmer**) rather than *more*.

   (E)   a mattress to a bed frame with ropes and then tightening the ropes to make the mattress firmer
   - This answer contains the singular nouns **mattress** and **frame** used logically with the plural noun **ropes**. It also contains the expression **tightening**, which is parallel to the expression *securing*, and the correctly formed comparison **firmer**.

It Works! GMAT Sentence Correction

11. This question tests **wordiness**, **awkwardness**, **idioms**, **clarity**, and **modifiers**.

    In a survey of the 1,000 words that are used most frequently in English, it was found that what the percentage was that had Old English origins was roughly 61.7 percent.

(A) In a survey of the 1,000 words that are used most frequently in English, it was found that *what the percentage was that had Old English origins* was roughly 61.7 percent.
   - The idea *what the percentage was that had Old English origins* is overly wordy and complex. The stylistic preference on GMAT is for more concise and simpler language.

(B) In a survey covering the 1,000 most frequently used words in English, researchers found *the percentage* of the words with Old English origins *was* *something close to* 61.7 percent.
   - The conjunction *that* has been omitted in front of the subject and verb *the percentage...was*. The stylistic preference on GMAT is to include the conjunction **that**
   - The idiomatic expression *something close to* is too casual for formal writing. It is stylistically preferable to use the more formal expression **close to**.

(C) A *survey* of the 1,000 most frequently used English words *found* that *the percentage with Old English origins was roughly 61.7 percent*.
   - The meaning of *found* is illogical. It does not make sense that a *survey...found* something.
   - The idea *the percentage with Old English origins was roughly 61.7 percent* is overly wordy and repetitive. The stylistic preference on GMAT is for more concise and less repetitive language.

(D) A researcher conducting a survey of the 1,000 words that are most frequently used in English found that roughly 61.7 percent had Old English origins.
   - This answer avoids the problems with wordiness, awkwardness, idioms, clarity, and modifiers that are found in some of the other answers.

(E) *Based on a survey of the 1,000 most frequently used English words,* *researchers* have determined the percentage of words with Old English origins to be approximately 61.7 percent.
   - The use of *researchers* following the comma (,) creates a sentence with a dangling modifier, *Based on a survey of the 1,000 most frequently used English words*. An introductory adjective should modify the subject of the main clause directly following the comma (,). In this sentence, the expression *Based on a survey of the 1,000 most frequently used English words* should modify **the percentage of words** and not *researchers*.

12. This question tests **wordiness**, **awkwardness**, and **verbs**.

   In *The Wealth of Nations*, Adam Smith (1723-1790) laid out the various philosophical *foundations* and *bases* of modern *capitalism* and the modern *market society*.

(A) Adam Smith (1723-1790) laid out the various philosophical *foundations* and *bases* of modern *capitalism* and the modern *market society*
   • The word *bases* is redundant because its meaning is included within the word *foundations*.
   • The expression *market society* is redundant because its meaning is included within the word *capitalism*.

[(B)] Adam Smith (1723-1790) laid out the varied philosophical bases of the modern capitalist society
   • This answer contains the correct simple past tense verb **laid** and avoids the problems with wordiness and awkwardness that are found in some of the other answers.

(C) an outline of the philosophical *foundations* *at the core* of the modern market society *were laid out* by Adam Smith (1723-1790)
   • The expression *at the core* is redundant because its meaning is included within the word *foundations*.
   • The passive voice *were laid out* is unnecessary here. The more direct active voice would be stylistically preferable on GMAT.

(D) various philosophical *foundations* and *bases* of the modern capitalist society *had been laid out* by Adam Smith (1723-1790)
   • The word *bases* is redundant because its meaning is included within the word *foundations*.
   • The passive voice *had been laid out* is unnecessary here. The more direct active voice would be stylistically preferable on GMAT.

(E) Adam Smith *(1723-1790)* *lay* out an outline of the philosophical foundations of *capitalism* and the modern *market society*
   • The simple present tense *lay* is used incorrectly. The simple past tense **laid** is needed because the time frame of the sentence is in the past *(1723-1790)*.
   • The expression *market society* is redundant because its meaning is included within the word *capitalism*.

GMAT-Style Tests
TEST 5

Choose the letter of the answer to each question that best reflects the style and accuracy of standard written English. Then, study the explanations on the pages that follow.

1. The Ford Motor <u>Company had already been building the ingeniously simple</u> Model T Ford for five years when its engineers developed the idea for assembly line production.

    (A) Company had already been building the ingeniously simple
    (B) Company, having already built the ingenious and simple
    (C) Company has built already the ingeniously simple
    (D) Company, already building the ingeniously simple
    (E) Company had been building already the ingenious and simple

2. The lens of the human <u>eyes grow with age; however, as it becomes larger, it also becomes less pliable and can not focus well</u>.

    (A) eyes grow with age; however, as it becomes larger it also becomes less pliable and can not focus well.
    (B) eye grows with age, however at the same time it also becomes less pliable and can not focus well
    (C) eyes grow with age; however, at the same time they have lost pliability and are less able to focus well
    (D) eye grows with age; however, as it becomes larger, it also becomes less pliable and less able to focus well
    (E) eye grow with age, however it also becomes larger, less pliable, and less able to focus well

3. Only now are scholars beginning to develop an appreciation for the size and wealth of the empires that flourished in sub-Saharan Africa before the arrival of the Europeans.

   (A) Only now are scholars beginning to develop an appreciation for
   (B) Scholars are only developing now an appreciation of
   (C) Since scholars are only now coming to appreciate
   (D) Only now that scholars are developing an appreciation of
   (E) Scholars are only now coming to appreciate

4. Contractions commonly begin to occur in the stomach 12 to 24 hours after food was last ingested; these hunger pains result from individual contractions that last in the neighborhood of 30 seconds each and occur in a series that may last for 30 to 45 minutes.

   (A) these hunger pains result from individual contractions that last in the neighborhood of 30 seconds each and occur in a series that may last for 30 to 45 minutes
   (B) an individual hunger pain can last around 30 seconds and occur in a series that often continues for 30 to 45 minutes
   (C) these hunger pangs result from an individual contraction lasting around 30 seconds and continuing for 30 to 45 minutes
   (D) these hunger pangs are the result of individual contractions lasting around 30 seconds each in a series that can continue for 30 to 45 minutes
   (E) an individual hunger pang is a contraction that lasts around 30 seconds and most likely is part of a series of contractions that continue for perhaps 30 to 45 minutes

5. In 1914, movie theaters became extremely popular in America, and movie attendance surged, which led some owners to bring in graduates of West Point for the purpose of training ushers in the logistics of moving large numbers of people through small spaces.

(A) surged, which led some owners to bring in graduates of West Point for the purpose of training ushers in the logistics of moving large numbers of people
(B) surged up, which caused some owners to hire West Point graduates as trainers for their ushers to teach them to move large groups of people
(C) surged, something that lead some owners to hire West Point graduates to train their ushers in moving large amounts of people
(D) surged, an occurrence that caused some owners to hire West Point graduates to train their ushers to move large groups of people
(E) surged up, an occurrence that led some owners to bring in graduates of West Point in order to train their ushers to move large amounts of people

6. While heroin works on receptor sites in the brain which are stimulated by the drug to rapidly produce pain-relieving and mood-enhancing chemicals, cocaine works by stimulating the central nervous system.

(A) While heroin works on receptor sites in the brain which are stimulated by the drug to rapidly produce pain-relieving and mood-enhancing chemicals
(B) Heroin works by stimulating receptor sites in the brain to rapidly produce mood-enhancing chemicals
(C) Unlike heroin, which works by stimulating receptor sites in the brain to produce pain-relieving and mood-enhancing chemicals rapidly
(D) Unlike the role of heroin, which works on receptor sites in the brain which is stimulated by the drug to produce chemicals that are both pain-relieving as well as mood-enhancing
(E) Heroin works on receptor sites in the brain which are stimulated by the drug to produce pain-relieving as well as mood-enhancing chemicals

7. The Vikings, who maintained a colony on the southwestern coast of Greenland for more than four centuries beginning in 982 made regular voyages to North America to obtain wood because of the lack of this necessity on Greenland.

    (A) beginning in 982 made regular voyages to North America to obtain wood because of the lack of this necessity
    (B) starting originally in 982 were travelling on a regular basis to North America for the purpose of obtaining wood, which was lacking
    (C) in 982 had been making voyages to North America by boat on a regular basis because they needed to obtain the wood that was lacking
    (D) in 982 made regular voyages to North America to obtain a much-needed product, wood, a product that was lacking
    (E) beginning originally in 982, had been making regular sea voyages to North America to obtain wood because of the lack of this product

8. According to many language experts, the most difficult kind of phrase to create is a palindrome, a sentence or group of sentences that read the same both backwards and forwards, such as, "Red rum, sir, is murder."

    (A) that read the same both backwards and forwards
    (B) that reads the same both backward and forward
    (C) that reads similarly backwards and forwards
    (D) with the characteristic that they read similarly both backward and forward
    (E) with the characteristic that it reads the same both backward and forward

9. Also known as prestidigitation or legerdemain, sleight of hand encompasses a variety of techniques used by magicians to control cards, coins, and other objects covertly.

   (A) sleight of hand encompasses a variety of techniques used by magicians to control cards, coins, and other objects covertly
   (B) magicians and card manipulators use various sleight of hand techniques to control cards, coins, and other objects covertly
   (C) the use of sleight of hand is comprised of various techniques that magicians use to covertly control cards, coins, and other objects
   (D) sleight of hand comprises a variety of techniques magicians and card manipulators use to control cards, coins, and other objects covertly
   (E) sleight of hand is comprised of various techniques used by magicians to covertly control cards, coins, and other objects

10. Art forger Madame Latour was so skilled at her craft that many art experts were made to feel foolish and, in addition, some artists were made to question which paintings were actually theirs.

   (A) Art forger Madame Latour was so skilled at her craft that many art experts were made to feel foolish and, in addition, some artists were made to question which paintings were actually theirs.
   (B) So skilled at her craft was art forger Madame Latour that her forgeries fooled many an art expert and even caused some artists that she copied to question which paintings were actually theirs.
   (C) Art forger Madame Latour had acquired such good forging skills that she had managed to fool many art experts and even fooled some artists she copied into questioning which paintings were theirs.
   (D) So skilled was art forger Madame Latour at her craft that her forgeries had fooled many supposed art experts and even forced the questioning by some artists of which paintings they had actually made.
   (E) Art forger Madame Latour had undergone the acquisition of so much skill that she was able to fool both many art experts as well as some artists she copied, who questioned which paintings were theirs.

11. Tests of <u>the solvency that a firm regularly exhibits necessarily focuses both on its ability to retire the principle in a timely manner and</u> also its ability to pay interest on its debts.

    (A) the solvency that a firm regularly exhibits necessarily focuses both on its ability to retire the principle in a timely manner and
    (B) the solvency that a firm regularly exhibits must necessarily focus on not only its ability to retire the principal in a timely manner and
    (C) a firm's solvency must focus on not only its ability to retire the principal in a timely manner but
    (D) a firm's solvency must focus necessarily on both its ability to retire the principle in a timely fashion and
    (E) the solvency regularly exhibited by a firm must focus both on its ability to retire the principal in a timely fashion and

12. The tectonic forces that created East Africa's Great Rift Valley created a rash of volcanoes, one of which erupted magnificently around two and a half million years ago <u>to create</u> the nineteen-kilometer-wide Ngorongoro Crater.

    (A) to create
    (B) and created
    (C) and resulted in the creation of
    (D) to result in the creation of
    (E) with a force that resulted in the creation of

EXPLANATIONS

1. This question tests **sentences**, **verbs**, and **modifiers**.

   The Ford Motor <u>Company had already been building the ingeniously simple</u> *Model T Ford* for five years *when its engineers developed* the idea for assembly line production.

   (A) Company had already been building the ingeniously simple
   - This answer contains the subject and verb **Company had...been building**, the correct past perfect progressive tense **had...been building**, and the correctly positioned modifier **already**.

   (B) *Company*, *having* already *built* the ingenious and simple
   - This sentence is a fragment because the main clause subject *Company* lacks a verb. *Having...built* is a participle and is not a verb.

   (C) Company *has built* *already* the ingeniously simple
   - The present perfect tense *has built* is used incorrectly. The present perfect tense should be used when an action occurs in the period from the past to the present. The action in this sentence is in the past *when its engineers developed*.
   - The modifier *already* is positioned incorrectly because an adverb cannot be positioned between a verb *has built* and its direct object *Model T Ford*.

   (D) *Company*, already *building* the ingeniously simple
   - This sentence is a fragment because the main clause subject *Company* lacks a verb. *Building* is a participle and is not a verb.

   (E) Company *had been building* *already* the ingenious and simple
   - The modifier *already* is positioned incorrectly because an adverb cannot be positioned between a verb *had been building* and its direct object *Model T Ford*.

2. This question tests **agreement**, **diction**, **sentences**, and **parallelism**.

   The *lens* of the human eyes grow with age; however, as it becomes larger, it also becomes less pliable and can not focus well.

(A) eyes grow with age; however, as it becomes larger it also becomes less pliable and can not focus well
   - The plural noun *eyes* does not make sense when used with the singular noun *lens*.
   - The plural verb *grow* does not agree with the singular subject *lens*.
   - The expression *can not* is always incorrect. Use **cannot** instead.

(B) eye *grows* with age, *however* at the same time *it* also *becomes* less pliable and *can not* focus well
   - This answer creates a run-on sentence because the two subjects and verbs *lens...grows* and *it...becomes* are connected with only a comma *(,)*. A comma cannot be used to connect two subjects and verbs without a conjunction, and *however* is an adverb and is not a conjunction.
   - The expression *can not* is always incorrect. Use **cannot** instead.

(C) eyes grow with age; however, at the same time they *have lost pliability* and *are less able* to focus well
   - The plural noun *eyes* does not make sense when used with the singular noun *lens*.
   - The plural verb *grow* does not agree with the singular subject *lens*.
   - The expression *have lost pliability* is not parallel to the expression *are less able*. The structure *and* indicates that these expressions should be parallel.

[(D)] **eye grows** with age; however, as it becomes larger, it also becomes less pliable and less able to focus well
   - This answer contains the correct singular noun **eye** and the correct singular verb **grows** to agree with the singular subject *lens*. It also avoids the problems of run-on sentences and parallelism found in some of the other answers.

(E) eye *grow* with age, *however it* also *becomes* larger, less pliable, and less able to focus well
   - The plural verb *grow* does not agree with the singular subject *lens*.
   - This answer creates a run-on sentence because the two subjects and verbs *lens...grow* and *it...becomes* are connected with only a comma *(,)*. A comma cannot be used to connect two subjects and verbs without a conjunction, and *however* is an adverb and is not a conjunction.

3. This question tests **wordiness**, **modifiers**, and **sentences**.

   Only now are scholars beginning to develop an appreciation for the size and wealth of the empires that flourished in sub-Saharan Africa before the arrival of the Europeans.

   (A) Only now are scholars *beginning* to *develop* an appreciation for
   - The word *beginning* is redundant because its meaning is included within the word *develop*.

   (B) Scholars are *only* developing *now* an appreciation of
   - The modifier *only* is positioned incorrectly because it is not directly in front of the word *now*, which it modifies.

   (C) *Since* scholars are only now *coming* to appreciate
   - This sentence is a fragment because the subject and verb *scholars are...coming* are introduced by the subordinate conjunction *Since*, creating a subordinate clause rather than a main clause.

   (D) Only now *that* scholars are developing an appreciation of
   - This sentence is a fragment because the subject and verb *scholars are developing* are introduced by the subordinate conjunction *that*, creating a subordinate clause rather than a main clause.

   (E) Scholars are only now coming to appreciate
   - This answer has a complete main clause subject and verb **Scholars are...coming** and has **only** correctly positioned in front of **now**. It also avoids the problem of redundancy found in one of the other answers.

4. This question tests **idioms**, **clarity**, and **agreement**.

Contractions commonly begin to occur in the stomach 12 to 24 hours after food was last ingested; these hunger pains result from individual contractions that last in the neighborhood of 30 seconds each and occur in a series that may last for 30 to 45 minutes.

(A) these *hunger pains* result from individual contractions that last in the neighborhood of 30 seconds each and occur in a series that may last for 30 to 45 minutes
   - The expression *hunger pains* is an incorrect idiom. Use **hunger pangs** instead.

(B) an individual *hunger pain* can last around 30 seconds and occur in a series that often continues for 30 to 45 minutes
   - The expression *hunger pain* is an incorrect idiom. Use **hunger pang** instead.

(C) these hunger pangs result from *an individual contraction lasting around 30 seconds and continuing for 30 to 45 minutes*
   - The expression *an individual contraction lasting around 30 seconds and continuing for 30 to 45 minutes* is illogical. It is not possible for one contract to last for 30 seconds and also continue for 30 to 45 minutes. It is an individual contraction that lasts for 30 seconds and a series of contractions that lasts for 30 to 45 minutes.

(D) these hunger pangs are the result of individual contractions lasting around 30 seconds each in a series that can continue for 30 to 45 minutes
   - This answer contains the correct idiom **hunger pangs** and avoids the problems with clarity and agreement found in some of the other answers.

(E) an individual hunger pang is a contraction that lasts around 30 seconds and most likely is part of *a series* of contractions *that continue* for perhaps 30 to 45 minutes
   - The plural verb *continue* does not agree with the subject *that*, which refers to the singular noun phrase *a series*.

5. This question tests **pronouns**, **wordiness**, **verbs**, and **nouns**.

In 1914, movie theaters became extremely popular in America, and *movie attendance* surged, which led some owners to bring in graduates of West Point for the purpose of training ushers in the logistics of moving large numbers of people through small spaces.

(A) *surged,* which led some owners to bring in graduates of West Point *for the purpose of training* ushers in the logistics of moving large numbers of people
  - The relative pronoun *which* is used incorrectly. This relative pronoun should be used to refer to a specific noun and not to a complete idea such as *movie attendance surged*.
  - The idea *for the purpose of training* is overly wordy and complex. The stylistic preference on GMAT is for more concise and simpler language.

(B) *surged* up, *which* caused some owners to hire West Point graduates as trainers for their ushers to teach them to move large groups of people
  - The word *up* is redundant because its meaning is included within the word *surged*.
  - The relative pronoun *which* is used incorrectly. This relative pronoun should be used to refer to a specific noun and not to a complete idea such as *movie attendance surged up* (should be **surged**).

(C) surged, something that *lead* some owners to hire West Point graduates to train their ushers in moving large *amounts* of *people*
  - The simple present tense *lead* is used incorrectly. The simple past tense (**led**) is needed because the time frame is of the sentence is *In 1914*.
  - The uncountable quantifier *amounts* is used incorrectly. This uncountable quantifier should not be used with the countable noun *people*. Use **numbers** instead.

(D) surged, an occurrence that caused some owners to hire West Point graduates to train their ushers to move large groups of people
  - This answer avoids the problems with pronouns, wordiness, verbs, and nouns that are found in some of the other answers.

(E) *surged* up, an occurrence that led some owners to bring in graduates of West Point *in order to train* their ushers to move large *amounts* of *people*
  - The word *up* is redundant because its meaning is included within the word *surged*.
  - The idea *in order to train* is overly wordy and complex. The stylistic preference on GMAT is for more concise and simpler language.
  - The uncountable quantifier *amounts* is used incorrectly. This uncountable quantifier should not be used with the countable noun *people*. Use **numbers** instead.

6. This question tests **modifiers**, **sentences**, **comparisons**, **agreement**, and **parallelism**.

   While heroin works on receptor sites in the brain which are stimulated by the drug to rapidly produce pain-relieving and mood-enhancing chemicals, *cocaine works* by stimulating the central nervous system.

(A) While heroin works on receptor sites in the brain which are stimulated by the drug to *rapidly* produce pain-relieving and mood-enhancing chemicals
   - The modifier *rapidly* is positioned incorrectly because an adverb cannot be used between the two parts of an infinitive (*to* and *produce*). This is called a split infinitive.

(B) *Heroin works* by stimulating receptor sites in the brain to *rapidly* produce mood-enhancing chemicals
   - This answer creates a run-on sentence because the two subjects and verbs *Heroin works* and *cocaine works* are connected with only a comma (,). A comma cannot be used to connect two subjects and verbs without a conjunction.
   - The modifier *rapidly* is positioned incorrectly because an adverb cannot be used between the two parts of an infinitive (*to* and *produce*). This is called a split infinitive.

(C) Unlike heroin, which works by stimulating receptor sites in the brain to produce pain-relieving and mood-enhancing chemicals rapidly
   - This answer contains the correctly used comparison **Unlike** and the correctly positioned modifier **rapidly**. It also avoids the problems with sentences, agreement, and parallelism found in some of the other answers.

(D) *Unlike the role of heroin*, which works on receptor *sites* in the brain *which is* stimulated by the drug to produce chemicals that are *both* pain-relieving *as well as* mood-enhancing
   - The expression *the role of heroin* is not parallel to the expression *cocaine*. The comparitive expression *Unlike* indicates that these expressions should be parallel.
   - The singular verb *is* does not agree with the subject *which*, which refers to the plural noun *sites*.
   - The expression *as well as* is used incorrectly. *Both...and* is a paired conjunction. Use **and** -- and not *as well as* -- with *both*.

(E) *Heroin works* on receptor sites in the brain which are stimulated by the drug to produce pain-relieving as well as mood-enhancing chemicals
   - This answer creates a run-on sentence because the two subjects and verbs *Heroin works* and *cocaine works* are connected with only a comma (,). A comma cannot be used to connect two subjects and verbs without a conjunction.

7. This question tests **wordiness**, **clarity**, and **verbs**.

The Vikings, who maintained a colony on the southwestern coast of Greenland *for more than four centuries beginning in 982 made regular voyages to North America to obtain wood because of the lack of this necessity* on Greenland.

(A) beginning in 982 **made** regular voyages to North America to obtain wood because of the lack of this necessity
  - This answer contains the correct simple past tense **made** and avoids the problems with wordiness and clarity found in some of the other answers.

(B) *starting originally* in 982 were travelling on a regular basis to North America *for the purpose of obtaining* wood, *which was lacking*
  - The word *originally* is redundant because its meaning is included within the word *starting*.
  - The idea *for the purpose of obtaining* is overly wordy and complex. The stylistic preference on GMAT is for more concise and simpler language.
  - The idea *which was lacking* is overly wordy and complex. The stylistic preference on GMAT is for more concise and simpler language.

(C) *in 982 had been making* voyages to North America *by boat* on a regular basis because they needed to obtain the wood that was lacking
  - The meaning of *in 1982* is illogical. It does not make sense that something occurred *for more than four centuries in 1982*.
  - The past perfect tense *had been making* is used incorrectly. The past perfect tense should be used when one past action is completed prior to another. The time expression *in 982* indicates that this past action was not prior to another past action.
  - The expression *by boat* is redundant because its meaning is included within the word *voyages*.

(D) *in 982* made regular *voyages* to North America to obtain *a much-needed product, wood, a product that was lacking*
  - The meaning of *in 1982* is illogical. It does not make sense that something occurred *for more than four centuries in 1982*.
  - The idea *a much-needed product, wood, a product that was lacking* is overly wordy and complex. The stylistic preference on GMAT is for more concise and simpler language.

(E) *beginning originally* in 982, *had been making* regular *sea* voyages to North America to obtain wood because of the lack of this product
  - The word *originally* is redundant because its meaning is included within the word *beginning*.
  - The past perfect tense *had been making* is used incorrectly. The past perfect tense should be used when one past action is completed prior to another. The time expression *in 982* indicates that this past action was not prior to another past action.
  - The word *sea* is redundant because its meaning is included within the word *voyages*.

8. This question tests **agreement**, **idioms**, and **wordiness**.

According to many language experts, the most difficult kind of phrase to create is a palindrome, *a sentence or group of sentences* that read the same both backwards and forwards, such as, "Red rum, sir, is murder."

(A) that read the same both backwards and forwards
- The plural verb *read* does not agree with the subject *that*, which refers to the singular noun *a sentence or group*.
- The idiomatic expression backwards and forwards is too casual for formal writing. Use **backward and forward** instead.

(B) that reads the same both backward and forward
- This answer contains the correct singular verb **reads** and the more formal idiomatic expression **backward and forward**. This answer also avoids the problem with wordiness found in some of the other answers.

(C) that reads similarly backwards and forwards
- The idiomatic expression backwards and forwards is too casual for formal writing. Use **backward and forward** instead.

(D) with the characteristic that they read similarly both backward and forward
- The idea with the characteristic is overly complex. The stylistic preference on GMAT is for simpler language.
- The plural subject and verb they read do not agree with the singular noun *a sentence or group*, to which they refer.

(E) with the characteristic that it reads the same both backward and forward
- The idea with the characteristic is overly complex. The stylistic preference on GMAT is for simpler language.

9. This question tests **modifiers**, **diction**, and **awkwardness**.

   Also known as prestidigitation or legerdemain, sleight of hand encompasses a variety of techniques used by magicians to control cards, coins, and other objects covertly.

   (A) sleight of hand encompasses a variety of techniques used by magicians to control cards, coins, and other objects covertly
   - This answer contains the subject **sleight of hand** following the comma to avoid the problem of a dangling modifier that is found in some of the other answers. It also avoids the problems with split infinitives, the use of *comprise,* and awkwardness that are found in some of the other answers.

   (B) *magicians and card manipulators* use various sleight of hand techniques to control cards, coins, and other objects covertly
   - The use of *magicians and card manipulators* following the comma (,) creates a sentence with a dangling modifier, *Also known as prestidigitation or legerdemain.* An introductory adjective should modify the subject of the main clause directly following the comma (,). The expression *Also known as prestidigitation or legerdemain* should modify **sleight of hand** and not *magicians and card manipulators.*

   (C) *the use of sleight of hand is comprised of* various techniques that magicians use *to covertly control* cards, coins, and other objects
   - The use of *the use of sleight of hand* following the comma (,) creates a sentence with a dangling modifier, *Also known as prestidigitation or legerdemain.* An introductory adjective should modify the subject of the main clause directly following the comma (,). The expression *Also known as prestidigitation or legerdemain* should modify **sleight of hand** and not *the use of sleight of hand.*
   - The expression *is comprised of* -- which means "makes up" and not "is made up of"-- is illogical in this context. Use **comprises** -- which means "is made up of" -- instead.
   - The modifier *covertly* is positioned incorrectly because an adverb cannot be used between the two parts of an infinitive, *to* and *control.* This is called a split infinitive.

   (D) sleight of hand *comprises* a variety of techniques *magicians and card manipulators use* to control cards, coins, and other objects covertly
   - The conjunction *that* has been omitted in front of the subject and verb *magicians and card manipulators use.* The stylistic preference on GMAT is to include the conjunction **that**.

   (E) sleight of hand *is comprised of* various techniques used by magicians *to covertly control* cards, coins, and other objects
   - The expression *is comprised of* -- which means "makes up" and not "is made up of"-- is illogical in this context. Use **comprises** -- which means "is made up of" -- instead.
   - The modifier *covertly* is positioned incorrectly because an adverb cannot be used between the two parts of an infinitive, *to* and *control.* This is called a split infinitive.

It Works! GMAT Sentence Correction

10. This question tests **awkwardness**, **verbs**, **idioms**, **wordiness**, and **parallelism**.

    Art forger Madame Latour was so skilled at her craft that many art experts were made to feel foolish and, in addition, some artists were made to question which paintings were actually theirs.

(A) Art forger Madame Latour was so skilled at her craft that many art experts were made to feel foolish and, in addition, some artists were made to question which paintings were actually theirs.
   - The passive voice in the expressions art experts were made to feel foolish and some artists were made to question is unnecessary here. The more direct active voice would be stylistically preferable on GMAT.

[(B)] So skilled at her craft was art forger Madame Latour that her forgeries fooled many an art expert and even caused some artists that *she copied* to question which paintings were actually theirs.
   - This answer contains **that** in front of the subject and verb *she copied*. It also avoids the problems with the passive voice, gerunds (*-ing* verbal nouns), past perfect verb tenses, idioms, wordiness, and parallelism found in some of the other answers.

(C) Art forger Madame Latour had acquired such good forging skills that she had managed to fool many art experts and even fooled some artists she copied into questioning which paintings were theirs.
   - The past perfect tense *had managed* is used incorrectly. The past perfect tense should be used when one past action is completed prior to another. The action *had managed* did not take place before *fooled*.
   - The expression *fooled...into* is an incorrect idiom. A better idiom to use here would be **tricked...into**.
   - The conjunction *that* has been omitted in front of the subject and verb *she copied*. The stylistic preference on GMAT is to include the conjunction **that**.

(D) *So skilled was* art forger Madame Latour at her craft that her forgeries had fooled many supposed art experts and even forced the questioning by some artists of which paintings they had actually made.
   - The past perfect tense *had fooled* is used incorrectly. The past perfect tense should be used when one past action is completed prior to another. The action *had fooled* did not take place before *So skilled was....*
   - The part of the answer *the questioning by some artists* is awkward. The stylistic preference on GMAT is to avoid unnecessary gerunds (*-ing* verbal nouns).

(E) Art forger Madame Latour had undergone the acquisition of so much skill that she was able to fool *both* many art experts as well as some artists she copied, who questioned which paintings were theirs.
   - The part of the answer *had undergone the acquisition of so much skill* is overly wordy. The stylistic preference on GMAT is for more concise language.
   - The expression *as well as* is used incorrectly. Both...and is a paired conjunction. Use **and** -- and not *as well as* -- with *both*.
   - The conjunction *that* has been omitted in front of the subject and verb *she copied*. The stylistic preference on GMAT is to include the conjunction **that**.

11. This question tests **wordiness**, **parallelism**, and **diction**.

   Tests of the solvency that a firm regularly exhibits necessarily focuses both on its ability to retire the principle in a timely manner and *also its ability to pay* interest on its debts.

(A) *the solvency that a firm regularly exhibits* necessarily focuses *both on its ability* to retire the *principle* in a timely manner *and*
   - The idea *the solvency that a firm regularly exhibits* is overly wordy and complex. The stylistic preference on GMAT is for more concise and simpler language.
   - The expression *on its ability* is not parallel to the expression *its ability* following *also*. The structure *both...and also* indicates that these expressions should be parallel.
   - The word *principle* -- which means "rule or belief" and not "original investment" -- is illogical in this context. Use **principal** -- which means "original investment" -- instead.

(B) *the solvency that a firm regularly exhibits* must *necessarily* focus on *not only* its ability to retire the principal in a timely manner *and*
   - The idea *the solvency that a firm regularly exhibits* is overly wordy and complex. The stylistic preference on GMAT is for more concise and simpler language.
   - The word *necessarily* is redundant because its meaning is included within the word *must*.
   - The word *and* is used incorrectly. *Not only...but (also)* is a paired conjunction. Use **but** (**also**) -- and not *and* -- with *not only*.

(C) a firm's solvency must focus on *not only* its ability to retire the principal in a timely manner *but*
   - This answer contains **its ability to retire** following *not only*, which is parallel to *its ability to pay* following *but also*. It also avoids the problems with wordiness and diction that are found in some of the other answers.

(D) a firm's solvency *must* focus *necessarily* on both its ability to retire the *principle* in a timely fashion and
   - The word *necessarily* is redundant because its meaning is included within the word *must*.
   - The word *principle* -- which means "rule or belief" and not "original investment" -- is illogical in this context. Use **principal** -- which means "original investment" -- instead.

(E) *the solvency regularly exhibited by a firm* must focus *both on its ability* to retire the principal in a timely fashion *and*
   - The idea *the solvency regularly exhibited by a firm* is overly wordy and complex. The stylistic preference on GMAT is for more concise and simpler language.
   - The expression *on its ability* is not parallel to the expression *its ability* following *also*. The structure *both...and also* indicates that these expressions should be parallel.

12. **This question tests clarity.**

    The *tectonic forces* that created East Africa's Great Rift Valley created a rash of volcanoes, one of which *erupted magnificently* around two and a half million years ago <u>to create</u> *the nineteen-kilometer-wide Ngorongoro Crater.*

(A) *to create*
   - This answer has a misused infinitive of purpose *to create* that makes the sentence illogical. According to this answer, *tectonic forces* had the purpose of creating *the nineteen-kilometer-wide Ngorongoro Crater*. However, *tectonic forces* cannot experience a sense of purpose.

(B) *and created*
   - The expression *and created* creates an answer that is imprecise. This answer states that a volcano *erupted magnificently...and created the nineteen-kilometer-wide Ngorongoro Crater*. However, it was the eruption, and not the volcano, that created the crater.

(C) *and resulted in the creation of*
   - The expression *and resulted in the creation of* creates an answer that is imprecise. This answer states that a volcano *erupted magnificently...and created the nineteen-kilometer-wide Ngorongoro Crater*. However, it was the eruption, and not the volcano, that resulted in the creation of the crater.

(D) *to result* in the creation of
   - This answer has a misused infinitive of purpose *to result* that makes the sentence illogical. According to this answer, *tectonic forces* had the purpose of resulting in the creation of *the nineteen-kilometer-wide Ngorongoro Crater*. However, *tectonic forces* cannot experience a sense of purpose.

(E) with a **force** that *resulted in the creation of*
   - This answer states precisely that it was the **force** of the eruption that *resulted in the creation* of the crater.

GMAT-Style Tests
TEST 6

Choose the letter of the answer to each question that best reflects the style and accuracy of standard written English. Then, study the explanations on the pages that follow.

1. Conceptual skills refer to a person's ability to think in the abstract, to diagnose and analyze different situations, <u>and to see beyond the present situation and understand the possibilities</u>.

    (A) and to see beyond the present situation and understand the possibilities
    (B) to see beyond what the present situation is and understand what could of been
    (C) and seeing beyond the present situation and understanding what could of been
    (D) and see beyond the present situation and understand what is possible
    (E) and see beyond what the present situation is and understand what is possible

2. <u>The amount of myths and folklore that has grown up around the story of Blackbeard truly attests</u> to the fascination the public holds for the pirate.

    (A) The amount of myths and folklore that has grown up around the story of Blackbeard truly attests
    (B) The number of myths and folklore that have grown up around the story of Blackbeard truly attest
    (C) The number of myths and the amount of folklore that have grown around the story of Blackbeard truly attest
    (D) The number and amount of myths and folklore that has grown around the story of Blackbeard truly attests
    (E) The number of myths and amount of folklore that has grown up around the story of Blackbeard truly attests

3. Becquerel's curiosity was peaked after, in 1896, he left a photographic plate and a container with uranium salts together in a drawer and noticed that the photographic plate had fogged.

   (A) Becquerel's curiosity was peaked after, in 1896, he left a photographic plate and a container with uranium salts together in a drawer and noticed that the photographic plate had fogged.
   (B) In 1896, Becquerel left a photographic plate and a container with uranium salts in a drawer; his curiosity was piqued when he noticed that the plate had become fogged.
   (C) In 1896, there was a piquing of Becquerel's curiosity after he left a photographic plate and a container with uranium salts in a drawer and the plate fogged up.
   (D) After Becquerel left a photographic plate and a container with uranium salts in a drawer in 1896, his curiosity was peaked when he became aware that there was fog on the photographic plate.
   (E) Becquerel had had his curiosity piqued when he left a photographic plate in a drawer with some uranium salts, resulting in the plate becoming fogged.

4. Tinnitus—a relentless and often life-changing ringing in the ears known to disable soldiers exposed to blasts, unwary listeners of too-loud music, and there are millions of others -- quite possibly result from the under-inhibition of key neural pathways in the brain's auditory center.

   (A) there are millions of others -- quite possibly result from
   (B) millions of others -- quite possibly results from
   (C) millions of others of them -- quite possibly results from
   (D) millions of others of them -- quite possibly as a direct result of
   (E) millions of others -- quite possibly resulting from

5. Life expectancy at birth for Americans was a mere 34.5 years for males and 36.5 years for females when the presidency was assumed by George Washington in 1789.

   (A) the presidency was assumed by George Washington
   (B) George Washington initially assumed the presidency
   (C) the presidency had initially been assumed by George Washington
   (D) George Washington had initially assumed the presidency
   (E) George Washington assumed the presidency

6. Believing that people were motivated by self-interest, Macchiavelli wrote *The Prince* in 1513 as advice for the leadership of Florence, recommending that leaders use fear, but not hatred, to maintain control.

   (A) Macchiavelli wrote *The Prince* in 1513 as advice for the leadership of Florence, recommending that leaders use
   (B) Macchiavelli's *The Prince* was written in 1513 to provide advise for the leaders of Florence, recommending that leaders use
   (C) *The Prince* was written in 1513 by Macchiavelli with advice for the leadership of Florence, he recommended in it that the leaders use
   (D) Macchiavelli wrote *The Prince* in 1513 as advice for the leaders of Florence; in it he recommended the leaders use
   (E) Macchiavelli wrote *The Prince* in 1513 with advise for the leaders of Florence, recommending that the leaders use

7. Though the largest planet, Jupiter incontrovertibly has the shortest day since it only makes one complete revolution around its axis in nine hours and fifty-five minutes.

    (A) Jupiter incontrovertibly has the shortest day since it only makes one complete revolution
    (B) Jupiter has undeniably a day that is shorter than the other planets since it makes only one complete revolution
    (C) it is irrefutable that Jupiter has the shortest day for the reason that it only makes one complete revolution
    (D) Jupiter undeniably has the shortest day since it makes only one complete revolution
    (E) Jupiter's day is incontrovertibly shorter than the days on other planets in that Jupiter makes only one complete revolution

8. Management by objectives is a system of setting of collaborative goals that extend from the top of an organization to the bottom of it.

    (A) a system of setting collaborative goals that extend from the top of an organization to the bottom of it
    (B) a systematic setting of collaborative goals that extend from the bottom to the top of an organization
    (C) a system of collaborative goal setting that extends from top to bottom in an organization
    (D) a system of collaborative goal setting that extend from bottom to top and everywhere in between
    (E) a collaborative goal-setting system consisting of extensions from the top of it to the bottom of it

9. Infants in the Chinook tribe were strapped between boards until the infants were about a year old so that they would have a fashionably flat skull.

    (A) they would have a fashionably flat skull
    (B) they had fashionably flat skulls
    (C) they had a flat skull that was fashionable
    (D) their skulls would be flat in a fashionable way
    (E) they would have fashionably flat skulls

10. Egypt's rulers of the Early Dynastic period were worshiped as gods after their deaths, a situation that caused ordinary Egyptians on the whole to consider their kings as their link to the invisible gods of the universe.

    (A) after their deaths, a situation that caused ordinary Egyptians on the whole to consider their kings as
    (B) after they died, something that caused ordinary Egyptians to consider their kings
    (C) after they died, which resulted in ordinary Egyptians on the whole considering their kings to be
    (D) following their deaths, and, as a result, it was ordinary Egyptians who regarded their kings to be
    (E) following their deaths, which caused most ordinary Egyptians to regard their kings as

11. Antoine de Saint-Exupéry began writing *The Little Prince* during World War II, after Germany's invasion of France <u>had forced him to give up aviation and flee to New York, thus the novel's nostalgia for childhood indicates not only Saint-Exupéry's desiring to</u> return to France and his hope to return to a time of peace.

    (A) had forced him to give up aviation and flee to New York, thus the novel's nostalgia for childhood indicates not only Saint-Exupéry's desiring to
    (B) had forced him to give up aviation and flee to New York; thus, the nostalgia for childhood in the novel is an indication of both Saint-Exupéry's wish to
    (C) had put him in a position where it was necessary to leave aviation behind and flee to New York; the nostalgia for childhood that is a key theme in the novel demonstrates not only Saint-Exupéry's desire to
    (D) made him understand the necessity of having to give up aviation and fleeing to New York; thus, the novel's nostalgia for childhood is an indication both of Saint-Exupéry's strong desire to
    (E) made him give up aviation and flee from France to New York, thus the nostalgia from childhood expressed in the novel demonstrates both Saint-Exupéry's wish

12. The role of marketing research is <u>to considerably increase the competitiveness of a firm by creating an understanding of the relationship between</u> the firm's stakeholders, its marketing variables, environmental considerations, and marketing decisions.

    (A) to considerably increase the competitiveness of a firm by creating an understanding of the relationship between
    (B) to considerably increase a firm's competitiveness by understanding the various relationships between
    (C) to increase considerably the competitiveness of a firm by creating an understanding of the various relationships among
    (D) to increase a firm's competitiveness considerably by understanding the relationship among
    (E) to increase the competitiveness of a firm considerably by creating an understanding of the various relationships among

EXPLANATIONS

1. This question tests **parallelism**, **wordiness**, and **diction**.

   Conceptual skills refer to a person's ability *to think* in the abstract, *to diagnose and analyze* different situations, <u>and to see beyond the present situation and understand the possibilities</u>.

   (A) and to see beyond the present situation and understand the possibilities
   - This answer contains the conjunction **and** and the parallel expression **to see**. It also avoids the problems of wordiness and diction found in some of the other answers.

   (B) to see beyond what the present situation is and understand what could of been
   - Though *to see* is parallel to *to think* and *to diagnose and analyze*, the conjunction **and** is needed in front of *to see* to create the parallel structure ___, ___, and ___.
   - The part of the answer *what the present situation is* is overly wordy and complex. The stylistic preference on GMAT is for simpler and more concise language.
   - The expression *could of* is always incorrect. Use **could have** instead.

   (C) and seeing beyond the present situation and understanding what could of been
   - The expressions *seeing* and *understanding* are not parallel to the expressions *to think* and *to diagnose and analyze*. The structure ___, ___, and ___ indicates that these expressions should be parallel.
   - The expression *could of* is always incorrect. Use **could have** instead.

   (D) and see beyond the present situation and understand what is possible
   - The expression *see* is not parallel to the expressions *to think* and *to diagnose and analyze*. The structure ___, ___, and ___ indicates that these expressions should be parallel.

   (E) and see beyond what the present situation is and understand what is possible
   - The expression *see* is not parallel to the expressions *to think* and *to diagnose and analyze*. The structure ___, ___, and ___ indicates that these expressions should be parallel.
   - The part of the answer *what the present situation is* is overly wordy and complex. The stylistic preference on GMAT is for simpler and more concise language.

2. This question tests **nouns**, **wordiness**, and **agreement**.

The amount of myths and folklore that has grown up around the story of Blackbeard truly attests to the fascination the public holds for the pirate.

(A) The *amount* of *myths* and folklore that has *grown up* around the story of Blackbeard truly attests
- The uncountable quantifier *amount* should not be used with the countable noun *myths*.
- The word *up* is redundant because its meaning is included within the word *grown*.

(B) The *number* of myths and *folklore* that have *grown up* around the story of Blackbeard truly *attest*
- The countable quantifier *number* should not be used with the uncountable noun *folklore*.
- The word *up* is redundant because its meaning is included within the word *grown*.
- The plural verb *attest* does not agree with the singular subject *number*.

(C) The number of *myths and* the amount of *folklore* that have grown around the story of Blackbeard truly attest
- This answer contains the correctly used quantifiers **number** with *myths* and **amount** with *folklore* and the correct plural verbs **have grown** and **attest** to agree with the plural subject **number** *and* **amount**. It also avoids the redundant *up* found in some of the other answers.

(D) The *number and amount* of *myths* and folklore that *has grown* around the story of Blackbeard truly *attests*
- The countable quantifier *number* and the uncountable quantifier *amount* cannot be used jointly this way with the countable noun *myths* and the uncountable noun *folklore*.
- The singular verb *has grown* does not agree with the subject *that*, which refers to the plural expression *number and amount*.
- The singular verb *attests* does not agree with the plural subject *number and amount*.

(E) The *number* of myths *and amount* of folklore *that has grown up* around the story of Blackbeard truly *attests*
- The singular verb *has grown* does not agree with the subject *that*, which refers to the plural expression *number...and amount*.
- The word *up* is redundant because its meaning is included within the word *grown*.
- The singular verb *attests* does not agree with the plural subject *number...and amount*.

3. This question tests **idioms** and **awkwardness**.

    Becquerel's curiosity was peaked after, in 1896, he left a photographic plate and a container with uranium salts together in a drawer and noticed that the photographic plate had fogged.

(A) Becquerel's *curiosity was peaked* *after, in 1896, he left* a photographic plate and a container with uranium salts together in a drawer and noticed that the photographic plate had fogged.
   - The expression *curiosity was peaked* is an incorrect idiom. Use **curiosity was piqued** instead.
   - The part of the answer *after, in 1896, he left,* is awkward. The stylistic preference on GMAT is for a more natural-sounding way of expressing this idea.

(B) In 1896, Becquerel left a photographic plate and a container with uranium salts in a drawer; his curiosity was piqued when he noticed that the plate had become fogged.
   - This answer contains the correct expression **curiosity was piqued** and the more formal **had become fogged** and avoids the problems with awkwardness found in some of the other answers.

(C) In 1896, there was *a piquing* of Becquerel's curiosity after he left a photographic plate and a container with uranium salts in a drawer and the plate *fogged up*.
   - The part of the answer *a piquing* is awkward. The stylistic preference on GMAT is to avoid unnecessary gerunds (-*ing* verbal nouns) if possible.
   - The idiomatic expression *fogged up* is too casual for formal writing. It is stylistically preferable to use the expression **became fogged**.

(D) After Becquerel left a photographic plate and a container with uranium salts in a drawer in 1896, his *curiosity was peaked* when he became aware that there was fog on the photographic plate.
   - The expression *curiosity was peaked* is an incorrect idiom. Use **curiosity was piqued** instead.

(E) Becquerel *had had his curiosity piqued* when he left a photographic plate in a drawer with some uranium salts, *resulting in the plate becoming fogged*.
   - The part of the answer *had had his curiosity piqued* is awkward. The stylistic preference on GMAT is for a more natural-sounding way of expressing this idea.
   - The part of the answer *resulting in the plate becoming fogged* is awkward. The stylistic preference on GMAT is for a more natural-sounding way of expressing this idea.

4. This question tests **parallelism**, **agreement**, **clarity**, and **sentences**.

   Tinnitus—a relentless and often life-changing ringing in the ears known to disable *soldiers* exposed to *blasts*, unwary *listeners* of too-loud music, *and* there are millions of others -- quite possibly result from the under-inhibition of key neural pathways in the brain's auditory center.

(A) there are millions of others -- quite possibly result from
   - The expression *there are millions of others* is not parallel to the expression *soldiers* and *listeners*. The structure ___, ___, *and* ___ indicates that these expressions should be parallel.
   - The plural verb *result* does not agree with the singular subject *Tinnitus*.

(B) millions of others -- quite possibly results from
   - This answer includes the expression **millions of others**, which is parallel to *soldiers* and *listeners*, and the correct singular verb **results** to agree with the subject *Tinnitus* and make the sentence complete. It also avoids the pronoun *them* with the unclear referent.

(C) millions of others of *them* -- quite possibly results from
   - The referent of the pronoun *them* is unclear. This pronoun could refer to either *soldiers*, *blasts*, *listeners*, or something else.

(D) millions of others of *them* -- quite possibly as a direct *result* of
   - The referent of the pronoun *them* is unclear. This pronoun could refer to either *soldiers*, *blasts*, *listeners*, or something else.
   - This answer creates a fragment because the main clause subject *Tinnitus* lacks a verb. *Result* is a noun and is not a verb.

(E) millions of others -- quite possibly *resulting* from
   - This answer creates a fragment because the main clause subject *Tinnitus* lacks a verb. *Resulting* is a present participle and is not a verb.

5. This question tests **awkwardness**, **wordiness**, and **verbs**.

   Life expectancy at birth for Americans was a mere 34.5 years for males and 36.5 years for females when <u>the presidency was assumed by George Washington</u> in 1789.

(A) the presidency *was assumed* by George Washington
   - The passive voice *was assumed* is unnecessary here. The more direct active voice would be stylistically preferable on GMAT.

(B) George Washington *initially* assumed the presidency
   - The word *initially* is redundant because its meaning is included within the word *assumed*.

(C) the presidency *had* *initially* *been assumed* by George Washington
   - The past perfect tense *had...been assumed* is used incorrectly. The past perfect tense should be used when one past action is completed prior to another. The time expression *in 1789* indicates that the past action was not prior to this year.
   - The passive voice *had...been assumed* is unnecessary here. The more direct active voice would be stylistically preferable on GMAT.
   - The word *initially* is redundant because its meaning is included within the word *assumed*.

(D) George Washington *had* *initially* *assumed* the presidency
   - The past perfect tense *had...assumed* is used incorrectly. The past perfect tense should be used when one past action is completed prior to another. The time expression *in 1789* indicates that the past action was not prior to this year.
   - The word *initially* is redundant because its meaning is included within the word *assumed*.

(E) George Washington **assumed** the presidency
   - This answer contains the active voice verb **assumed** in the correct simple past tense and avoids the problems with awkwardness and wordiness that are found in some of the other answers.

It Works! GMAT Sentence Correction

6. This question tests **modifiers**, **awkwardness**, **diction**, and **sentences**.

   Believing that people were motivated by self-interest, Macchiavelli wrote *The Prince* in 1513 as advice for the leadership of Florence, recommending that leaders use fear, but not hatred, to maintain control.

(A) Macchiavelli wrote *The Prince* in 1513 as advice for the leadership of Florence, recommending that leaders use
   - This answer avoids the dangling modifier and the unnecessary passive voice found in some of the other answers and correctly uses the word **advice**.

(B) Macchiavelli's *The Prince* was written in 1513 to provide advise for the leaders of Florence, recommending that leaders use
   - The use of *Macchiavelli's the Prince* following the comma *(,)* creates a sentence with a dangling modifier, *Believing that people were motivated by self-interest.* An introductory adjective should modify the subject of the main clause directly following the comma *(,)*. The expression *Believing that people were motivated by self-interest* should modify **Macchiavelli** and not *Macchiavelli's The Prince*.
   - The passive voice *was written* is unnecessary here. The more direct active voice would be stylistically preferable on GMAT.
   - The word *advise* -- which is a verb -- is inappropriate in this context. Use **advice** -- which is a noun -- instead.

(C) *The Prince* was written in 1513 by Macchiavelli with advice for the leadership of Florence, he recommended in it that the leaders use
   - The use of *The Prince* following the comma *(,)* creates a sentence with a dangling modifier, *Believing that people were motivated by self-interest.* An introductory adjective should modify the subject of the main clause directly following the comma *(,)*. The expression *Believing that people were motivated by self-interest* should modify **Macchiavelli** and not *The Prince*.
   - The passive voice *was written* is unnecessary here. The more direct active voice would be stylistically preferable on GMAT.
   - This answer creates a run-on sentence because the two subjects and verbs *The Prince was written* and *he recommended* are connected with a only comma *(,)*. A comma cannot be used to connect two subjects and verbs without a conjunction.

(D) Macchiavelli wrote *The Prince* in 1513 as advice for the leaders of Florence; in it he recommended the leaders use
   - The conjunction *that* has been omitted in front of the subject and verb *the leaders use*. The stylistic preference on GMAT is to include the conjunction **that**.

(E) Macchiavelli wrote *The Prince* in 1513 with advise for the leaders of Florence, recommending that the leaders use
   - The word *advise* -- which is a verb -- is inappropriate in this context. Use **advice** -- which is a noun -- instead.

It Works! GMAT Sentence Correction

7. This question tests **modifiers**, **comparisons**, **wordiness**, and **awkwardness**.

   Though the largest planet, Jupiter incontrovertibly has the shortest day since it only makes one complete revolution around its axis in nine hours and fifty-five minutes.

(A) Jupiter incontrovertibly has the shortest day since it *only* makes *one* complete revolution
   - The modifier *only* is positioned incorrectly because it is not directly in front of the idea *one,* which it modifies.

(B) Jupiter *has undeniably* a *day* that is *shorter than the other planets* since it makes only one complete revolution
   - The modifier *undeniably* is positioned incorrectly because an adverb cannot be positioned between a verb *has* and its direct object *day.*
   - The expression *the other planets* is not parallel to the expression *day.* The comparison *shorter than* indicates that these expressions should be parallel.

(C) *it is irrefutable* that Jupiter has the shortest day *for the reason that* it *only* makes one complete revolution
   - The use of *it is irrefutable* following the comma (,) creates a sentence with a dangling modifier, *Though the largest planet.* An introductory adjective should modify the subject of the main clause directly following the comma (,). The expression *Though the largest day* should modify **Jupiter** and not *it is irrefutable.*
   - The idea *for the reason that* is overly complex. The stylistic preference on GMAT is for simpler language.
   - The modifier *only* is positioned incorrectly because it is not directly in front of the idea *one,* which it modifies.

[(D)] Jupiter undeniably has the shortest day since it makes only one complete revolution
   - This answer begins with **Jupiter** to avoid the problem of a dangling modifier. It also contains the correctly positioned modifiers **undeniably** and **only** and avoids the problems with comparisons, wordiness, and awkwardness found in some of the other answers.

(E) *Jupiter's day* is incontrovertibly shorter than the days on other planets *in that* Jupiter makes only one complete revolution
   - The use of *Jupiter's day* following the comma (,) creates a sentence with a dangling modifier, *Though the largest planet.* An introductory adjective should modify the subject of the main clause directly following the comma (,). The expression *Though the largest planet* should modify **Jupiter** and not *Jupiter's day.*
   - The expression *in that* is considered stylistically awkward and overly formal on GMAT. The stylistic preference on GMAT is for a more natural-sounding way of expressing this idea.

8. This question tests **agreement** and **clarity**.

Management by objectives is <u>a system of setting of collaborative goals that extend from the top of an organization to the bottom of it</u>.

(A) a *system* of setting collaborative goals *that* extend from the top of an organization to the bottom of it
  • The plural verb extend does not agree with the subject *that*, which refers to the singular noun *system*.

(B) a systematic *setting* of collaborative goals *that* extend from the bottom to the top of an organization
  • The plural verb extend does not agree with the subject *that*, which refers to the singular noun *setting*.

(C) a *system* of collaborative goal setting *that* **extends** from top to bottom in an organization
  • This answer contains the correct singular verb **extends** to agree with the subject *that*, which refers to the singular noun *system*. It also avoids the problems with clarity that are found in some of the other answers.

(D) a *system* of collaborative goal setting *that* extend from bottom to top and everywhere in between
  • The plural verb extend does not agree with the subject *that*, which refers to the singular noun *system*.
  • The expression *from top to bottom and everywhere in between* is imprecise. It is not clear that this expression refers to an organization.

(E) a collaborative goal-setting system consisting of extensions from the top of it to the bottom of it
  • The expression *from the top of it to the bottom of it* is imprecise. It is not clear that this expression refers to an organization.

9. This question tests **agreement**, **verbs**, and **wordiness**.

   Infants in the Chinook tribe *were strapped* between boards until the *infants were* about a year old *so that* they would have a fashionably flat skull.

   (A) they would have a fashionably flat skull
   - The singular noun skull does not make sense when used with the plural noun *infants*.

   (B) they had fashionably flat skulls
   - The simple past tense had is used incorrectly. Because the verbs *were strapped* and *were* preceding *so that* are in the simple past tense, the verb following *so that* should be in the conditional (**would have**) tense to indicate purpose.

   (C) they had a flat skull that was fashionable
   - The simple past tense had is used incorrectly. Because the verbs *were strapped* and *were* preceding *so that* are in the simple past tense, the verb following *so that* should be in the conditional (**would have**) tense to indicate purpose.
   - The singular noun skull does not make sense when used with the plural noun *infants*.
   - The part of the answer a flat skull that was fashionable is overly wordy. The stylistic preference on GMAT is for more concise language.

   (D) their skulls would be flat in a fashionable way
   - The part of the answer be flat in a fashionable way is overly wordy. The stylistic preference on GMAT is for more concise language.

   (E) they would have fashionably flat skulls
   - This answer contains the correct verb tense **would have** following *so that* and the correct plural noun **skulls** to agree with *infants*. It also avoids the problem of wordiness found in some of the other answers.

10. This question tests **idioms**, **pronouns**, and **wordiness**.

Egypt's rulers of the Early Dynastic period *were worshiped as gods* after their deaths, a situation that caused ordinary Egyptians on the whole *to consider* their kings *as* their link to the invisible gods of the universe.

(A) after their deaths, a situation that caused ordinary Egyptians on the whole to consider their kings as
- The expression *considered...as* is an incorrect idiom. The word *considered* should never be followed by either *as* or *to be*. Use **considered** (without *as* or *to be*) instead.

(B) after they died, something that caused ordinary Egyptians to consider their kings
- This answer contains the word **something** to avoid the problem of the incorrectly used relative pronoun *which* found in some of the other answers. It also contains the verb **consider** used correctly without *as* or *to be* and avoids the problem with wordiness found in one of the other answers.

(C) *after they died*, which resulted in ordinary Egyptians on the whole considering their kings to be
- The relative pronoun *which* is used incorrectly. This relative pronoun should be used to refer to a specific noun and not to a complete idea such as *Egypt's rulers...were worshiped as gods after they died*.
- The expression *considered...to be* is an incorrect idiom. The word *considered* should never be followed by either *as* or *to be*. Use **considered** (without *as* or *to be*) instead.

(D) following their deaths, and, as a result, it was ordinary Egyptians who regarded their kings to be
- The idea *and, as a result, it was ordinary Egyptians who* is overly wordy and complex. The stylistic preference on GMAT is for more concise and simpler language.
- The expression *regarded...to be* is an incorrect idiom. The word *regarded* should be followed by **as** and not *to be*. Use **regarded...as** instead.

(E) *following their deaths*, which caused most ordinary Egyptians to regard their kings as
- The relative pronoun *which* is used incorrectly. This relative pronoun should be used to refer to a specific noun and not to a complete idea such as *Egypt's rulers...were worshiped as gods following their deaths*.

11. This question tests **sentences**, **parallelism**, **awkwardness**, and **wordiness**.

Antoine de Saint-Exupéry began writing *The Little Prince* during World War II, after Germany's invasion of France <u>had forced him to give up aviation and flee to New York, thus the novel's nostalgia for childhood indicates not only Saint-Exupéry's desiring to</u> return to France *and his hope to return* to a time of peace.

(A) had forced him to give up aviation and flee to New York, thus the novel's nostalgia for childhood indicates not only Saint-Exupéry's desiring to

- This answer creates a run-on sentence because the two subjects and verbs *Antoine de Saint-Exupéry began* and *nostalgia...indicates* are connected with only a comma (,). A comma cannot be used to connect two subjects and verbs without a conjunction, and *thus* is an adverb and is not a conjunction.
- The expression *not only* is used incorrectly. *Not only...but (also)* is a paired conjunction. Use **both** -- and not *not only* -- with *and*.
- The part of the answer *desiring* is awkward. The stylistic preference on GMAT is to avoid unnecessary gerunds (*-ing* verbal nouns) if possible.

(B) had forced him to give up aviation and flee to New York; thus, the nostalgia for childhood in the novel is an indication of both Saint-Exupéry's wish to

- This answer avoids the problems with sentences, parallelism, awkwardness, and wordiness that are found in some of the other answers.

(C) had put him in a position where it was necessary to leave aviation behind and flee to New York; the nostalgia for childhood that is a key theme in the novel demonstrates not only Saint-Exupéry's desire to

- The idea *a position where it was necessary to leave aviation behind* is overly wordy and complex. The stylistic preference on GMAT is for more concise and simpler language.
- The expression *not only* is used incorrectly. *Not only...but (also)* is a paired conjunction. Use **both** -- and not *not only*-- with *and*.

(D) made him understand the *necessity* of having to give up aviation and fleeing to New York; thus, the novel's nostalgia for childhood is an indication both of Saint-Exupéry's strong desire to

- The expression *having to* is redundant because its meaning is included within the word *necessity*.
- The expression *of Saint-Exupéry's strong desire* is not parallel to the expression *his hope to return*. The structure *both...and* indicates that these expressions should be parallel.

(E) made him give up aviation and flee from France to New York, thus the nostalgia from childhood expressed in the novel demonstrates both Saint-Exupéry's wish

- This answer creates a run-on sentence because the two subjects and verbs *Antoine de Saint-Exupéry began* and *nostalgia...demonstrates* are connected with only a comma (,). A comma cannot be used to connect two subjects and verbs without a conjunction, and *thus* is an adverb and is not a conjunction.

12. This question tests **modifiers**, **agreement**, **diction**, and **clarity**.

The role of *marketing research* is <u>to considerably increase</u> the competitiveness of a firm by creating an understanding of the *relationship between* the firm's *stakeholders*, its marketing *variables*, environmental *considerations*, and marketing *decisions*.

(A) to *considerably* increase the competitiveness of a firm by creating an understanding of the *relationship between*
- The modifier *considerably* is positioned incorrectly because an adverb cannot be used between the two parts of an infinitive, *to* and *increase*. This is called a split infinitive.
- The singular noun *relationship* does not make sense when used with the plural nouns *stakeholders, variables, considerations,* and *decisions*.
- The word *between* -- which should be used when two people or objects are related -- is incorrect in this context, in which *stakeholders, variables, considerations,* and *decisions* are related.

(B) to *considerably* increase a firm's competitiveness *by understanding* the various relationships *between*
- The modifier *considerably* is positioned incorrectly because an adverb cannot be used between the two parts of an infinitive, *to* and *increase*. This is called a split infinitive.
- The meaning of *by understanding* is illogical. It does not make sense that *marketing research* can experience a sense of understanding.
- The word *between* -- which should be used when two people or objects are related -- is incorrect in this context, in which *stakeholders, variables, considerations,* and *decisions* are related. Use **among** -- which is used when three or more people or objects are related -- instead.

(C) to *increase considerably* the *competitiveness* of a firm by creating an understanding of the various relationships among
- The modifier *considerably* is positioned incorrectly because an adverb cannot be positioned between a verb *increase* and its direct object *competitiveness*.

(D) to increase a firm's competitiveness considerably *by understanding* the *relationship* among
- The meaning of *by understanding* is illogical. It does not make sense that *marketing research* can experience a sense of understanding.
- The singular noun *relationship* does not make sense when used with the plural nouns *stakeholders, variables, considerations,* and *decisions*.

(E) to increase the competitiveness of a firm **considerably by creating an understanding** of the various **relationships among**
- This answer contains the correctly positioned modifier **considerably**, the logical expression **creating an understanding**, the logical plural noun **relationships**, and the correctly used word **among**.

www.ingramcontent.com/pod-product-compliance
Lightning Source LLC
Chambersburg PA
CBHW080455110426
42742CB00017B/2893